Dickenson Publishing Company, Inc.
Encino, California & Belmont, California

The Foreign Policy of the USSR: Domestic Factors

Morton Schwartz
University of California, Riverside

TO MY MOTHER AND FATHER

327.47
Sch 9f
94868
oct 1975

1

ISBN—0—8221—0145—9
Library of Congress Catalog Card Number: 74-27743

Printed in the United States of America

Printing (last digit): 9 8 7 6 5 4 3 2 1

Contents

Foreword

The COMPARATIVE FOREIGN RELATIONS SERIES is designed for foreign policy courses that employ a comparative approach, as well as for courses in comparative politics and international relations that survey the foreign relations of key states. Because the basic literature is lacking, few courses today are able to make a genuinely comparative examination of national actors in the international system, in the manner increasingly adopted for the study of domestic politics. This series has been prepared to fill the need for such a basic literature.

The series presents an analytical model and case materials for beginning a comparative study of foreign relations. As a method of studying foreign relations phenomena, comparison allows us to investigate the differences and similarities among states in relation to the international system, and thereby generate or test propositions about the external relations of states.

In order to compare cases, an analytical model or framework should be used—that is, the same set of subjects and questions should be used to arrange and present information about each case. The analytical model of the series is presented in the core volume, *Comparative Foreign Relations: Framework and Methods,* which outlines a framework for describing the international situation and foreign policy of a state, explaining its current policy, analyzing its current problems, and projecting its future problems and policy alternatives.

The books in the series make comparison possible by presenting material of the same nature about each case; however, the actual comparisons must be made by the reader. Some ways in which the series might be used to further the comparative study of foreign relations are presented in the preface to the core volume.

David O. Wilkinson
Lawrence Scheinman

Preface

"There is not a single question of any importance which could at present be solved without the Soviet Union or against its will. . . ." So spoke Andrei Gromyko at the 24th Congress of the Communist Party of the Soviet Union (April, 1971). "Moreover," said the Soviet Foreign Minister, "it is precisely our proposals . . . which are in the center of political discussions." Discounting for some exaggeration and a measure of puffery, it is difficult to fault Mr. Gromyko's assessment. The USSR today does play a key role in world politics; its influence in a great many parts of the globe—Eastern Europe, the Middle East, South Asia, the Far East, the Caribbean—is considerable and, in places, even crucial. Even its foremost dissident critic, the novelist Alexander Solzhenitsyn, grudgingly admitted the Soviet regime's foreign policy successes in his bitterly critical letter of September 1973 to the Soviet leaders. "Soviet diplomacy," he wrote,

> . . . knows how to make demands, exact concessions, simply get things in ways that Tsarism never knew. In terms of its actual achievements it might even be regarded as brilliant; in fifty years, with only one large-scale war, which it won from a position no more advantageous than that of the other participants, it rose from a country riven by civil strife to a superpower before which the entire world trembles.[1]

The crucial role currently played by the Soviet Union would by itself justify another study of Soviet foreign policy. However, we have additional reasons. The USSR is not just another Great Power with vast external interests and influence. For the United States, it is what sociologists refer to as our "relevant other." Since the end of the Second World War, the United States has been embroiled in a major and at times highly dangerous military confrontation with the USSR. The struggle between these two Great Powers quickly became what Sir Bernard Lewis has called "the overriding reality" of the post-war political scene to which all other problems and conflicts are "subordinate and secondary." Though the tense and grim days of the Cold War seem to have given way to a more hopeful era of what Soviet leaders have labeled "peaceful coexistence," the political confrontation between the two superpowers is still very much with us.

The foreign policy of the USSR is worthy of our attention for yet another reason. The Russian Revolution, in the words of George F. Kennan, is one of "the greatest political events of the present century." According to Kennan, it merits this description not only because of its extraordinary impact on the lives of the Russian people but, more importantly for our purposes, because of "the profound exemplary effect it had across great portions of the globe." The Soviet Union, a self-acclaimed revolutionary power from the very outset, the center of a world-wide revolutionary movement dedicated to the socialist transformation of the world, has long been considered a disturber of international order and a threat to the community of nations. In fact, whether by its overt revolutionary activity or its revolutionary example, Soviet Russia's presence has considerably accelerated the international forces for change. While not precisely in the ways the founding fathers of the Bolshevik Revolution had dreamt, the establishment of a Communist state in Russia has had a profound impact on both the style and content of international political life; it has helped promote the revolutionary climate in which the nations and peoples of the world now find themselves.

Given the Soviet Union's enormous importance, especially for the United States, and its distinctive contribution to contemporary world politics, it is not surprising to find that research and writing on the USSR, especially in this country, has been prodigious. As has often been noted, more has been written about the Russian Revolution and the fifty-odd years of Soviet rule than about any comparable development in history.

How useful, it can fairly be asked, has this sizable outpouring been? How close are we to the "truth" about Russia? How far have we come since Churchill's famous characterization of Russia as "a riddle wrapped in a mystery inside an enigma"? Though perhaps abundant in their outpourings and sophisticated in their judgment, writers on Soviet foreign policy have been neglectful of the needs of the student. The single greatest weakness in this literature has been the absence of an analytic perspective. Virtually all Western texts on Soviet foreign policy are primarily historical or monographic. Thus, among the best of the recent wave of writing are such first-rate studies as Thomas Wolfe's *Soviet Power and Europe, 1945–1970*, Adam Ulam's *Expansion and Co-existence, A History of Soviet Foreign Policy, 1917–1967*, and Robert Wesson's *Soviet Foreign Policy in Perspective*—all essentially histories.

The present study represents a small effort to help overcome this deficiency. Focusing on what in Moscow would be called the "motive forces" which have shaped Soviet foreign policy, it strives for a general analytic perspective lacking elsewhere. Furthermore, to stimulate students with wider interests and especially those who find the comparative perspective fruitful, it strives for some degree of unity of approach with other volumes in the Comparative Foreign Relations Series. Evaluation of the domestic roots of Soviet foreign policy in contrast with those of other countries will, it is hoped, thereby be encouraged.

The problems involved in writing a book of this kind are several. First, the analyst of Soviet foreign policy who concentrates his attention on the internal bases of Soviet international behavior is necessarily taken away from his normal concerns. Rather than examining the diplomatic and military activities of the USSR, the focus of analysis is on economic, historical, ideological, and domestic political circumstances and trends. Such a perspective, while perhaps a departure from the more traditional methods of foreign policy analysis, is the natural product of the multidisciplinary "area" approach to the Soviet Union. Such, indeed, has been my training and is my bias. To the extent the material presented here is a contribution, let it be seen as reflecting the insights of this occasionally beleaguered but still worthy tradition. However, while familiar with the general contours of these various dimensions of Soviet life, I do not, as a political scientist, pretend to any special competence in other academic disciplines. Given my professional limitations, I have had to rely to an extent perhaps somewhat greater than usual on the contributions of others. Thus, I owe a particular intellectual debt to my many brethren in the vast and varied vineyards of Soviet studies.

Another general problem confronting most analysts of Soviet national policy is the reticence of the Soviet political leadership to reveal details about Soviet economic and political life. Though prone to incessant speechmaking and ever boasting of the number of books, pamphlets, journals and newspapers published each year in the USSR and the circulation records that are constantly being set, the Kremlin is curiously silent about many highly important features of Soviet public affairs. For example, Soviet publications and official pronouncements contain very little news about relationships among the members of the Politburo's "collective leadership." Such "negative phenomena" as accidents and natural catastrophes are only reluctantly reported. Crime statistics are not publicly available. The activities and fate of internal dissident groups and individuals receive virtually no official attention. Information regarding grain reserves is considered too sensitive to be revealed publicly. There are also numerous accounts of false reporting. For example, recent press accounts have conceded that a huge Siberian power generator, recorded as having been "put in service" in 1968—an event hailed as "the beginning of a technological revolution"—had not in fact been installed at all, having burned out on the factory floor.[2] Furthermore, data published regarding Soviet defense spending is grossly misleading. While the Soviet authorities conceal such information from their own population, they are especially concerned to control and manipulate what is revealed to foreign audiences.

Soviet reluctance to reveal information about themselves borders on the bizarre. According to a former Soviet journalist, publishing house censors in the USSR are bound by a "top secret" instruction manual (bearing the title "Index of Information Not to be Published in the Open Press,") not to allow publication of the following types of newsmatter without special authorization in each individual case: "information about earthquakes, avalanches and other natural disasters within the territory of the USSR; news about fires, explosions, train or plane crashes, naval and mine disasters; any comparison of the budgets of Soviet citizens or the retail price of goods; any reports of increasing living standards anywhere outside the socialist countries; any average statistical information about the USSR as a whole not taken from official reports of the Central Statistical Administration; data on the salary or earnings of party and government workers; reports on food shortages in the USSR; the names of any members of the State Security Committee (KGB), apart from that of the Chairman, and any references whatsoever to the censorship organs or to the jamming of foreign radio broadcasts."[3]

Analysts of Soviet policy, therefore, have rather uncertain and usually highly tendentious official information to guide them. Their predicament was very well described by Sir William Hayter, former British Ambassador to Moscow, when he wrote:

> So we are reduced to groping in the dark, trying to guess by the feel of the odd objects we touch or dimly discern what the shape of the whole surrounding space must be, conscious that large areas of it must escape our observation and that other observers, bumping into something else, may form different views, probably just as valid, about what is going on in the dark void all round.[4]

However, to the extent that Western observers have been reduced to the condition of the proverbial Indian blindmen seeking to describe the elephant, the responsibility for this unfortunate state of affairs has not been theirs.

A final word about approach. All textbooks, whatever their field, should provide the student with a foundation for further reading and whet his appetite for more. In pursuit of these purposes, the author should be guided by two main objectives: He first should attempt to piece together the facts and interpretations of modern scholarship in his field. Second, he should organize these essential facts around a theme or themes. Mere collection of information only dulls the appetite for knowledge. Further, if you include all possible interpretations you are bound at least to have mentioned the right one—but little of significance will have emerged. Undigested information and the spectrum of interpretations have little explanatory power.

The pages that follow contain unabashedly "digested" information and interpretation. Where possible, I try to present all sides to the argument. At the same time, I do not shrink from setting forth my own position—hopefully, with persuasive explanations for the conclusions reached. In the event I am not entirely reasonable, or am even incorrect, I am sure, along with Leonardo da Vinci, that critics hoping I make mistakes will be more useful than friends trying to conceal them.

I should like to express my special appreciation to two groups of people. First, I am indebted to my professional colleagues, Sidney Ploss and Alexander Dallin, who graciously read the whole manuscript. The rigorous standards which they set in their own work and their specific comments on mine were a challenge and an inspiration. For their wise counsel, my grateful thanks. I benefited as well from the valuable comments of Michael M. Stoddard. Errors of fact or interpretation are, of course, my responsibility. Thanks are also due to my wife, Runa, and my sons, David and Jonathan, who with unfailing cheerfulness have shared many of the burdens which preparation of this book has entailed. For their patience and forbearance, my profound gratitude.

Notes

[1]A. Solzhenitsyn, "Letter to the Soviet Leaders," September 3, 1973; published in the *Sunday Times* (London), March 3, 1974, p. 33.

[2]*The New York Times*, June 15, 1973.

[3]*The Right to Know, Report of the Presidential Study Commission on International Radio Broadcasting* (Washington, D. C.: Government Printing Office, 1973), Appendix C. "Impediments to the Free Flow of Information and Ideas in The Soviet Union", p. 69.

[4]Sir William Hayter, *Russia and the World* (New York: Taplinger Publishing Company, 1970), p. x.

Introduction

Western specialists on Soviet foreign policy can be divided into two major schools: those who stress the role of domestic factors in explaining Soviet behavior and those who focus on the determining role of the international environment. The emphasis in each case is rather different. The former or "microanalytic" approach explains Soviet foreign policy primarily in terms of internal needs. Placing great stress on such factors as the role of Marxist–Leninist ideology, the nature of the Communist political system, the distinctive character of Russia's cultural traditions, and the personalities of its political leaders, this view generally insists that these internal forces exert powerful demands which Soviet policymakers cannot escape in their foreign policy choices.

The second school stresses the "macroanalytic" approach, focusing on variables external to the Soviet Union. Rejecting the view that, because of its internal arrangements or circumstances, the USSR is a unique phenomenon, this school usually considers the Soviet Union as a traditional power striving to survive in the hard and at times brutal international political environment. Its basic foreign policy objectives—national security, defense of strategic frontiers, national economic well-being, international prestige—are seen as conventional rather than unique. Much depends on the particular shape of the international environment, on the specific possibilities and dangers confronting them. Thus, rather than ask the questions, What *must* the USSR do? or What do domestic circumstances demand of the Kremlin?, this approach is concerned with the question, What do the Soviet leaders think the USSR *can* do?[1]

The particular approach adopted to analyze Soviet behavior has significant policy consequences. If one assumes that the "microanalytic" approach is the more persuasive, this implies, as William Zimmerman has suggested, that Soviet policy tends to be both preprogrammed and resistant to change.[2] For example, if one assumes that the internal political dynamics of a Communist regime or an authoritarian system of government imposes an aggressive thrust on Soviet foreign policy, this suggests that changes in Kremlin behavior are not likely until the nature of the Soviet regime is substantially altered. The policy alternatives available to outside powers are, therefore, quite limited. Until the Soviet leaders abandon their ideological convictions as expressed in the old Russian couplet

> Eat pineapple, gorge on grouse,
> Your last day is coming, bourgeois louse

the Western powers can do little but maintain a strong military posture and carefully guard their interests against this congenitally hostile foe.

The "macroanalytic" school, sees Soviet policy as largely reactive and, therefore, subject to some degree of influence. Policy alternatives here are much greater in that the changing shape of the international environment and the policies of other states—especially the other major world power (the United States), traditional and new sources of danger (Germany and China), and Russia's allies (the East European Communist states)—are seen as exerting significant influence on Soviet behavior. Kremlin policy choices and behavior therefore can be modified without waiting for profound changes in the internal political system or for transformations in deeply embedded political attitudes and values. Policy options in dealing with the USSR are more open and flexible. In this sense, the Soviet Union is a "normal" power to be treated much as any other large power.

Most Western analysts of Soviet foreign policy, scholars with "area studies" training and diplomatic officials who have served in the Soviet Union, have overwhelmingly adhered to the "microanalytic" approach. To some extent, this has been a product of the Cold War. The marked deterioration in Soviet–American relations after World War II led many observers to explain the hostility they saw in Soviet international behavior as somehow the result of the distinctive character of Russian society and, especially, the Soviet political system. The authoritarian structure and the messianic ideology of the Communist state were seen to be the source of Moscow's aggressive foreign policy. External expansion was believed to have been necessary to the survival of the Soviet regime.

Concentration on "microanalytic" factors, however, has also been the product of the natural and somewhat self-serving prejudices of all area specialists. Trained experts and diplomats who have devoted their lives to the study of China, for example, are fully persuaded that the object of their attentions and affections is distinctive in important ways. So with Soviet area specialists who, even before the Cold War, tended to the view that only with a proper understanding of the national character of the Russian people, their cultural traditions, and their unique historical experience could one understand Moscow's behavior. The key to Russia's political system and her foreign policy—whatever the regime—was what used to be called "the Russian soul." Many still hold, along with the poet Tyutchev, that

> Russia is not to be grasped with the mind,
> There is no stick by which she can be measured.
> She has her own particular character.
> In Russia—one can only believe.

This study is in the "microanalytic" tradition. That is to say, it concentrates on the domestic variables and forces which shape foreign policy behavior. Hopefully, it is free of both Cold War biases and the prejudices of the "Russianists." However, it does assume that Soviet decisionmakers do not deal with the external world *in vacuo* but that they see threats and opportunities, choose their goals and their methods in the context of an ideological-cultural-political milieu which, along with their country's economic and military resources, conditions their attitudes and goals and shapes their policy choices.

In a very discerning work, C. A. W. Manning wrote that "among the various forms of 'reductionism' against which we do well to be warned is the one which sees international politics as involving the behavior only, hence the relationship only, of fleshly human beings."[3] Manning's point is very well taken. While it is wise to remember that in politics, as in all human activity, it is men that act and decide and not abstractions called "the Soviet Union" or "the United States," it is profoundly wrong to think of the political universe solely in such terms. The USSR, like all countries, consists of men with passions and prejudices, interests and fears, attitudes and priorities. However, these men are Soviet men whose behavior is strongly influenced by Soviet traditions, experiences and interests. Despite the ultimate commonality of their concerns, Soviet politicians, diplomats, generals, and industrialists are indeed different from their counterparts elsewhere. Their country's historical experiences, geographic circumstances, and internal political arrangements place specific demands and impose particular needs and interests on the Kremlin authorities. Such factors profoundly shape their conception of the external world as well as their role in it. In this sense, Soviet men act distinctively, if not differently from other men.

The purpose of this study is less to argue the position of the "microanalytic" approach than to utilize its insights for an understanding of Soviet behavior. Obviously, domestic factors do influence the foreign policy of the USSR. Even the most hard-bitten "macroanalyst" could not dispute this. However, it is the author's position that neither domestic nor external factors alone best explain Soviet policy but, rather, the interplay of both.

The analysis begins with an examination of the so-called objective factors of international politics. Environmental (geographic size, location, resource endowment), demographic, and economic strengths and weaknesses (tracing both the pattern of Soviet economic growth and recent economic performance as well as economic problems affecting foreign policy) are treated in Chapter One. Soviet military capabilities (conventional forces, levels and trends in strategic force levels) are considered in Chapter Two. Chapters Three and Four deal with Soviet political beliefs, the attitudes and values of the Soviet political leadership regarding the Soviet role in world affairs. This profoundly important subject is examined from the perspectives of historical (pre-1917) Russian traditions and of more recent influences such as the official ideology of the Soviet state, Marxism–Leninism.

Chapters Five and Six are concerned with Soviet political processes. They concentrate on the particular character of the Soviet political system, the internal dynamics of Communist Party rule, the institutions of foreign policy decisionmaking, and the ever-shifting pattern of Soviet internal politics. Chapter Seven seeks to evaluate the trends in the internal development of the Soviet Union and to assess their implications for Soviet foreign policy. It also offers some speculations on the basic question, To what extent is Soviet foreign policy an extension of Soviet internal political processes?

Notes

[1]William Zimmerman, "The Sources of Soviet Conduct: A Reconsideration," paper presented to the Annual Meeting of the American Political Science Association, Washington, D. C., September 5–9, 1972 (mimeo), pp. 4ff. and Charles Gati, "X Plus 25: What Containment Meant," *Foreign Policy*, No. 7 (Summer 1972), p. 2. For an earlier statement of the "power politics calls the tune" approach, see Barrington Moore, Jr., *Soviet Politics—The Dilemma of Power* (Cambridge: Harvard University Press, 1950), chs. 16–17.

[2]Zimmerman, *op. cit.*, p. 5.

[3]C. A. W. Manning, *The Nature of International Society* (London: G. Bell and Sons, Ltd., 1962), p. 65.

1

Capabilities

That we begin our discussion with an analysis of Soviet economic and military power reflects an important assumption about the basic character of international society. We assume, as many scholars have observed, that world politics is basically anarchic—that it lacks a supranational authority capable of regulating and adjusting differences and preventing military conflict and war. Thus, men continue to belong to a multiplicity of legally sovereign states without any international institution standing above them, without a common law or an impartial and effective international police force.

The relative primitiveness of international society has important consequences, one of the most significant being a highly inegalitarian (or oligarchic) order where "the powerful prevail over the weak." Though all of the more than one hundred forty independent nation-states are legally sovereign and formally equal, in fact the more powerful nations settle the important affairs of the world. Stalin's question (said to have been asked during the Second World War), "How many divisions has the Pope?", reflects his appreciation of the fact that, for the statesmen of the world, power is the currency of international relations.[1]

The sad fate of Czechoslovakia in the twentieth century provides a vivid example of the inegalitarian character of world politics. On two separate occasions, in 1938 and again in 1968, Czechoslovakia faced invasion from enormously powerful neighbors. In both instances, the Czech army and citizenry offered no military resistance. To avoid threatened mass destruction, great bloodshed, and certain defeat at the hands of the Nazi and Soviet armies, the Czechoslovaks meekly stood by and watched while the tanks of their adversaries swept through their cities.

The basic lesson to be drawn from the Czechoslovak experience (countless other examples could have been cited) is obvious. As David O. Wilkinson suggests in the core volume to this series, "Strength in capability resources . . . makes ambitious projects feasible and increases their chance of success; weakness constrains, restrains, and limits choices and independence."[2] Hitler and Brezhnev as well as the hapless Czechoslovaks could all be called in as character witnesses in support of Wilkinson's observation.

Thus, Great Power status in world politics is clearly a function of both terms, "great" and "power." And, as appropriate to leaders of a nation which has long aspired to such a role, the men in the Kremlin have been acutely sensitive to the relative economic and military strengths and weaknesses of their country. Even the most casual reader of the Soviet press cannot but be struck by the frequency with which the phrase "correlation of forces" appears in official pronouncements. In contrast to "idealists" who, it is said, seek to explain international political behavior in terms of intangible factors such as the skills and personality of leaders, public morale, and historical accident, the Kremlin leaders stress the critical role of economic and military power. Accepting this "realistic" perspective, our analysis begins with an examination of the political implications of the USSR's power capabilities.

Geography

Good things, it is said, come in small packages; power, however, is almost always associated with size. The biggest kid in the neighborhood is usually the strongest (and often the meanest) while the largest plane is invariably the most powerful one (it would have to be, given the laws of aerodynamics). Shortly after Soviet-led forces had occupied his country, a Czechoslovak writer wistfully acknowledged the importance of size in world politics. "A large nation," he wrote,

> . . . does not question the reason and justification for its existence; with a crushing inevitability it simply exists. It rests in its largeness and often indulges in it as if this itself were a valuable accomplishment . . . A small nation, on the other hand, if it is of any significance in the world has to keep building it up. As soon as a small nation stops producing values, it loses the right to exist, and may actually cease to exist, because it is frail and destructible.[3]

In international as in human affairs, size affects psychological outlook. Leaders of large nations tend to think and act big because they are big; they can generally do pretty much as they please—unless challenged by another large power. On the other hand, small nations act within narrow constraints. The leaders of such countries know that their fortunes generally lie with—not against—the dominant forces in their area.

Size is so often linked with power that Russia is usually assumed always to have been a Great Power. This misconception has a logical root in that Russia is by far the largest country in the world in physical size. It occupies 8,647,000 square miles and is more than twice the size of each of its major rivals, China and the United States. The country is so vast that it sprawls across large portions of two continents, Europe and Asia. (It is about a ten-day train trip across the 5,700 miles which separate Chop on the western border with Czechoslovakia from the tip of Siberia in the east.) In strictly territorial terms, the USSR is Asian, for the bulk of the country lies east of the Ural mountains, generally considered the dividing line between Europe and Asia. However, despite considerable population migrations eastward since the beginning of the Second World War, three-quarters of the USSR's people still live in the European part. Thus, of all major neighboring areas, Europe "is nearest the Soviet 'effective national territory,' [and] has always had the closest contact with it. . . ."[4] Thus Russia is fundamentally European.

Soviet Russia's very vastness has been both an asset and a liability. As Napoleon and Hitler found, much to their dismay, great size allowed Russia's generals considerable latitude for maneuver. It proved impossible for the French and German armies to deliver a decisive blow. Taking advantage of its geographic flexibility, Russia used a defense-in-depth strategy, dispersing and regrouping its forces ever eastward. Thus, while Napoleon actually took Moscow, and Hitler's forces reached the gates of the capital city, the invading but overextended armies were defeated on Russia's wintry plains. During the Russo–Japanese War (1904–1905), however, Russia itself had great difficulty supplying its armies. Japan's victory over Tsarist Russia was in no small measure a result of the fact that while Russia had to move men and munitions more than six thousand miles on the recently completed, single-track Trans-Siberian Railway, Japanese forces were operating close to their sources of supplies and equipment.

Clearly, vast size allows for military maneuverability. However, it also poses serious transportation problems with important economic consequences. Though Russia has vast mineral and energy resources, there is "a striking lack of coincidence" between the location of most of these resources and the centers for their consumption. "At least two-thirds of the population and industry are in European Russia, including the Urals, whereas at least four-fifths of the energy resources are in Siberia."[5] (According to another source, while 82 percent of the USSR's power output comes from European Russia, Soviet Asia contains approximately 90 percent of the country's total energy reserves.[6]) Thus, though well-endowed with resources, the country's enormous size creates serious problems and requires an efficient transportation system.

Less obvious than the USSR's huge size is its "high latitude position." Virtually all of the Soviet Union lies north of the 45° parallel (latitude). Moscow, the Soviet capital, is further north than Edmonton, Alberta, the most northerly Canadian city of any significance, while Leningrad, Russia's second largest city, is on the latitude of southern Alaska. Only the southern part of the Ukraine, the area of the Caucasus and Soviet Central Asia, are in the same latitude zones as the northern part of the United States. This "high latitude position" has a number of important consequences. First, this location is the source of the severe climate which benumbed ill-prepared invading French and German armies in the nineteenth and twentieth centuries. Here, "General Frost" joined "General Distance" to blunt the offensive drives of both Napoleon and Hitler. It also helps explain why, with such an enormous territory at its disposal, the USSR still confronts serious agricultural problems. Severe climate means good farm land is relatively scarce—only ten percent of the USSR's eight and one-half million square miles is arable—and the growing season in all but a few regions is extremely short. Russia's bitter cold also means that mining in Siberia is often extremely difficult and costly.

A second consequence stemming from this high latitude position relates to the USSR's maritime activity. Given its northerly position, virtually the whole Soviet coast is ice-locked during the winter. The ice is so thick as to make commercial or naval activity unthinkable for much of the year. Even Odessa and Vladivostok, Russia's great southern port cities, are troubled by ice in the winter, though they manage to keep open. (Paradoxically, though Murmansk lies within the Arctic Circle, it is warmed by the Gulf Stream and is completely ice-free as are the Baltic ports.) Given these conditions, it is easy to understand why "with the longest coastline of any country, a maritime, naval or trading tradition has hardly developed."[7] It also helps explain Russia's historic drive for warm-water ports and her particular interest in the Turkish Straits. Given Tsarist Russia's involvement in European trade, a secure outlet to the sea was an economic necessity. As we shall see, the trading pattern and dependence on warm-water ports has been quite different since 1917.

Topography has endowed the USSR with a rather distinctive physical setting. Put very crudely, the central and western portions of the country are an extensive flat plain, only a few hundred feet above sea level. In the south and the east, Russia is bound by high mountains and rugged plateaus. The primary major mountains in the western part of the country are the Urals. Elevations generally no more than two thousand feet (with the greatest heights no more than six thousand feet) offer no barrier to transportation or, should they ever come that far, to invading armies.

This topographic configuration is of the greatest political significance. The presence or absence of natural barriers—oceans or mountains—affect the accessibility of a nation. While easy access may be beneficial to the development of trade and cultural ties, as between the United States and Canada, it could easily become a major liability in time of war. In the Soviet case, access from the south and the east is severely limited by the Black and Caspian Seas, the Caucasus Mountains, the

Hindu Kush Range, the Pamirs, the Tyan Shans, and the Altai, which include ranges reaching elevations well above twenty thousand feet. The largely impassable and forbidding Arctic Circle protects the USSR's northern frontier. In the west, however, especially in the area between the Baltic Sea and the Carpathian Mountains, the great East European plain spills over into the western territories of the Soviet Union—the Baltic States, Byelorussia, and the Ukraine.

The USSR's long border with the rest of Europe lies totally unprotected. As a result of this vulnerability, the western frontier has long been Russia's neuralgic zone. The Kremlin rulers have always been especially concerned that the countries bordering on this area be in friendly hands. This is true for two reasons. First, they border on Russia's most exposed frontier. Second, since the sixteenth century, the technologically more advanced nations of Europe have spawned numerous expansionist leaders—Napoleon and Hitler, to mention the most recent—who have sought to fulfull their ambitions by wresting control of Russian lands.

Thus, of the twelve nations with which the USSR is in direct land contact—Norway, Finland, Poland, Czechoslovakia, Hungary, Rumania, Turkey, Iran, Afghanistan, China, Mongolia, North Korea—the Soviet leaders are especially concerned with those in the west, especially the four East European states and Finland. (The Norwegian border is very small and so far north as to be largely inaccessible to major military activity.) Devoid of any natural barriers, this area has been the major invasion route of countless European armies. On the south and east, with the exception of China, most of Russia's neighbors are both militarily and politically weak and deterred by topographic obstacles from attempting such ventures.

The importance attributed to topography must be qualified somewhat. The significance of natural barriers has been severely diminished by the development in recent years of faster means of transportation and highly sophisticated weaponry. The USSR's frozen arctic frontier is no obstacle at all to American intercontinental missiles. Further, a determined, well-equipped Chinese military force could (and recently did) cause the Kremlin considerable anxiety on her eastern border. (The numerous border conflicts, which exploded into pitched battles in 1969, were political rather than military in nature. Neither side intended to cross the border in force to conquer large sections of "enemy territory.") Nevertheless, given Russia's unfriendly historical environment, her leaders have continued to worry primarily about the need to establish secure and defensible frontiers in the west.

A geographer has observed that Russia's boundaries in this "fracture zone" on its western frontier "have been subject to wide oscillations as major power blocs have shifted in the background." In fact, the precise location of Russia's western border usually indicates its relative international position. From the fourteenth through the seventeenth centuries, and again after the Treaty of Brest–Litovsk in the Soviet period, the country was weak; the border was thus pushed to the east with a powerful

Poland occupying much of what we know today as Byelorussia, the Ukraine and even parts of western Russia proper. In the eighteenth and nineteenth centuries, and again after World War II, when Russia was powerful, the situation was reversed, the boundary again shifted to the west, and these lands were reincorporated into Russia.[9]

Moscow's acute sensitivity to its vulnerability in the west helps explain the harsh character of Soviet behavior toward Finland in the late 1930s. With the rise of Hitler to power in Germany, Stalin grew increasingly concerned with protecting his country's security position. This problem was particularly acute in the northwest. Leningrad, the second largest city in the USSR, its most important seaport, and a major industrial center, was situated only fifteen miles from the Finnish border. Given the fact that Finland and the Baltic states were small, weak and politically hostile to the USSR, Stalin feared that they could become a springboard for a possible German attack.

To protect Russia's former capital, the city of Peter and Lenin, Stalin demanded that the Finns agree to move the frontier back a distance of forty-three miles and to allow the Soviets to establish naval and military bases in the Gulf of Finland and on the mainland. Such actions, claimed the Kremlin leaders, would allow them "to guarantee the sea and land approaches" to Leningrad. When Finland refused to accept the Soviet demand, the Red Army attacked in November, 1939. After some initial difficulties, Soviet forces were victorious. In March, 1940, an armistice was signed which ceded the entire Karelian isthmus including the city of Vyborg to the USSR. As a result, the Soviet–Finnish border was pushed back about one hundred miles from Leningrad. (The Soviet Union also acquired a thirty-year lease on a naval base in the Gulf of Finland.) Thus, to secure greater defense in depth on his exposed northwestern flank, Stalin resorted to force of arms.[10]

In terms of natural resources, the USSR is extremely well endowed. Soviet scientists claim that it contains 58 percent of the world's coal deposits, 58.7 percent of its oil, 41 percent of its iron ore, 25 percent of all timberland, 83 percent of its manganese, 54 percent of its potassium salts, and nearly one-third of its phosphates.[11] However, much of these mineral riches is located east of the Urals, distant from the major industrial users, and often present problems of access. The same situation exists regarding energy supplies. Geographers agree that "the USSR may well have greater total reserves of energy—coal, oil, gas, and water—than any other country."[12] Here, too, the problem is not one of physical scarcity but of conquering vast distances and coordinating the enormous supplies in the east with the needs of the large industrial centers situated mainly in the western regions. Nevertheless, however awkwardly located, whatever the mining difficulties, the high transportation costs, and the less than first-class quality of some of the deposits, "it now appears that the Soviet Union has adequate reserves of virtually all the raw materials needed for modern industry on its own doorstep, which cannot be said for any other country."[13]

Demography

As important as the USSR's physical setting are its human resources. Like size, great numbers can be a rather mixed blessing. A relatively large population is essential to man the economic and military instruments which determine a nation's power. At the same time, enormous numbers can be a major economic burden, as in a country like India where scarce resources must be invested in agriculture so that its ever-growing population has sufficient food to eat. In assessing the strengths and weaknesses of a population base, much depends on the particular demographic mix—the size of the population, distribution, cultural and educational levels, technological skills and cohesiveness.

With its 241.7 million people, according to the 1970 census,[14] the USSR has the third largest population in the world, and easily the largest in Europe. This has been a significant factor in European politics. Though not always the best trained or equipped, the very size of Russia's armies has alone kept Russia among the ranks of the major World Powers. In World War I, for example, Russia's major asset was its huge population which consisted of approximately 171 million people in 1913. (Its nearest European rivals were Germany with 65 million, Austria–Hungary with 50 million, Great Britain, 45 million, and France, 39 million.) Given these enormous numbers, Russia could and did muster huge armies. By the beginning of 1917, her army had 13 million men, a figure representing less than half her 30 million men between the ages of twenty and forty.[15]

Despite these great demographic resources, the USSR today is far below, in numerical terms, what its population should be. Another glance at the figures—170.8 million in 1913 and 241.7 million in 1970, an increase of only 70 million in 57 years—should indicate that something is amiss. In the same period, the population of the United States grew from 97 million in 1913 to over 200 million in 1970, an increase of more than 100 million. The United States has therefore been closing "the population gap." In 1913, Russia's population was 43 percent greater than that of the United States; in 1970 it is only 17 percent greater.[16]

This rapid improvement in the American position is not the result of greater American know-how or fertility but, rather, of catastrophic Russian population losses. Between 1917 and 1957, the USSR lost, according to various estimates, between 48 and 56 million people.[17] "The losses in human lives which the population of the Soviet Union had suffered between 1914–45," according to Richard Pipes, "exceed those of any other people in modern times except European Jewry."[18] It is the estimate of one demographer that "had the 1917 population on what is now Soviet territory increased at the rate of 2 percent a year, which then was the normal rate for a rural country, there would have been 325 million Soviet citizens by 1950; instead there were 178.5 million."[19] Therefore, the USSR has a population deficit of about 150 million people.

The devastation inflicted during the Second World War still exerts a profound impact on Soviet population statistics. The losses were so heavy that the chart used by demographers to show poulation distributions, which is normally shaped like a pyramid, shows deep and irregular indentations. This is particularly true on the male side, as Chart 1 indicates. Of the twenty million killed in World War II, fifteen million were estimated to have been males.[20] According to the most recent census, there were still almost twenty million more women than men in the Soviet population—130,321,000 women as compared to 111,399,000 men. This "sex gap" is wholly in the forty-plus age group where there are 50,448,000 women and 40,416,000 men.[21]

These severe population losses, particularly among the relatively young people of childbearing age, have seriously depressed the Soviet birth rate. Though other factors, including industrialization and urbanization, are involved, the relatively low birth rate is a continuing and in some instances a worsening problem. In fact, in 1968 the crude Soviet birth rate showed an increase of only 2.2 million, smaller than for any other year since 1950.

The current demographic situation has the leadership worried. Soviet demographers share the view that "a country's position in the world, all other things being equal, is determined by its population."[22] They are especially concerned that an inadequate population base will lead to a weakening of the economy. Such, indeed, has begun to occur. As a result of the decline in the Soviet birth rate, the Soviet labor force has been growing very slowly. In 1939, the number of men and women in the twenty-nine to thirty-nine age group was sixty-three million. Twenty years later there were only six million more people who could be included in this age group—an increase of less than 10 percent in twenty years! In 1970, the figure was still only 69 million. There has been no growth in the size of this most productive age group in the Soviet labor force in the past eleven years! The future looks even more bleak. According to one Soviet source, "whereas 35,700,000 were born in the years 1955–1959, 20,800,000 were born in 1965–69. This means that the number of young people entering the work-age group will be considerably greater in 1971–75 than in 1981–85."[23]

The USSR is running short on labor reserves. While the size of the Soviet industrial work force increased by about 20 percent during the Eighth Five-Year Plan (1965–1970)—primarily by attracting older persons and housewives into industry—the Ninth Five-Year Plan (1971–1975) plans an increase of only 4 percent. Therefore, considerable labor shortages are in prospect. Soviet officials calculate that the rise in the number of workers required in the Russian Republic during the Ninth Five-Year Plan "will outstrip the growth of labor reserves . . . by about 20%."[24]

The implications of these acute labor shortages are ominous. Increases in overall Soviet economic growth depend either on growth in the size of the labor force or on increases in the productivity of individual Soviet workers. Faced with the prospect of a declining labor supply in the years ahead, the government has placed great emphasis on the need to

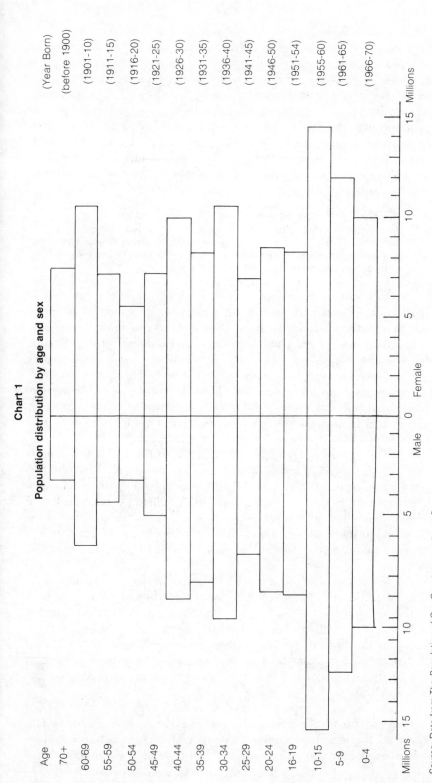

Chart 1

Population distribution by age and sex

Age	(Year Born)
70+	(before 1900)
60-69	(1901-10)
55-59	(1911-15)
50-54	(1916-20)
45-49	(1921-25)
40-44	(1926-30)
35-39	(1931-35)
30-34	(1936-40)
25-29	(1941-45)
20-24	(1946-50)
16-19	(1951-54)
10-15	(1955-60)
5-9	(1961-65)
0-4	(1966-70)

Male   Female

Millions   15   10   5   0   5   10   15   Millions

Source: Data from *The Population of Our Country*, *op. cit.*, p. 5.

improve the efficiency of the current work force. To this end, the Soviet authorities have been waging a vigorous campaign "to strengthen labor discipline." For example, the daily press has been stressing curtailment of absenteeism, reduction of excessive job shifting, and increased diligence on the part of the existing labor force. The Kremlin's effort, begun under Khrushchev, to improve living standards is also geared to increasing labor productivity. As Soviet planners discovered long ago, economic incentives—wages convertible into consumer goods of reasonable quality and variety, better housing and other consumer services—are one of the most effective stimuli to increased labor output. As the Soviet minister for internal trade recently observed:

> The more goods there are in the stores, the wider their assortment and the better their quality . . . the more perceptible the reality of the working people's well-being is, the greater the influence of consumption on the increased productivity of social labor and on a further upsurge in the entire national economy becomes. . . .[25]

In addition, the Soviet authorities clearly hope that accelerated importation of advanced Western technology—as provided for by agreements recently concluded with the United States and a number of countries in Western Europe—will help stimulate labor productivity. Finally, the Kremlin leaders are apparently hopeful of overcoming the existing "unfavorable demographic situation." To this end, "birth rate incentives" —bonuses, special allowances for "heroine mothers"—are being employed. In the words of one Soviet official, "to increase the birth rate is one of our country's urgent problems." Only then, it is suggested, will it be possible to achieve "a more balanced labor situation."[26]

The pattern of population distribution in the USSR also reflects the growing impact of industrialization. The majority of Soviet citizens now live in cities. At present, 136 million people (56 percent) are classified as living in urban areas and only 105.7 million (44 percent) live in rural communities. This represents a major change in the structure of the Soviet population. As recently as 1959—the last census—more than half of the population was classified as rural while in 1939 the figure was 68 percent.[27]

While the absolute and relative weight of the rural population is declining, it is still quite large for modern industrial economy, particularly when compared to that of the United States. In contrast to the Soviet figure of 44 percent, 26.5 percent are considered to live in rural areas in the U.S. Further, of the 77.9 million people employed in the United States, only 3.6 million (about 4.6 percent), work in agriculture, while in the USSR the figure is 26.5 million (25 percent) out of a total labor force of 104.9 million.

As one might expect of a nation so large in expanse, the USSR is not a homogeneous state. Since the growth of the Russian Empire mainly occurred through the accretion of peripheral lands usually peopled by non-Slavic indigenous cultures, the USSR is today a vast multinational state including over two hundred non-Russian nationality groups. According to official census figures, the Soviet population is composed primarily of the following nationalities: Russians, 129 million; Ukrainians, 40.7 million; Uzbeks, 9.1 million; Byelorussians, 9 million; Tatars, 5.9 million; Kazakhs, 5.3 million; Azerbaidjanis, 4.4 million; Armenians, 3.5 million, Georgians, 3.2 million; Moldavians, 2.7 million; Lithuanians, 2.6 million; Jews, 2.2 million; Tadjiks, 2.1 million; Germans, 1.8 million; Chuvash, 1.7 million; Turkmenians, 1.5 million; Kirgiz, 1.5 million; Latvians, 1.4 million, and many other lesser nationalities.[28]

As these figures reveal, about three-quarters of the Soviet population are ethnically Slavic: Russian, Ukrainian, and Byelorussian. However, it is among the Slavs and in the three Baltic republics that the decline in the birth rate is being most sharply felt. In fact, in some areas of the Russian Republic, absolute population is actually beginning to decline. In Central Asia, however, the birth rate is sharply increasing.

Table 1

Births/thousand population (1968)

All-Union	17.3
Russian Republic	14.2
Ukraine	14.9
Byelorussia	16.5
The Five Central Asian Republics	over 30
(Tadjikistan)	37.3

According to 1970 census figures, the population of the Central Asian Republics increased by 40 percent or more between 1959 and 1970, while that of the Russian, Ukrainian and Byelorussian republics increased by about 11 percent, 5 percent below that of the USSR as a whole.[29]

The existence of such nationality diversity, which, at least in numerical terms, is growing, generally has little influence on Soviet economic or military capabilities. In two areas, however, this may prove to be a factor of some importance. First, a far smaller proportion of the population enters the industrial labor force from Central Asia (where the local citizens prefer to stay in the villages) than from the industrialized western regions of the country. Thus, to the extent that an increase in the birth rate is forthcoming, the regions where this will occur, namely Central Asia and the Caucasus, are not expected to contribute a very sizable number of workers to the industrial labor force. Therefore, the prospect of a serious labor shortage looms ahead.

Second, the existence of considerable national diversity raises the specter of lack of internal cohesion, especially during a period of crisis. The Soviet leadership has been very sensitive to this danger. Fearing possible disloyalty during the Second World War, the Volga Germans, the Crimean Tatars, the Chechen-Ingush, the Kalmyks, and other small nationalities were deported en masse from their national territories and dispersed in distant Central Asia. It is reported that more than five million people were victims of Stalin's policy of mass deportation.

The concern of the regime about the threat of divided loyalties has hit the Soviet Jewish population especially hard. Though not the only factor involved, one reason for Moscow's harsh policy toward Israel after 1948, and the stark increase in domestic Soviet anti-Semitism then displayed, was the affection and enthusiasm displayed by many Russian Jews for the newly created state of Israel. The Soviet leadership became increasingly suspicious especially after the first Israeli Ambassador to the USSR, recent Prime Minister Golda Meir, was greeted excitedly by the Jewish populations of Moscow and Leningrad. An unbridled anti-Semite (as his daughter, Svetlana, has confirmed), Stalin became convinced that Soviet Jews were untrustworthy. Further, ties with their numerous brethren abroad (in Israel and in the United States) proved to him that they were potential traitors.

To protect the state against such dangerous influences, Stalin launched a vicious anti-Semitic campaign whose impact reached into the highest echelons of the Soviet literary world and the political leadership itself.[30] Though conditions have dramatically changed, internally and externally, the "anti-Zionist" campaigns of the 1960s and 1970s reflect a similar distrust on the part of the Kremlin toward its Jewish population. Svetlana reports that, as late as 1966, Foreign Minister Gromyko rejected the candidacy of a talented, specially trained young man for a post in the Soviet Embassy in Washington for the sole reason that he was Jewish.[31]

Moscow is also very much concerned about the loyalty of Ukraine. A people with a long and distinctive history, the Ukrainians have, on occasion, demonstrated strivings for greater national autonomy and even for independence. With German help and encouragement, Ukrainian nationalists actually did break away during the Russian Civil War and set up an independent government for a brief time. During those chaotic times, Georgia, Finland and the Baltic States (Estonia, Latvia and Lithuania) also broke away from Moscow's control and established themselves as separate republics. Of these four regions, only Finland managed to retain its independence. Georgia and the Ukraine were reincorporated in the early 1920s, while the Baltic states were retaken just prior to the beginning of the Second World War.

Stalin's apprehension about Ukrainian separatist tendencies was heightened during the early days of the Second World War when considerable numbers of Ukrainians collaborated with the Nazis. According to Khrushchev's speech of February 1956 against Stalin, the latter wanted to "liquidate" the Ukrainian people—as he had other "traitorous" minorities—but he found it too numerous. Fearful that a Ukrainian enclave outside Soviet borders might establish an "independent Ukraine," Stalin forced Czechoslovakia at the end of the war to cede its easternmost territories, populated by Ruthenians who are kinsmen of the Ukrainians. This region was then incorporated into the Ukrainian USSR. During this period, Stalin also reasserted Moscow's control over the Baltic States,

Bessarabia, and Eastern Poland, territories lost during the Civil War (1917–1921). All potential irredentist claims were thus terminated.

In the view of some observers, Soviet national diversity is an important source of weakness. Many Soviet national minorities were incorporated into the Russian Empire as recently as the nineteenth century.[32] Given the surging wave of national consciousness the world over, it would be surprising if they continued to accept complete Russian rule without demanding greater autonomy. However, the Soviet regime has managed to control nationalist aspirations. Though the national minorities have some right of self-regulation—according to the USSR Constitution—the tightly centralized Soviet political system has thus far ensured a high degree of internal cohesion. Where manifestations of "bourgeois nationalism" have appeared (as in Lithuania in the early 1970s), they have thus far been successfully arrested. Nevertheless, Party documents still note the continued existence of "nationalism, chauvinism, and ethnic bigotry," especially among Ukrainians, Georgians, and in the Baltic and Central Asian republics.[33]

Recent events also indicate serious problems regarding the Soviet Jewish population. The Kremlin leaders, sometime probably in 1970, took the unusual step of allowing considerable numbers of Soviet Jews to emigrate. Originally adopted to appease Western public opinion, this Soviet emigration policy has backfired for it has raised Jewish consciousness in the USSR. Between 1971 and 1973, the demand for exit visas grew at a rapid rate. By the end of 1973, approximately 80,000 Jews had left the USSR, mainly for Israel. Thus, though still very much under control, the "nationality problem" in the Soviet Union persists.

One aspect of Soviet population statistics deserves special mention. This relates to the factor of "quality." As a result of its vast population base, Russia historically has been able to field enormous armies; yet Moscow has found it very difficult to translate this into military advantage. In 1904–1905, the numerically superior Russians were defeated by tiny Japan. Again during the First World War, despite its need to fight both in the east, against Russia, and in the west, against France and England, Imperial Germany defeated the considerably larger Russian forces.

Despite its numerical superiority, Russia's armies were of limited military effectiveness. Moscow found it very difficult to supply and feed its troops during World War I; only half the total manpower available was called to arms. Furthermore, such forces as were mobilized were poorly supplied and equipped. Fighting often without rifles or even sidearms, the Russian infantry employed a "human wave" offensive, hoping thereby to inundate enemy forces. Such tactics were of little avail and resulted in enormous casualty figures.[34]

The internal disintegration of the Russian Empire contributed to the poor showing of the Russian armies. The Tsarist autocracy, which was to crack under the strain in February–March 1917, simply proved unable to supply and equip its armies and to feed its population. By 1916, large segments of the diverse but overwhelmingly peasant army lost their will to fight. Hearing reports of chaotic conditions and dire food shortages in the cities and the villages, many simply quit the front and tried to make their way home.

The situation was vastly different in World War II when Soviet forces fought extremely well. Though often fighting under extremely difficult circumstances, the Red Army did not crack. Only a relatively small number proved disloyal. In the defense of Leningrad, and in the battles of Moscow, Kursk, and Stalingrad, Soviet troops fought valiantly and victoriously. Nazi armies seized much of Russia's industrial and agricultural heartland, killed or captured millions of Russian soldiers and civilians, and reached the gates of Leningrad, Moscow, and Stalingrad; yet in June, 1945, a Soviet general controlled Berlin.

How can the difference in outcome be explained? While important economic changes had taken place since the revolution, and Russia's industrial base in 1941 was far larger than it had been in 1914, economic considerations were not decisive. In fact, especially in the early period of the Second World War, shortages of munitions and equipment often plagued Soviet commanders who, ordered by Stalin not to retreat, again used the human assault tactics of the First World War—with similarly disastrous results.[35]

The difference in performance and outcome is best explained by the qualitative changes which had occurred within the Soviet population since the revolution. Through the application of both persuasion and coercion, the Soviet authorities led by Stalin integrated the diverse population of the USSR as perhaps never before in history. Using a vastly expanded educational system, a sophisticated indoctrination machine, and the totalitarian political instruments created for this purpose, Kremlin authorities by the 1930s had provided an effective government and a high degree of national unity. National and patriotic sentiments, which had been manipulated by the regime to bind the nation together during the stresses of the industrialization and collectivization drives of the 1930s, were cultivated with renewed vigor during the war. Stressing the expolits of national heroes such as Peter the Great and of Tsarist generals such as Suvorov and Kutuzov, achieving a *modus vivendi* with the Orthodox Church, and emphasizing the need to save the nation and repel the Nazi invaders from Russia's soil, Stalin successfully transformed the struggle against Germany into "the Great Fatherland War," as it is still known in Soviet textbooks.

In 1914, as Richard Pipes has observed, a large proportion of Russia's rural population "lacked an elementary sense of citizenship or of national identity. Some peasants even wondered in August 1914 whether the declaration of war affected their villages."[36] Thus, when Bolshevik agitators later urged the overwhelmingly peasant army to desert the ranks and head back to the villages, there was little sense of national identity or patriotic sentiment to which the government could appeal. By 1941, the country had been sufficiently integrated, politically and socially, for Stalin to capitalize successfully on the genuine national upsurge which the Nazi invasion evoked and to galvanize the Soviet peoples into a disciplined, resourceful and militarily effective fighting force.

Since 1945, this situation has further improved. The factors assumed to create increased social cohesion and vitality—level of education, rising living standards, a balanced and integrated economic, transportation, and communications system—have grown enormously in recent decades. In regard to changes in educational levels, the figures in the chart below are most instructive.

Table 2

	1928		1966	
Percent Literate	49.8		99.6	
Total School Enrollment (per capita)	12,592,000	(.08)	50,208,000	(.21)
Primary School Enrollment (per capita)	10,981,000	(.07)	41,371,000	(.18)
Secondary School Enrollment (per capita)	1,354,000	(.008)	4,623,000	(.019)
University Enrollment (per capita)	257,000	(.002)	4,214,000	(.018)

Source: Reprinted from *Cross-Polity Time Series Data,* by Arthur S. Banks by permission of The M.I.T. Press, Cambridge, Massachusetts. Copyright © 1971 by The M.I.T. Press.

The population is more highly educated than ever, particularly in the non-Slavic areas. In Central Asia, where cultural and educational standards have historically been extremely low, large elements of these populations have since 1917 been brought up to a level comparable to nation-wide standards.[37] In the area of the five Central Asian Republics, there were only 136,000 pupils in primary and secondary schools in 1914–1915, representing less than 0.5 percent of the total student population of 9.6 million in all Russia. By 1955–1956, enrollment was up to 3.59 million, an increase of more than twenty-five times, which was equal to about 13 percent of the total student enrollment for these grades (or about the same proportion of the population of Central Asia as of the Soviet population as a whole.)[38] The literacy rate (which in Tadjikistan was 4 percent in 1926) is now considered close to 100 percent.

In some societies, the rise of educational and cultural standards has created serious problems and generated social tensions. In the USSR, expansion of educational opportunities has helped integrate Soviet society. Soviet technicians and engineers, who are often one or perhaps two generations off the farm, tend overwhelmingly to identify with the system which gave them opportunities for social advancement. This is especially true in the minority regions. Given recent improvement in the physical environment—rising living standards, improved housing, expansion of cultural facilities in the rural areas—it would be fair to conclude that Soviet society as a whole—its workers and peasants, its educated cadres, its consumers and national minorities—are more cohesively united than ever before. Though there are indications of grievances and even disaffection among certain minority groups, as noted earlier, and, to some degree, among elements within the scientific and creative intelligentsia, the

Soviet population as a whole strongly indentifies with and supports its political leadership. Soviet collapse from within, often predicted by outside observers, seems increasingly remote.

Economic Capabilities

The pattern of Soviet economic growth

In early 1940, Benito Mussolini observed that "in spite of her extent and her population, Russia is not a power but a weakness."[39] This remark, while undoubtedly self-serving, reflected an assessment of the USSR's military power then generally accepted throughout Europe. Badly beaten in World War I, severely bled during the Civil War, tormented by major social turmoil accompanying the 1917 Revolution and the great social transformations of the 1930s (the Five Year Plan, collectivization of agriculture, and the Great Purge), Russia, it was assumed, could not survive a major assault.

The Soviet leaders, in the late 1920s, were themselves very concerned about the military and economic situation in which they found themselves. For Stalin, weakness had dire political implication. "In our times," he wrote in 1934, "it is not the custom to give any consideration to the weak—consideration is only to the strong."[40] Power, in his view, was the key to Russia's past and Russia's future. The country's long history of suffering at the hands of foreigners, he observed in 1931, was the result of weakness. Old Russia, he noted, was continually beaten—by the Mongols, the Turks, the Swedes, the Poles, the Lithuanians, the French, the British, the Japanese—because of her backwardness.

> Such is the law of the exploiters—to beat the backward and the weak. It is the jungle law of capitalism. You are backward, you are weak—therefore you are wrong; hence, you can be beaten and enslaved. You are mighty—therefore you are right; hence, we must be wary of you. That is why we must no longer lag behind.[41]

To end Russia's weakness and backwardness and to provide the USSR with the strength to protect its basic security interests, Stalin decided upon a program of rapid industrialization. "We are fifty or one hundred years behind the advanced countries," he declared. "We must make good this distance in ten years. Either we do it, or we shall be crushed."[42]

The famous Five-Year Plans, first inaugurated in 1928, were designed to make the USSR competitive—to transform this relatively backward, overwhelmingly peasant nation into an economically self-sufficient and technologically advanced industrial power. Stalin assumed that political power on the world scene was a function of economic and military strength and that the latter depended largely on the former. To create a powerful economic base for the Soviet military machine, the Kremlin leaders launched their program of forced march industrialization.

While Stalin's task was considerable, too much can be made of Russia's backwardness. It would be a mistake to assume that the Communists in 1917 had taken over a wholly underdeveloped and illiterate country with a stagnant economy. Though it developed very slowly in some years, pre-1917 Russian industrial output grew rapidly in others. From 1891 to 1900, for example, industrial production more than doubled. (In 1900, Russia's oil production was the highest in the world.) According to Soviet estimates, during the fifty-year period 1860–1910, the world's industrial production increased by a factor of six; that of Great Britain increased only two and one-half times, Germany by six, and Russia by ten.[43]

Though her industrial growth compared favorably to that of her main rivals, Russian industry was still woefully inadequate. As the following table indicates, the pre-1914 industrial economy was still far below the level of the other major powers.

Table 3

Comparative industrial production (1913)

	Russia	USA	UK
Electricity (billion Kilowatts)	2.0	25.8	4.7
Coal (million tons)	29.2	517.8	292.0
Oil (million tons)	10.3	34.0	—
Pig Iron (million tons)	4.2	31.5	10.4
Steel (million tons)	4.3	31.8	7.8
Cotton Textiles (billion meters)	1.9	5.7	7.4

Source: *Promyshlennost' SSSR* (Moscow: 1964), pp. 112 –116; reproduced in Alec Nove, *An Economic History of the USSR* (London: Allen Lane, The Penguin Press, 1969), p. 14.

Despite considerable efforts and real economic growth, Moscow did not make much headway in her efforts to catch up with the advanced countries. In the fifty years from 1860 to 1910, Russia's industrial performance fell to tenth place among the major Western industrial powers, behind that of Spain and Italy.

Thus, though relatively weak industrially, Russia was still a ranking World Power in 1913, capable of competing economically and militarily with at least some of her rivals of the time—especially Austria–Hungary and the Ottoman Empire. However, during the First World War and the years of the Civil War, the country suffered enormous destruction. By the time the first Five-Year Plan began in 1928, the economy had just barely recovered to its prewar levels.

Through a costly and sometimes bloody process, Soviet industry was greatly expanded and modernized during the first two Five-Year Plans and agriculture was collectivized. Between 1928 and 1940, Soviet industrial production grew between 250 and 450 percent with the Soviet Gross National Product increasing at about 12 percent a year. Soviet achievements under the prewar Five-Year Plans are indicated by the following table:

Table 4

The growth of Soviet heavy industry (1913–1940)

	1913	1921	1928	1940
Steel (million metric tons)	4.2	.2	4.2	18.3
Coal (million metric tons)	29.1	9.5	35.5	165.9
Oil (million metric tons)	9.2	3.8	11.6	31.1
Cement (million metric tons)	1.8	.1	1.9	5.7
Electricity (billion kilowatt hours)	2.0	.5	5.0	48.3

Source: Harry Schwartz, *An Introduction to the Soviet Economy* (Columbus, Ohio: Charles E. Merrill Publishing Co., 1968), p. 21.

Despite these enormous efforts and the great progress achieved, the USSR in 1941 was economically and militarily weaker than its Nazi attackers. Key Soviet industries were in the exposed western portion of the country; the eastern territories were still industrially underdeveloped. In addition, the USSR's defense industry had been particularly hard hit by Stalin's political purges of the 1930s. Numerous first-rate military planners, designers, and managers were imprisoned and executed and many of their replacements were not qualified. The affairs of the defense industry were so poorly managed that important decisions were made slowly and then were often wrong-headed. As a result of managerial incompetence, Red Army forces began the war with obsolete planes and tanks and grave shortages of automatic weapons and anti-tank guns.[44]

Germany thus began the war with considerable advantages. In addition, it swiftly occupied vast territories in the western parts of the country which contained most of the USSR's industrial plants. Nevertheless the Soviet Union succeeded in producing the military wherewithal necessary to defeat the Germans. By large-scale redeployment of plants to the the Urals, strictly centralized direction of both materials and manpower, and considerable improvisation, the arms industry turned out sufficient tanks, planes and guns to equip the Red Army.[45] The industrial achievements of wartime Russia match the heroic performance of the Red Army, and were the foundation for the USSR's triumph. The Soviet Union produced the bulk of its own war materials, most of which, especially its tanks, were more than a match for the Germans. The vast majority of the best weapons were of Soviet manufacture. Western military assistance (mainly through American Lend–Lease) supplied mainly road transport, especially automobiles, but comparatively few armaments.[46]

Paradoxically, the eventual victory of the Red Army was, in some measure at least, a function of Russia's backwardness. As the military historian Basil Liddell Hart has written, the country's primitiveness, the "toughness of her people and soldiers—their capacity to endure hardships and shortages that would have been paralyzing to Western peoples and Western armies" was a very important factor in determining the war's final outcome. "A greater asset still," he notes,

... was the primitiveness of the Russian roads. Most of them were no better than sandy tracks. The way they dissolved into bottomless mud, when it rained, did more to check the German invasion than all the Red Army's heroic sacrifices. If the Soviet regime had given Russia a road system comparable to that of Western countries, she would have been overrun almost as quickly as France.[47]

Furthermore, though only rarely and grudgingly recognized by Soviet sources, the military activities of the Western Allies helped contribute in various ways to the final Soviet victory. For example, although the Anglo-American bombing campaign in 1943 and 1944 failed to disrupt German war production as had initially been hoped, its most important effect was to "draw off an increasingly large part of the German air force from the Eastern front to the Western thus aiding the Soviet advance."[48]

Though victory was achieved, the economic and human costs of the war were extremely heavy. In addition to the twenty million deaths mentioned previously, the Soviet industrial plant was shattered. The western half of European Russia and virtually all the Ukraine and Byelorussia were devastated. Official Soviet sources list the following statistics on material damages resulting from the war: 1,700 towns and 70,000 villages destroyed; over 6,000,000 buildings gutted; more than 31,000 industrial enterprises demolished; 1,000 coal mines and 300 oil wells ruined.[49] Furthermore, destruction of livestock, farm equipment, railway machinery, bridges and other facilities of the civilian economy was enormous.

Despite the severely damaged and physically exhausted state of the country at the war's end, Stalin quickly turned the Soviet people to the task of rebuilding the country's economic base. As he declared in his famous "Election Speech" early in 1946, the immediate aim of his regime was "to rehabilitate the ravaged areas of the country, to restore the pre-war levels in industry and agriculture, and to surpass this level in more or less substantial measure."[50] Stalin's policy was successful; in the period from 1946 to 1950, the Soviet economy by and large succeeded in reconstructing the productive capacity of basic Soviet industry. Industrial progress in these difficult years is indicated by the following performance record:

Table 5

Soviet industrial productivity, 1940–1950

	1940	1950
Steel (million tons)	18.3	27.3
Oil (million tons)	31.1	37.9
Coal (million tons)	166.0	261.1
Electricity (billion kilowatts)	48.3	91.2
Machine tools (thousands)	58.4	70.6

Source: Compiled from table in *Kommunist*, No. 11, 1967; reproduced in Nove, *op. cit.*, p. 387.

As the table indicates, recovery in heavy industry was substantially completed by 1950. However, in light and consumer goods industries and in agriculture recovery took substantially longer. In favoring heavy industry, Stalin continued to operate on the basis of the original priorities which underlay his industrialization drive: to strengthen the sinews of national power. Thus, 87.9 percent of industrial investments in 1945 through 1950 were given over to the producers' goods sector of the economy with only 12.1 percent to light and food industries.[51] The fate of the Soviet consumer in this difficult early postwar period was especially grim. In agriculture, for example, per capita grain output in 1952 barely reached 1928 figures, while livestock output was well below that level. Considering that even before the war the Russian diet was one of the poorest in Europe and that urban housing was now one-fifth of what it had been in the 1920s, the lot of the average Russian citizen was bleak.

Recent Soviet economic performance

As has often been noted, Stalin's post-war economic objectives were more than fulfilled. The seemingly high industrial targets set in 1946 to be achieved by 1960 were met. And, for that matter, in the years since Stalin's death the consumer has received an increasing share of the growing economic pie.

Table 6

Stalin's postwar economic objectives and attainments

	1945	1960 (estimate)	1960 (actual)
Steel (million tons)	12.25	60	65
Coal (million tons)	149.3	500	513
Oil (million tons)	19.4	60	148

Source: Nove, *op. cit.*, p. 290.

The overall achievements of the Soviet economy can best be appreciated by examining recent levels of accomplishment and comparing Soviet with U.S. economic performance. The Soviet economy is the second largest in the world, some two and one-half times that of Japan. According to a recent study, the total dollar value of the Soviet Gross National Product (GNP) is about $365 billion, or approximately 47 percent of the U.S. level. (Given its larger population base, however, the Soviet position is considerably poorer in per capita terms.)[52]

Table 7

USSR and selected market economies, comparative gross national product in 1967 (1966 U.S. dollars)

Ranked by Total GNP (billions)		Ranked by GNP per capita	
US	$777	US	$3,902
USSR	365	Germany	2,377
Japan	153	France	2,293
Germany	142	UK	2,092
UK	116	USSR	1,552
France	114	Japan	1,530
Italy	78	Italy	1,482

Source: Stanley H. Cohn, "General Growth Performance of the Soviet Economy," *Economic Performance and The Military Burden in the Soviet Union*, Joint Economic Committee, Congress of the United States Washington: GPO, 1970, p. 13.

The changes which have taken place in the relationship of the Soviet economy to that of the United States can be roughly summarized in the following table:

Table 8

USSR and United States: comparative trends in GNP (in billions of 1966 U.S. dollars)

	1950	1955	1958	1960	1965	1967	1968	1969
US	414	508	519	565	711	777	815	838
USSR	140	185	230	253	326	365	386	395
Difference	275	322	289	312	385	412	417	443
USSR as % of US	33.8	36.4	44.3	44.8	45.8	47.0	47.4	47.1

Source: Cohn, *op. cit.*, p. 14.

Thus, in its proportion of the United States economy, the USSR has apparently come from about 34 percent in 1950 to around 45 to 47 percent. While the relationships between the economies seem to have stabilized during the 1960s, the absolute margin of the U.S. economy over the Soviet has been steadily widening.

In absolute terms, Soviet economic progress has been considerable. This is particularly true in industry where output over the past two decades has been most impressive. While the Soviet economy as a whole is much smaller than that of the United States, this is less true for the industrial sector. Here the USSR in some instances actually leads the U.S. The striking progress in this area is a result of deliberate policy. Today, as under Stalin, heavy industry receives the lion's share of the funds invested in industry as a whole. In October, 1967, the Soviet leaders began to reverse fields somewhat when they announced that the rate of growth planned for consumer goods in 1968 would be slightly larger than that for heavy industry: 8.6 percent to 7.9 percent. In absolute terms, however, heavy industry remained favored by a large margin —planned goals for 1970 came to 250 billion rubles of output for producers' goods compared with 100 billion for consumers' goods.[53]

Continuous attention to heavy industry has paid off dramatically. The following statistics indicate the striking progress achieved by Soviet industry since the first Five-Year Plans.

Table 9

Soviet industrial growth, 1928–1966

	1928	1940	1950	1960	1966
Steel (million tons)	4.3	18.3	27.3	65.3	96.9
Oil (million tons)	11.6	31.1	37.9	147.9	265.1
Coal (million tons)	35.5	166.0	261.1	509.6	585.6
Electricity (billion kilowatt hours)	5.0	48.3	91.2	292.3	544.6
Gas (billion cubic meters)	0.3	3.4	6.2	47.2	144.7
Machine Tools (thousands)	2.0	58.4	70.6	155.9	192.1
Motor Vehicles (thousands)	0.8	145.4	362.9	523.6	675.2
Tractors (thousands)	1.3	31.6	116.7	238.5	382.5
All fabrics (billion meters)	3.0	4.5	4.5	8.2	9.4
Leather footwear (million pairs)	58	211	203	419	522
Radios (thousands)	—	160	1072	4165	5842
Television sets (thousands)	—	6.3	11.9	1726	4412
Domestic refrigerators (thousands)	—	3.5	1.2	529	2205

Source: *Kommunist*, No. 11, 1967, compiled from Nove, *op. cit.*, p. 387. Taken from an article celebrating the fiftieth anniversary of the Bolshevik revolution, these figures tend to highlight the fastest growing sectors.

Though industrial growth continues at a significant rate, the early expansion rate of 12 percent a year has fallen off considerably in recent years. In the immediate post-war period, the considerable growth rate of 7 to 8 percent a year was achieved. By the late 1950s, growth rates began to fall more sharply. In the six-year period ending with 1964, aggregate outputs rose at an annual rate of 5 to 6 percent. The Soviet economy therefore suffered about a one-fifth to one-fourth decline in its rate of expansion. In fact, the overall rate of growth in recent years is generally lower than at any time since the Five-Year Plans began in 1928 (excluding the war years).

Table 10

USSR: percentage of growth rates of gross national product for selected years, 1950–1969

1959 ....4.5	1967 ....4.9	
1960 ....5.1	1968 ....5.8	
1961 ....6.3	1969 ....2.3(preliminary)	
1962 ....3.3		
1963 ....2.2	1951–55 ....5.9	
1964 ....7.6	1956–60 ....6.5	
1965 ....5.5	1960–65 ....5.0	
1966 ....5.4	1966–69 ....4.8	

Source: Cohn, *op. cit.*, p. 9.

Fluctuations in growth rates are explained by several factors. First, the sharp drop in rates of expansion which occurred in the 1960s (1963, 1965, 1967, 1969) is the result, in considerable measure, of serious crop failures. The poor harvest of 1972, in which grain production fell almost 30 million tons below target, caused a decline in the overall economic growth rate to its lowest point in ten years—since the catastrophic crop failure of 1963.[54] In 1973, when a record grain harvest of 222.5 million tons helped boost total agricultural production by 14 percent over the dismal 1972 levels, Soviet industrial production increased markedly (7.4 percent).[55] This pattern reflects the continued importance of agriculture in the Soviet economy. Employing about one-quarter of the total labor force, agriculture accounts for over one-fifth of the GNP—a disproportionately large figure for a modern, industrialized economy. Poor performance in agriculture seriously affects the general health of the economy.[56]

A second factor, one closer to our immediate concerns, relates to Soviet defense expenditures. Though there is some uncertainty about the precise nature of the processes involved, most economists agree that there is an inverse correlation between overall economic growth level and the size of the Soviet military budget. That is to say, the larger the share of investment funds going to defense, the slower the rate of economic growth. This pattern seems to be confirmed by the Soviet experience of the 1950s and 1960s. As the figures below indicate, the rapid economic growth of the 1950s seemed directly related to high levels of capital investment and low defense expenditures. During the 1960s when capital investment figures declined and the size of the defense budget increased, growth rates tended to fall.[57]

Table 11

Growth trends in capital investment and defense allocations (average annual rates in percent)

	Capital Investment	Defense	GNP
1951–55	12.5	5.5	5.8
1956–60	12.8	.4	6.5
1961–65	6.3	8.5	5.2
1966–67	7.9	7.9	5.6

Source: Derived from Cohn, *op. cit.*, p. 10. According to this source, "no other major economy has increased rates for defense expenditures at the rate of the Soviet Union between 1960 and 1965."

Increases in military spending are seen to affect overall growth in two ways. First, high investment in defense (and in recent years in consumer goods) means resources are being drained away from producers' goods, the sector of the economy generally considered the most productive of long-term growth. Investment shortfalls in producers' goods, combined with other problems such as the relatively low growth of labor productivity and continued reliance on obsolete equipment, have all contributed to a decline in growth rates. This has even affected heavy industry, normally the most rapidly growing sector of the economy. Expansion of industrial output fell from 10 percent a year in 1967, to 8.1 percent in 1968, to 7 percent in 1969.[58]

The second factor explaining the negative correlation between overall growth rates and the size of the military budget is qualitative rather than quantitative. Intensive Soviet defense activities imposes great demands on Soviet scientific and technological manpower. In particular, it concentrates the innovative energies of engineers, scientists, and managers on military rather than civilian production. While the total number of engineers graduated since 1960 has risen by 83 percent, the growth rate of specialties related to defense has been considerably more rapid (electrical engineering and electro-instrument making, 306 percent; radio technology and communications, 151 percent) and the defense industry has received the most talented of the skilled personnel available as well as first call on all raw material resources.[59]

This situation has an obvious impact on the civilian economy. Aggregation of the country's most highly educated and skilled manpower, its scarce capital, most modern equipment and managerial and technological resources in the defense sector works a strongly negative influence on the civilian economy. As much was admitted by Premier Kosygin when he declared in 1971 that shortcomings in the Soviet economic activity during the Eighth Five-Year Plan Period (1966–1970) were the results of "a certain diversion of resources and manpower" which had been required by the need to take "additional measures in the field of defense."[60]

The problems created by high levels of military spending are particularly serious for the USSR where, according to a Soviet military analyst, "the state is compelled to allocate extensive resources to defense."[61] Although the Soviet government remains rather shy about revealing the full extent of its military expenditures—the announced budget of the Soviet Ministry of Defense for 1974 was only 17.6 billion rubles (23.5 billion dollars), or just over one-quarter of the 85.2 billion dollar budget of the U.S. Defense Department—most analysts agree that actual Soviet defense outlays are equal, in relative if not absolute terms, to those of the United States. (According to a Soviet economist, 40 percent of the Soviet economy is either controlled by military agencies or harnessed in one way or another to the defense sector.)[62] Such circumstances clearly hinder balanced economic development. In fact, according to official Soviet sources, American imperialist circles have in the past hoped to use the arms race to "bankrupt Russia."[63] Thus, though obviously a highly treasured asset internationally, Soviet military power has been a considerable burden to the economy as a whole.

Problems of organization and innovation

The very striking achievements in the Soviet economy during the last forty years are, in considerable measure, attributable to its system of organization. Virtually all economic activity in the USSR, from the production of sugar beets to the development of computers, is subject to centralized direction and control. Each sphere has its own five-year and one-year plans with goals, resources, and personnel allocated by central directive agencies, mainly the State Planning Committee (Gosplan), according to basic economic policy decisions made by the leadership of the Communist Party. Furthermore, the centralized political apparatus of the Communist Party and the economic ministries of the government also supervise the management of the economy to ensure that party policies and economic plans are actually being implemented.

The highly centralized nature of economic planning and management has allowed the USSR to achieve its basic objective—rapid economic growth especially in the production of capital goods—with striking speed. Though not without serious problems, a system of centralized decision-making greatly facilitates economic mobilization. A planned economy, reinforced by a centralized political apparatus, can more easily allocate manpower and material resources to heavy and defense-related industries than an unplanned, decentralized economy. Not only can energies and resources be better coordinated when decisions are centralized but resistance or opposition to such policies is less likely (particularly if, as during the early Five-Year Plans, the Communist Party and the secret police are used to discourage recalcitrants).

It was largely as a result of central planning that the USSR was able during the Second World War to deal with the gigantic problems of converting its economy to a wartime footing. As Alec Nove has pointed out:

> Mobilization for war was extremely thorough. Control over all resources was very strictly centralized, and both materials and labor were directed to serve the war effort to a degree unknown elsewhere. In 1940, 15 percent of the national income was devoted to "military purposes." In 1942 the figure had risen to 55 percent, perhaps the highest ever reached anywhere.[64]

Centralization was essential in all warring countries in order to mobilize resources effectively; it was absolutely vital in the USSR to help overcome the crippling economic losses of the first months of the war and to carry out the remarkable expansion of industrial production in the Urals.

Though very effective in achieving swift results during the early stages of industrialization, the USSR's highly centralized command economy has proved less than efficient in recent years. Centralized decisions facilitate the mobilization of resources and increase efficiency when the economy they guide is relatively small and uncomplicated. However, a large, complex, developed economy requires sophisticated planning and management. According to the Czech economist Ota Sik, a highly industrialized country like that of Czechoslovakia produces about one and one half million separate items which have to be taken into account by planners. However, he observed, during the peak years of centralization, the planning agencies had been able to include only a thousand to twelve hundred categories or articles in their calculations.[65] As diligent and resourceful as they may be, the central planners in Moscow can only deal in broad aggregates; they cannot allocate resources and coordinate supply and demand for all items in the economy. As a result of central planning, the economy suffers chronic imbalances, oversupply in some areas, shortages in others, and disequilibrium throughout.

The generally glowing accounts appearing in the Soviet press to the contrary notwithstanding, the Kremlin leaders are very much concerned with the inefficiencies and cumbersomeness of their economic system and the enormous waste of resources it continually engenders. (Prime Minister Kosygin did somewhat shyly note that during the Eighth Five-Year Plan, the Soviet economy suffered some "difficulties and shortcomings."[66]) In an attempt to deal with such problems, they have occasionally contemplated (though have never implemented) plans for some measure of economic decentralization.[67] The Kremlin leaders are particularly concerned that the Soviet economy be made more efficient, that high growth rates be sustained, and, above all, that it be modernized and kept competitive with the larger, more sophisticated economy of the United States.

In this regard, the Soviet leaders have in recent years been paying particular attention to what they refer to as "the scientific and technological revolution." In their view, improvement in both production techniques and more efficient management of the economy can directly contribute to higher growth rates. Through the introduction of modern methods and vigorous application of the results of scientific research, according to one official source, national income in some capitalist countries has increased by as much as 50 percent.[68] This, clearly, is a model to be emulated. Further, the "scientific and technological revolution" is also regarded as having potential political significance, particularly in terms of world-wide rivalry between the Soviet Union and the United States. As one Soviet analyst recently observed, "states having outstripped other countries in terms of industrial or scientific-technological development receive, by virtue of this one fact, not a few serious advantages in this competition."[69]

Moscow's continued stress on "the scientific and technological revolution" reflects the obvious but very painful fact that the USSR is in many sectors a technologically underdeveloped society. This is obviously not true of defense-related industries, where resources and scientific talent are concentrated. In nonmilitary sectors of the economy, however, the evidence of backwardness is overwhelming.

This is especially true in the countryside where, for example, the absence of an effective road system virtually paralyzes transportation during part of each year. The roads in the agricultural regions of the country are so poorly developed that during the spring thaws they become virtually impassable. As a result, children often cannot be transported to rural schools and mail is not delivered. In order to protect such roads as do exist from the annual onslaught of mud, the officials of Ivanovo province (200 miles northeast of Moscow) not long ago prohibited all traffic by heavy trucks and kept all other vehicles under a thirty-mile-an-hour speed limit. As a result, a forty mile trip on a good road took visitors about an hour and a half.[70]

The backwardness of the Soviet countryside can also be seen from the unusually large number of people which is required to produce a sufficient food supply. In the United States, just over 3.5 million people (less than 4 percent of the labor force) more than meet domestic needs while the 26.5 million collective and state farmers (24 percent of the total number of Soviet workers) fulfill their planned objectives only erratically. The disparity in performance is largely the result of the vastly greater labor productivity of the American farmer, a product of the far higher level of mechanization of U.S. agriculture, more sophisticated use of fertilizers and irrigation, and a much more effective system of economic incentives.

Soviet technological underdevelopment is also revealed in the fact that the USSR has not been able to produce advanced products capable of competing effectively on the world market. Soviet industrial and consumer goods are often of such poor quality that they simply are not competitive.[71] Moscow's inability to sell its goods in foreign markets reflects the technological backwardness of the Soviet civilian economy. It has been estimated that the overall technological level of the Soviet industrial economy in 1962 lagged on the average twenty-five years behind that of the United States; in some areas it was as much as forty years behind; in a few other, only five to seven years. As a result—and even Soviet official statistics admit this—output per worker in the USSR was only 40 to 50 percent of the United States level in 1963.[72] This "productivity gap" is largely the result of technological backwardness and the use of obsolete production processes. Given lower worker productivity and reliance on outdated techniques—a famous Soviet economist is quoted as having said that "approximately half of Soviet research discoveries are obsolescent by the time of their development"[73]—it is little wonder that Soviet goods are not competitive.

While this technological lag characterizes all but a few priority industries—in high speed aviation, rocketry, atomic power, and certain sections of the machine tool, iron and steel industries the USSR is as advanced or almost as advanced as the West[74]—it is especially true in the production and the utilization of computers. A recent report notes that there were 5,500 or 6,000 computers in the Soviet Union as against 24,000 in Western Europe and 63,000 in the United States. Not only does the USSR have far fewer computers but those they do have are less sophisticated than those operating in the U.S. Thus, the computers on Soviet spacecraft, presumably the very best available, are said to perform about 100,000 operations a second, while American spaceborne computers work at 500,000 to a million operations a second.[75]

Why this "technological gap"? Why is the economy of the USSR so backward? The lag is not due to lack of attention. The Kremlin devotes almost as much of its national product and its labor force to research and development as does the United States, while Western Europe lags far behind. A prime cause of the Soviet Union's relative technological backwardness is, in the judgment of most specialists, the centrally planned economic mechanism. Despite feverish efforts to stimulate technological development, "the centrally administered Soviet economy has no spontaneous mechanism that operates automatically to spur technological progress in the way that profit-seeking competition does, however imperfectly, in the West."[76] Instead of stimulating productivity, the bureaucratic planning mechanism and the centralized system of economic and political controls seem to deter innovation, to hinder rather than promote progress.[77]

Another factor retarding progress is the rigid compartmentalization of military and state activities from the civilian economy. Partly as a matter of secrecy and partly as a result of the great technological gap between them, the two economic sectors are virtually isolated one from the other. What this means is that the Soviets do not even attempt to apply new processes and products developed in the space program to the civilian economy.[78] (In the U.S., the civilian electronics, television, telephone, and numerous other industries have directly benefitted from space technology.) Given the talented personnel and special research and development facilities of the defense industries, a potentially important source of technological advancements for the civilian economy is ignored. The overall situation was aptly depicted by Zbigniew Brzezinski when he observed: "Whether it is a matter of computers, or transistors, or lasers, or pulsars, or plastic, or—equally important—management techniques, or the psychology of labor relations, or sociology, or economic theory, or systems analysis, the Soviet lag is unmistakable."[79]

Conclusion

The total picture of nonmilitary capability resources can be outlined as follows. In geographic and demographic terms, the position of the USSR is a strong one. It is a vast country, with well-protected borders, save on the west, whose enormous territories are relatively well-integrated by an extensive network of railways and airlines. In terms of raw materials and energy resources, the Soviet position is extremely good. While the United States must import such vital items as oil, manganese, chrome, and tin, the USSR is virtually self-sufficient in industrial raw materials. Demographically, the situation is also basically strong. The Soviet population is sizable, easily the largest in Europe, increasingly well-educated, and politically and socially cohesive. In terms of both size and technological sophistication, it is adequate to the task of maintaining and equipping large fighting forces with the most up-to-date weaponry.

Resources and talents seem to run thin in the civilian economy, however. The problem seems to be shortages of both skilled and unskilled manpower. The demographic catastrophes of the Soviet period have obviously created serious problems. Given a falling off of birth rates, Soviet industry will have a declining work force for the next two decades at least.

The pressures to tighten labor discipline so as to increase the productivity of the existing resources have begun to increase sharply.[80]

The economy, too, should be considered a major asset. The decision to concentrate resources and energies on rapid industrialization and to defer satisfaction of immediate consumer needs—a decision taken and sustained by a small political elite and forcibly imposed on the rest of the population—has resulted in the creation of the second largest industrial economy in the world. Further, the USSR is the equal of the United States in scientific and industrial areas related to defense. Nevertheless, the economy does have certain problems which could influence foreign policy behavior. Let me briefly mention just three: agriculture, the unevenness of overall economic growth, and technological under-development.

The weakness of Soviet agriculture is a special problem for the USSR because it plays a disproportionately large role in the Soviet economic picture. Agriculture has long been the single weakest sector of the economy. For example, during the twenty-five years of Stalin's rule, per capita production of agriculture actually declined. (Between 1928 and 1953, agricultural output increased by 10 percent but the population grew by 25 percent.) Since 1953, production per capita has been expanding at the rate of about 1 percent a year.[81] Given the continued importance of agriculture, serious crop failures, as in 1963 and 1972, gravely affect the economy as a whole. To protect against famine, major quantities of wheat have had to be imported from capitalist countries. (Despite imports, shortages in 1963 and 1965 were so bad that there was difficulty in supplying bread and flour and some agricultural areas became short of food.)

The lack of agricultural self-sufficiency and the need to import grain from the United States, Canada, and Australia were a considerable blow to the prestige of Khrushchev, who had earlier promised "to overtake and surpass" the United States in various agricultural and dairy products. Not only did it reveal the inferiority of "socialist" as compared to "capitalist" agriculture, which was particularly embarrassing because prerevolutionary Russia was a grain-exporting nation, but it also reminded the Soviet leaders that, in bad crop years, they were dependent on others for vital food supplies.

The vulnerability which this implied made the post-Khrushchev regime determined not to repeat the disastrous experience of 1963. To avoid future embarrassment, and the possibility of exposure to pressure from supplier nations, the farm sector has received somewhat more favored treatment under Brezhnev and Kosygin. Despite their efforts, however, the grain crop for 1972 was a very poor one. To help compensate for these losses, the Soviet government agreed to purchase $750 million worth of American grain, the biggest transaction of its kind of the history of the two countries.[82]

The enormity and diversity of the problems confronting the agriculture sector were glaringly exposed by Party Secretary Brezhnev when he disclosed that, despite a record harvest, grain losses in 1973 were "especially acute" due to shortages in storage, transportation and processing facilities. The "heroic efforts of farm workers," he bitterly complained, were being "reduced, to some extent, to naught."[83] Thus, even when agricultural output has been increased, waste, mismanagement and inadequate facilities have deprived the Soviet citizenry of the fruits of their labors.

The difficulties confronting Soviet agriculture reflect the more basic economic problem which, in a general way, affects the international position of the USSR. The slow growth recorded by Soviet agriculture is partly the result of lack of investment. Soviet collective farmers cultivate crop lands 71 percent greater in size than those of the United States with over seven times the manpower but with only 34 percent of the number of tractors, 33 percent of the trucks, 60 percent of the grain combines, 62 percent of the commercial fertilizer and 80 percent of the electric power used in U.S. agriculture.[84] This low level of agricultural mechanization and support reflects both the relative scarcity of investment resources, most of which have been concentrated in heavy and defense-related industries, and the low priority of agriculture in the value system of the Soviet leadership. The resources which were in the past left over for agriculture were obviously insufficient.

The lack of adequate investment in agriculture reflects the relative weakness of the Soviet economy as a whole, especially when compared to that of the United States. This even affects the defense sector. The total output from which the Soviet government must draw in making its military outlay is small by American standards. As noted earlier, Soviet GNP is currently running about 50 percent of that of the United States (only 40 percent when calculated per capita). In the words of a noted economist "the Soviet Government has been seeking to support a military establishment of the first class with an economy that by U.S. standards has been second class."[85]

This has not forced the USSR to a second-class position militarily. In fact, Soviet military power has grown enormously, especially in recent years. This growth, however, came at some cost to other sectors of the economy, and to the growth rate of the economy as a whole. Since national security expenditures must compete with demands for increased outlays for both consumption and investment, the pressure for these scarce resources necessarily acts as a restraint on the defense budget. This has been so in the past. For example, there is some evidence that the Soviet decision not to produce and deploy large numbers of intercontinental missiles after they had successfully tested the world's first ICBM and launched Sputnik, the first earth satellite, in the fall of 1957, was in some degree shaped by economic considerations.[86]

The point to be made here is that tight economic circumstances affect choices—in the area of national defense as elsewhere. While not always compelling, especially if basic security interests are seen to be involved, such stringencies are constraining. This may perhaps explain why the Soviet Union dropped out of the moon race and why its space program has generally lagged behind that of the United States. Further, in light of these considerable burdens, the Soviet leaders have a strong economic motivation to limit further arms expansion; this is one of the factors which persuaded the USSR to join the U.S. in May, 1972, in signing the Strategic Arms Limitation Talks (SALT) agreement which placed limits on the future deployment of missiles. The problems are certainly not such that the Soviet economy risks stagnation or breakdown; nevertheless, an arms limitation agreement would relieve the economy of a considerable burden and free resources for possible use elsewhere.

Finally, the Soviet government is particularly concerned, for reasons both of prestige and power, with maintenance of a strong military and industrial position. In view of this concern, the "technological gap" referred to earlier is a source of continued anxiety. Party General Secretary Leonid Brezhnev underlined the importance of this issue in a speech in Minsk in late 1968 when he declared:

> It can be said without exaggeration that in this particular field, the field of scientific-technological progress, now lies one of the main fronts of the historical competition of the two systems. For our party the further intensive development of science and technology and the wise introduction of the latest scientific-technological achievements, is not only the central economic task but also an important political task.[87]

The difficulties encountered in promoting technological innovation, some of which were briefly mentioned earlier, has tended to push the Soviet Union into somewhat closer relations with the West. From importing entire factories for the manufacture of synthetic fibers from Great Britain to extensive contracts with Fiat and Ford motor companies for the production of automobiles and trucks, the USSR has felt compelled to expand its economic and technological cooperation with the industrially advanced countries. Its concern to accelerate economic growth and improve living standards has also led to expansion of trade with the West—the USSR importing mainly Western machinery and, increasingly, clothing and and footwear and the machinery for their manufacture.[88] Enlarged foreign trade is considered desirable not only to increase the volume and variety of goods available but, perhaps more importantly, to help improve the quality of domestic output. In order to compete effectively, Soviet goods will have to meet the competitive requirements of the world market. Foreign trade, therefore, will act as a "reliable assessment" of the generally indifferent technical standards of Soviet industry.[89]

Relations with the United States are critical in the Soviet view. American achievements on this "main front of historical competition" are recognized and respected. The achievements of America's industrial technology—from the "fuller industrialization" of all sectors of the economy including agriculture, to the automation of management with the aid of electronic computers and the reduction of production costs in the processing industry—have caught Moscow's eye. In early 1974, negotiations were underway with one of the largest accounting firms in the United States to advise the Soviet government on such matters as auditing, business procedures, personnel training and management techniques.[90] "All this," notes a leading Soviet political analyst, "is of interest to us." Although he argues that "the development of all these processes is in large measure deformed by capitalist production relations," he goes on to note that "there is no doubt that the experience accumulated in this field by the leading capitalist countries, above all the USA, is of considerable interest to us."[91]

Such factors have had an important bearing on relations between Moscow and Washington in recent years. The decidedly friendly and cooperative posture of the Kremlin towards the United States in the early 1970s is clearly related to Moscow's need to borrow advanced production and management techniques and to meet growing popular pressure for a better life. While other factors are surely involved (especially anxiety regarding China), the lure of American capital, technology, and grain was obviously a vital element in the Soviet decision to receive President Nixon and to sign the SALT and other agreements which were part of the "Moscow summit" of May, 1972.

A discussion of the significance of economic factors for Soviet foreign policy is fittingly concluded with the words of the Soviet leaders themselves. In his speech to an international conference of Communist Parties in Moscow in June 1969, Party General Secretary Brezhnev declared that the influence of Soviet foreign policy on the world scene "to a large extent depends on how things develop within our country and on successes in Communist construction." The same point was made somewhat more vividly by Foreign Minister Andrei Gromyko at the 24th Party Congress when he declared

> Every lathe, every ton of metal, every new computer, and every quintal of grain produced in our country constitutes not only a contribution to achieving an upsurge in our economy and to the people's prosperity but also a contribution to our foreign policy.[92]

The Soviet leaders are clearly aware that economic capabilities create potential for military strength. They are also aware that economic and technological achievements help create and reinforce the USSR's reputation as a dynamic world power of the first rank. "In present day conditions," in the words of one Soviet analyst, "our country's level of economic development and its position in the international division of labor are becoming increasingly decisive in respect of its international standing."[93] It is small wonder, then, that so much effort is spent bolstering the Soviet position on "the economic front."

Notes

[1]For a perceptive analysis of this basic point, and inspiration for the above discussion, see Raymond Aron, "The Anarchical Order of Power," *Daedalus*, Vol. 95, No. 2 (Spring, 1966), pp. 479–502.

²David O. Wilkinson, *Comparative Foreign Relations: Framework and Methods* (Belmont, California: Dickenson Publishing Company, 1969), p. 27.

³Milan Kundera, "The Czech Destiny," *Listy*, Christmas Issue, 1968; reprinted in the *Times Literary Supplement* (London), January 2, 1969.

⁴David J. M. Hooson, *A New Soviet Heartland?* (Princeton, New Jersey: D. Van Nostrand Company, Inc., 1964), p. 9.

⁵*Ibid.*, p. 34.

⁶Robert C. Kingsbury and Robert N. Taffee, *An Atlas of Soviet Affairs* (New York: Frederick A. Praeger, Publishers, 1965), p. 58.

⁷Hooson, *op. cit.*, p. 8.

⁸Paul E. Lydolph, *Geography of the USSR*, 2d ed. (New York: John Wiley & Sons, 1970), p. 2.

⁹Cyril E. Black, "The Pattern of Russian Objectives," in Ivo J. Lederer, ed., *Russian Foreign Policy* (New Haven: Yale University Press, 1962), pp. 8–9.

¹⁰Leon Gouré, *The Siege of Leningrad* (Stanford: Stanford University Press, 1962), pp. 4–5.

¹¹S. H. Steinberg, ed., *The Statesman's Year-book* (New York: St. Martin's Press, 1968), p. 1527.

¹²Hooson, *op. cit.*, p. 34.

¹³*Ibid.*, p. 41.

¹⁴Report by the U.S.S.R. Council of Ministers' Central Statistical Administration, "The Population of Our Country—On the Age Structure, Level of Education, Nationality Composition, Languages and Sources of Livelihood of the Population of the USSR. According to Data of the January 15, 1970, All-Union Population Census." *Pravda* (April 17, 1971), pp. 1, 3; translated in the *Current Digest of the Soviet Press*, Vol. XXIII, No. 16 (May 18, 1971), p. 14. (The *Current Digest of the Soviet Press* hereinafter abbreviated as *CDSP*.)

¹⁵Pierre Sorlin, *The Soviet People and Their Society* (New York: Frederick A. Praeger, Publishers, 1968), p. 39. The total available manpower was never used because the country did not have the necessary means to transport, equip or feed all the men available.

¹⁶For 1913 population figures, see *Cross-Polity Time Series Data*, assembled by Arthur S. Banks (Cambridge, Mass.: The MIT Press, 1971), pp. 48, 50.

¹⁷According to Richard Pipes, Russia suffered some two million casualties in World War I, fourteen million during the Civil War and famine, ten million during collectivization, ten million during the purges and twenty million during the Second World War. *The Limitation of Strategic Arms*, Hearings before the Subcommittee on Strategic Arms Limitation Talks of the Committee on Armed Services, United States Senate, 91st Congress, 2d Session, March 18, 1970, Part I (Washington, D. C.: Government Printing Office, 1970), p. 23.

¹⁸*Ibid.*

¹⁹Murray Feshbach, "Observations on the Soviet Census," *Problems of Communism*, Vol. XIX, No. 3 (May-June, 1970), p. 58.

²⁰*Ibid.*

²¹"The Population of Our Country," *op. cit.*, p. 14.

²²*Literaturnaya gazeta*, (March 20, 1968), p. 11. Quoted in Helen Defosses Cohn, "Population Policy in the USSR," *Problems of Communism*, Vol. XXII, No. 4 (July-August 1973), p. 45.

²³A. Kvasha, "A Scientist's Forecast: The Generation of the Year 2000," *Literaturnaya gazeta* (March 22, 1972), p. 10; translated in *CDSP*, Vol. XXIV, No. 11 (April 12, 1972), p. 13.

²⁴A. Maikov, "Sources and Reserves of Manpower," *Sotsialisticheskaya industriya* (March 15, 1972), p. 2; translated *ibid.*, p. 14.

²⁵A. Struyev, "Soviet Trade: Results and Tasks," *Pravda*, February 27, 1973, p. 3. Translated in *CDSP*, Vol. XXV, No. 9 (March 28, 1973), p. 11. Translation copyright 1974 by the Current Digest of the Soviet Press; published weekly

at The Ohio State University by the American Association for the Advancement of Slavic Studies; reprinted by permission.

[26]Editor's Note to "A Statistical Commentary: It's Time to Marry," by Candidate of Economics V. Perevedentsev, *Literaturnaya gazeta* (April 21, 1971), p. 13; translated in *CDSP*, Vol. XXIII, No. 15 (May 11, 1971), p. 35. See also V. Guseinov and V. Korchagin, "Questions of Labor Resources," *Voprosy ekonomiki*, No. 2 (February, 1971), pp. 45–51; translated in *CDSP*, Vol. XXIII, No. 18 (June 1, 1971), p. 5.

[27]"The Population of Our Country," *op. cit.*, p. 14. The pace of "urbanization" has been swift. While the urban population "overtook" the rural population in 1962, in 1926 only 18 percent of the population lived in urban areas; in 1897 only 16 percent. Figures cited in *Abstract* "Will Increased Labor Productivity Cure the Falling Birthrate," *CDSP*, Vol. XXV, No. 10 (April 4, 1973), p. 21.

[28]*Ibid.*, pp. 16–18.

[29]*Ibid.*, p. 14.

[30]Mrs. Meir has recently recounted her conversation in 1948 with Mrs. Paulina Molotov, wife of the then Soviet Foreign Minister. For the "crime" of speaking to the Israeli Ambassador in Yiddish (Mrs. Molotov was herself Jewish), the Soviet Foreign Minister's wife was sent to prison for two years. *The New York Times* December 30, 1970, p. 25. For a fuller description of these grim developments, see Yehoshua A. Gilboa, *The Black Years of Soviet Jewry 1939–1950* (Boston: Little, Brown and Company, 1971).

[31]Svetlana Alliluyeva, *Only One Year* (New York: Harper and Row, 1969), p. 176.

[32]Tbilisi, capital of Soviet Georgia, fell to Russia in 1801; Baku, capital of the present Azerbaidjani SSSR, in 1806; and Yerevan, the Armenian capital, in 1828; the Central Asian city of Tashkent was captured in 1865; Bukhara and Samarkand in 1868; the Amur Province and the Maritime Province in the Far East were annexed in the 1850s and 1860s.

[33]See Theodore Shabad, "Migrants Worry Estonia, Latvia," *The New York Times*, March 13, 1972, and "Ideological Aberrations in Four Republics," *CDSP*, Vol. XXV, No. 11 (April 11, 1973), pp. 12–16.

[34]Between late 1914 and early 1917, the Russian Army suffered approximately four million casualties! Sorlin, *op cit.*, p. 43.

[35]Approximately seven million soldiers were killed, either in combat or in POW camps. *Ibid.*, p. 197.

[36]Richard Pipes, "Communism and Russian History," in Donald W. Treadgold, ed., *Soviet and Chinese Communism, Similarities and Differences* (Seattle, Washington: University of Washington Press, 1967), p. 14.

[37]See, for example, Alec Nove and J. A. Newth, *The Soviet Middle East* (New York: Frederick A. Praeger, Publishers, 1967).

[38]Alex Inkeles, "Soviet Nationality Policy in Perspective," in Abraham Brumberg, ed., *Russia Under Khrushchev* (New York: Frederick A. Praeger, Publishers, 1962), pp. 314–315.

[39]Louis Fischer, *Russia's Road from Peace to War; Soviet Foreign Relations, 1917–1941* (New York: Harper and Row, Publishers, 1969), p. 389.

[40]J. Stalin, *Problems of Leninism* (Moscow: Foreign Languages Publishing House, 1954), p. 592.

[41]*Ibid.*, pp. 455–456.

[42]*Ibid.*, p. 456.

[43]Alec Nove, *An Economic History of the USSR* (London: Allen Lane, The Penguin Press, 1969), pp. 11–13.

[44]*Ibid.*, p. 269.

[45]*Ibid.*, pp. 270–275. According to one source, the Soviet Union succeeded in outproducing Germany in the mechanized weapons of war in every year throughout the conflict. In 1941, the USSR produced 16,000 planes (10,000 after the invasion); in 1942, the USSR produced 23,000 tanks to Germany's 9,300;

25,000 airplanes to Germany's 14,700; 34,000 heavy guns to Germany's 12,000. Francis B. Randall, *Stalin's Russia* (Glencoe, Illinois: The Free Press, 1965), pp. 281–282.

[46]Nove, *op. cit.*, pp. 274–275.

[47]B. H. Liddell Hart, *History of the Second World War* (New York: G. P. Putnam's Sons, 1971), pp. 169–170.

[48]*Ibid.*, pp. 605–606.

[49]Information Bulletin (Embassy of the USSR, October 11, 1945); cited by D. F. Fleming, *The Cold War and Its Origins*, Vol. I, 1917–1950 (Garden City: Doubleday and Company, 1961), p. 252.

[50]J. V. Stalin, "Election Speech, February 9, 1946, "reprinted in Myron Rush, ed., *The International Situation and Soviet Foreign Policy* (Columbus, Ohio: Charles E. Merrill Publishing Company, 1970), p. 123.

[51]Nove, *op. cit.*, p. 290.

[52]These figures give only a rough sense of overall economic potential. If concern is with consumer welfare, the divergence is obviously wider. In 1968, for example, Soviet consumption per capita—including such things as textiles, food products, shoes, refrigerators, washing machines, health and education services— was estimated at about 33 percent of the U. S. level. (See David W. Bronson and Barbara S. Severin, "Consumer Welfare," *Economic Performance and the Military Burden in the Soviet Union*, Joint Economic Committee, Congress of the United States [Washington: Government Printing Office, 1970], p. 95. [Hereinafter cited as *Economic Performance . . .*]) If concern is with military potential, as ours is, the best indicator is industrial production, where the gap continues to narrow.

[53]*The Limitation of Strategic Arms, op. cit.*, Part II, May 20, 1970, p. 54. This shift in priority in favor of the consumer sector has continued. In the Economic Plan for 1969–1970, and, more recently, in the new Ninth Five–Year Plan approved by the 24th Congress of the Soviet Communist Party (April, 1971), larger growth rates were assigned to consumer goods industries. While industrial output as a whole is scheduled to increase from 42 to 46 percent during the period 1971–1975, the planned increase for producers' goods is set for 41 to 45 percent, and that for consumers' goods, 44 to 48 percent. *Resolution of the 24th Congress of the Communist Party of the Soviet Union on the C.P.S.U. Central Committee's Draft Directives of the 24th C.P.S.U. Congress for the Five-Year Plan for the Development of the USSR National Economy in 1971–1975*, April 11, 1971; translated in *CDSP*, Vol. XXIII, No. 18 (June 1, 1971), p. 12.

[54]*The New York Times*, December 14, 24, 1972.

[55]*Ibid.* January 26, 1974.

[56]Stanley H. Cohn, "General Growth Performance of the Soviet Economy," *Economic Performance . . .*, p. 9. This occasionally spotty performance should not be allowed to blind us to the obvious accomplishments of Soviet agriculture. In absolute terms, agriculture is continually growing. Thus, even with its relatively poor harvest, "Agricultural production in 1969 was 12 percent above the level achieved in 1964, the last year of the Khrushchev era." Terence E. Byrne, "Recent Trends in the Soviet Economy," *Economic Performance . . .*, p. 3. However, as a result of the 1972 crop failure, plans for heavy and especially consumer goods industries have been revised sharply downward. *The New York Times*, February 4, 1973.

[57]The reasons for the striking increase in military expenditures in the 1960s will be discussed in the next chapter.

[58]*The Limitations of Strategic Arms*, Part II, *op. cit.*, p. 55.

[59]Stanley H. Cohn, "The Economic Burden of Soviet Defense Outlays," *Economic Performance . . .*, p. 177.

[60]*The Directives of the 24th CPSU Congress for the Five-Year Plan for the Development of the USSR National Economy in 1971–1975*. Report by Comrade A. N. Kosygin, Chairman of the Council of Ministers, on April 6, 1971. *Pravda*

(April 7, 1971), pp. 2–7; translated in *CDSP*, Vol. XXIII, No. 15 (May 11, 1971), p. 5.

[61]Col. Yu. Vlasyevich, "On the Laws Governing the Dynamics of Military–Economic Costs," *Kommunist vooruzhennykh sil*, No. 16 (August, 1970); translated in *CDSP*, Vol. XXII, No. 44 (December 1, 1970), p. 6.

[62]*The Limitations of Strategic Arms*, Part II, *op. cit.*, p. 58. For a Western analysis of the Soviet defense budget, see *The Military Balance, 1972–1973* (London: International Institute for Strategic Studies, 1972), p. 9. According to this source, there was "virtual parity in defense spending between the two super-powers" in 1971. The great disparity between the announced budget figures and the actual level of military expenditures is explained by the fact that many items, such as the cost of nuclear warheads, research and development expenses, and the military elements of the space program, are hidden in the budgets of other ministries.

[63]L. I. Brezhnev, "The Interests of the People and Concern for their Welfare are the Supreme Meaning of the Party's Activity," *Pravda*, June 12, 1971; translated in *CDSP*, Vol. XXIII, No. 24 (July 13, 1971), pp. 18–19.

[64]Nove, *op. cit.*, p. 273.

[65]"Revolution—or Reform? A Conversation between Ota Sik and Raymond Aron," *Encounter*, Vol. XXXVI, No. 3 (March, 1971), p. 52. As a result of his own unhappy experience with central planning, Sik played an important role in the movement for economic reform in the mid-1960s in Czechoslovakia. His activity earned for Sik the title of "Father of Czechoslovakia's 'New Economic Model'."

[66]*The Directives of the 24th CPSU Congress . . .*, *op. cit.*, p. 5.

[67]See Nove, *op. cit.*, pp. 355–362.

[68]K. Mikulsky, "New Scientific and Technological Horizons in the CMEA Countries," *International Affairs*, No. 6 (June, 1970), p. 39.

[69]K. P. Ivanov, *Leninskie osnovy vneshnei politiki SSSR* (Moscow: Znanie, 1969), p. 51.

[70]*The New York Times*, April 2, 1973.

[71]Zbigniew Brzezinski, "The Soviet Past and Future," *Encounter*, Vol. XXXIV, No. 3 (March, 1970), p. 9.

[72]Gertrude E. Schroeder, "Soviet Technology: System vs. Progress," *Problems of Communism*, Vol. XIX, No. 5 (September–October 1970), p. 20.

[73]Brzezinski, *op. cit.*, p. 9, footnote 11.

[74]R. V. Burks, "Technology and Political Change," in Chalmers Johnson, ed., *Change in Communist Systems* (Stanford: Stanford University Press, 1970), p. 283. In 1972, for the second consecutive year, steel production in the USSR was greater than in the United States. *The New York Times*, February 26, 1973.

[75]"A Computer Lag by Russia Found," *The New York Times*, March 14, 1971. This report was based on the visit of a RAND Corporation computer expert to the Soviet Institute of Space Research in Moscow. See also, Schroeder, *op. cit.*, p. 21. According to a recent account, the Soviet Union has been running more than eight years behind the United States in the development of the third generation of computers. Introduced in the United States in 1964, these advanced models went into production only during 1972. *The New York Times*, May 5, 1971 and March 23, 1972.

[76]Schroeder, *op. cit.*, p. 21.

[77]This is the main argument of Vladimir Dudintsev's explosive novel of the mid-1950s, *Not By Bread Alone*. Though twenty years have elapsed, the conditions which inspired Dudintsev seem to be little changed.

[78]Brzezinski, *op. cit.*, p. 9.

[79]*Ibid.*

[80]Guseinov and Korchagin, *op. cit.*, pp. 5–7.

[81]Testimony of Joseph Berliner, *The Economic Basis of the Russian Military Challenge to the United States,* June 23 and 24, 1969, Hearings before the Subcommittee on Economy in Government of the Joint Economic Committee, Congress of the United States, 91st Congress, 1st Session, June, 1969, Part III, (Washington, D.C.: Government Printing Office, 1969), pp. 906–907.

[82]See *The New York Times,* July 9, 1972.

[83]Quoted in *The New York Times* and *The Washington Post,* March 6, 1974.

[84]Testimony of Joseph Berliner, *op. cit.,* p. 907.

[85]Testimony of Abram Bergson, *ibid.,* p. 901.

[86]Morton Schwartz, "The Cuban Missile Venture," in James B. Christoph and Bernard E. Brown, eds., *Cases in Comparative Politics,* 2d ed. (Boston: Little, Brown and Co., 1969), pp. 281–286.

[87]Quoted in Burks, *op. cit.,* p. 276.

[88]Robert S. Kovach and John T. Farrell, "Foreign Trade of the USSR," *Economic Performance . . .,* p. 106.

[89]See O. Bogomolov, "A Demand of Life," *Izvestiya* (February 26, 1974), p. 4 and *The New York Times,* February 5, 1974.

[90]*The New York Times,* March 19, 1974.

[91]N. N. Inozemtsev, "The U.S.A. Today and Soviet American Studies," *SShA,* No. 1 (January, 1970), p. 10.

[92]Speech by USSR Foreign Minister A. A. Gromyko at 24th Congress, *Radio Moscow* (April 25, 1971).

[93]V. Vasiliev, "Some Factors in International Life Today," *International Affairs,* No. 5 (May 1970), p. 60.

2

Soviet military power

Their impressive economic accomplishments have been a source of considerable pride to the Soviet leaders. Though purchased at great cost and much human suffering and denial,[1] the pace of economic progress has been impressive and has greatly added to Soviet prestige. Russia's reputation as a technologically advanced industrial power was greatly enhanced by the launching of Sputnik in 1957, a truly remarkable technological breakthrough. Backward Russia, home of the abacus, seemed to have "overtaken and surpassed" the world's leading scientific power. Many people around the world, including in the United States, viewed Sputnik as symbolizing a major turning point in the tide of world history; they believed, along with Mao Tse-tung, that "the East wind is prevailing over the West wind."

Despite the magnificent promise of Sputnik and of the spectacular flight into space of Yuri Gagarin a few years later, the USSR has not been able to sustain its image as a major scientific and technological innovator. For numerous reasons, the Russians lag behind the advanced technology of other leading industrial nations; yet Soviet prestige and influence continue to grow. Increasingly, however, the USSR's world reputation is a function of its military power. Soviet accomplishments in this area have been most impressive, especially in recent years. In absolute and relative terms, the current regime possesses military forces far greater in size and sophistication than those at the command of any previous Kremlin leader. Not only is Russia much stronger than ever but, for the first time in its history, its military position is equal of (and in some respects superior to) that of its major rivals.

Russia has long been considered a ranking world power militarily. Historically, this was true because of the country's vast land armies which compared very favorably, especially in size, with the military forces of its relatively small European neighbors. Recently, Moscow's prominent military position is a function of quality rather than quantity. It is in the sphere of weapons capabilities, especially strategic weapons such as intercontinental ballistic missiles, and naval forces, that Moscow's military eminence now rests. However, the Red Army remains a military force of considerable significance.

Soviet conventional forces

In terms of the number of men in uniform, the USSR has the largest military establishment in the world—Soviet armed forces in 1972 totaled about 3.4 million men (as compared with 2.3 million in the United States). These forces are distributed among five major service components: the ground forces (army); the naval forces; the strategic rocket forces; the air force; and the anti-air-defense forces. There are, in addition, about 175,000 uniformed border guards and 125,000 security troops. The manpower reserve pool that supplies the armed forces is potentially very large: there are approximately 50 million men between the ages of eighteen and forty-five in the USSR. The corresponding figure for the United States is 39 million; in China, however, the Soviet Union faces a manpower reserve of 170 million. (Total Chinese regular forces are currently estimated at only 2.9 million.)

The army is traditionally the most powerful element in the Soviet military hierarchy. Though its role has come under increasing challenge in recent years as the technologically more sophisticated components of the Soviet military apparatus play an increasingly important role in Soviet defense arrangements, the army is still the largest of the major services and represents a powerful force. The two million Soviet ground troops are currently (1973) composed of 164 divisions, the most important of which are said to be maintained at full strength—the 31 divisions in Central and Eastern Europe (including 20 in East Germany, 5 in Czechoslovakia, 4 in Hungary and 2 in Poland), many of the 60 divisions in European Russia, and about a third of the 45 divisions in the Far East. Soviet troops in position on the Sino-Soviet border have been continually reinforced ever since the bloody border clashes in 1969. The figure of 45 divisions cited above represents an increase of 12 divisions over the 1971 count of 33. A more recent source claims that this figure has now reached 49, i.e., 30 percent of all the active formations in the Soviet army are said to be manning the frontier with China.[2]

Since the end of the Second World War, Soviet ground forces have been transformed into a modern, sophisticated army. The quality of their tanks, artillery, and other weaponry is highly respected by Western military analysts. Further, Soviet troops are supported by over forty thousand tactical aircraft as well as tactical nuclear missile units. Though the primary mission of Soviet ground forces is defensive, gone are the days of the scorched earth policy and Russia's traditional strategy of "trading space for time." The Red Army is one of the world's great land forces capable of striking with extensive armor, mechanized forces, and paratroopers deep into an enemy's territory. Built around the notions of speed and fire power it will no longer be compelled to attempt to overwhelm its enemies by the brutal World War I tactic of human wave assaults. Soviet forces are well supplied with weapons. The Soviet-designed "Kalashnikov" is currently the world's most famous rifle, especially among irregular forces in the Middle East. Unlike their grandfathers in 1914, Russian troops will not have to go into battle without rifles or even sidearms.

From the evidence, one has the distinct impression of powerful conventional ground forces equipped with modern weapons and equipment, directed by efficient and well-trained officers, and supported by a self-sufficient and growing economy and by a sizable, cohesive, and well-motivated manpower base.[3] This last point is of critical importance. Lack of internal cohesion shattered the effectiveness of Russia's military forces during World War I, reducing their considerable numerical advantage to near insignificance. It was little wonder that Lenin in 1918 regarded his country as "a military zero."[4] However, in confronting the threat to its very existence posed by the invading German armies in 1941–1942, the Soviet army demonstrated a striking degree of unity, a fact dramatically illustrated by the heroic performance of Soviet civilian and military forces at the gates of Leningrad (where they withstood almost three years under siege) and in the grueling battles for Moscow and Stalingrad.

There were instances of disloyalty, especially during the early months of World War II, when a considerable number of Soviet troops defected to the Germans. (Some actually fought in Nazi military uniform or in separate anti-Soviet military forces such as the Vlasov army, named after the turncoat Soviet general who led them.[5]) As the war progressed, however, disloyalty became a relatively minor problem. The threat to the nation's survival represented by the German invaders and the cruel behavior of the occupying Nazi forces were by themselves sufficient to stir a patriotic response among the Soviet people. In addition, the Communist Party performed well, organizing and disciplining the Soviet population. The Party also performed gallantly in the armed services. Party–army relations were not without their difficulties; however, high devotion and political consciousness among Party members helped overcome the demoralization which infected Soviet forcces during the early bleak months of the war.[6] In general, then, both army and population supported the regime during this time of great internal stress.

The political loyalty of the Red Army, as that of the population as a whole, is now well established. Though military service is nearly universal—exemptions are only on medical or family hardship grounds with no provisions for deferment for reasons of religion or conscience[7]—and each male high school student is required to take two years of compulsory premilitary training as well as serve two years in the army or air force or three years in the Soviet navy, no draft cards have been burned in the Soviet Union nor have military officers been hooted off university campuses. The military is a high-prestige profession in the USSR and the terms of service, if only by comparison with prerevolutionary times, are not considered a great hardship. "In a country where a sardonic old soldiers' song with the lines 'Don't cry, don't cry, my beauty, We're parting for only twenty-five years,' is still remembered," a journalist remarked recently, being drafted for two or three years must not seem too onerous a burden.[8]

While the evidence of internal harmony and loyalty is impressive, we may be a victim of a lack of information. The fact that all seems well—if one reads *Pravda* or *Krasnaya zvezda (Red Star)*, the organ of the Defense Ministry—is not sufficient proof that all, in fact, is well. There are indications, even in the official press, that the Soviet leadership occasionally encounters critical attitudes regarding the military, especially among Soviet young people. There is evidence, for example, of problems relating to morale and the readiness with which military authority and leadership are accepted.

One finds in the official literature a growing anxiety over the attitudes which Soviet youth bring with them into the armed forces. Concern seems greatest over the suspected ideological laxity of the younger generation in general and, more particularly, its skeptical attitude towards the virtues of military life. Complaints can be found of young people who because they have not themselves experienced "the school of war" are said to "regard military service as a temporary and unfortunate nuisance" if not an actual waste of time.

Furthermore, Soviet military leaders in recent years have been overtly critical of what they see as pacifist and anti-military trends in Soviet art and literature. In February, 1964, for example, the military high command lectured Soviet writers and artists on the need for a heroic and romantic approach to the theme of war. Marshal Malinovskii attacked, in particular, the tendency of Soviet intellectuals to concentrate on the horrors and sufferings of war and on "abstract humanism" while ignoring the broader picture of the country's military past and its struggle to survive. According to the Soviet Defense Minister, various artistic works contain "pacifist themes and abstract negation of war."[9] More recently, Marshal Konev warned: "Great harm is done to the upbringing of young people by the fact that recently some writers have set about the revision of heroes on whom more than one generation of Soviet young people has been reared." He went on to implore Soviet novelists to applaud rather than play down the exploits of Soviet military heroes.[10]

The increasingly critical posture of Soviet youth and their apparent receptivity to nonmilitary themes can be ascribed, in part, to changes in their social background. Formerly, the overwhelming majority of young people, including those conscripted into the Soviet armed forces, was rural and poorly educated. Today, an increasingly more sophisticated, better-educated group of Soviet youths with wide and diverse interests arrive at the induction centers each autumn. While still patriotic in spirit, they tend to be more skeptical of the virtues of military life than their fathers and grandfathers.

To instill a properly martial spirit among Soviet young people, Khrushchev's successors have in recent years conducted an intensified campaign of "military-national glorification," during which millions of Russian school children visit historic battlefields where they receive lectures on the heroism of Soviet soldiers. In addition, so as to give draftees a proper send-off, patriotic celebrations are held on annual autumn Induction Day when the new conscripts are to report for duty. Furthermore, the press has seen a considerable tide of articles extolling military-patriotic virtues, love of country, and the Soviet regime.[11] An example of this effort can be seen in the recent novel, *What Do You Want?*, where the conservative writer, Vsevolod Kochetov, reprimands Soviet youth for their laxness. He writes:

> . . . you youngsters take everything lightly. Your efforts are all focused on pleasure, on enjoying yourselves—that is to say, on consumption. The passion for consumption! Of course, that is nice; it's pleasant. Have a good time. We didn't always have our noses to the grindstone, ourselves, you know. We weren't monks, either. Look at how many of you youngsters we produced. But we were not carefree, Felix, I can tell you that. Day and night, on weekdays and holidays, we prepared for the fact that sooner or later they would attack us. We learned how to fight and to defend our government and our system, our present and your future.[12]

These various measures to stir up patriotic virtues indicate the regime's concern over the moral fiber of its younger generation. However, the problem is a minor one, when compared to the high tide of anti-militarism running in many Western countries; it seems most unlikely to affect the military potential of the Soviet Union.[13]

Warsaw treaty allies

In considering Soviet military capabilities, brief mention should be made of the USSR's close allies in the Warsaw Treaty Organization (WTO). The organization's command structure indicates that the armed forces of the Warsaw Treaty countries are, in considerable degree, under the effective control of the Soviet High Command. The Commander-in-Chief of WTO military forces, currently Marshal Yakubovskii, (earlier Marshal Grechko, the current Soviet Defense Minister), has always been the Soviet senior officer; in fact, most of the alliance's whole top command have been Soviet. For most purposes, it would probably be accurate to consider them as part of the Soviet military contingent.[14]

The main contribution made by the six East European members —Bulgaria, Czechoslovakia, East Germany, Hungary, Poland, and Rumania—to the military power of the Communist bloc consists of ground forces. (While some of these countries have displayed tactical missile launchers, they do not seem to have been supplied with nuclear warheads for such weapons. Soviet Medium-Range Ballistic Missiles and other strategic weapons are based in the USSR and are under Soviet control.) Of the approximately four-and-one-half million troops in the Communist bloc, 3,425,000 are Soviet; the remaining one million come from Poland (280,000), Rumania (170,000), Czechoslovakia (190,000), Bulgaria (152,000), East Germany (132,000), and Hungary (103,000). Including Soviet troops, the alliance maintains about 1,220,000 men under arms in Europe, a numerically larger number than the 1,130,000 in NATO army and marine forces. (This omits Soviet and American forces on other continents.) These forces, according to recent reports, currently have considerably more operational tanks than NATO and more tactical aircraft.[15]

Whatever contribution these troops might make to augmenting the power of the Red Army has been offset to some extent by the political unrest which in recent years has characterized Eastern Europe. The regimes of several alliance members, especially Poland, Hungary, Czechoslovakia, and Rumania have, on various occasions, taken an independent course from the one prescribed by the Kremlin. One former member of the alliance, Albania, formally denounced the Warsaw Pact Treaty in September, 1968, having played no part in its activities since 1960. Hungary (in 1956) and Czechoslovakia (in 1968) were invaded by Soviet forces in order to ensure their continued loyalty. The military reliability of the armed forces of these countries and the independently oriented Rumanian contingents are clearly something Moscow cannot take for granted in time of military crisis.

Impressive as Soviet ground forces and those of the Warsaw Pact countries are, they afford Moscow rather little by way of political influence. Were its military arsenal to consist solely of such conventional forces, the USSR would be capable of using its military weight only on the European political stage. In recent years, however, the Kremlin's military capabilities have been expanded far beyond these rather limited dimensions. Today, the USSR's strategic forces—those capable of seriously damaging the military capabilities of potential enemies from whatever source and whatever distance—are a highly important factor in the world military balance of power.

Evolution of Soviet strategic power

Soviet military capabilities have developed erratically since the Second World War. In the immediate post-war period, Soviet forces were very considerably reduced. From a figure of 11,365,000 in May, 1945, Soviet armed forces were down to between 4,000,000 and 5,000,000 by 1947–1948. (The official figure given by Soviet sources is 2,874,000.[16])

This contraction, significant as it clearly was, still left the USSR with a considerable military establishment, as American forces were reduced from 12,000,000 on VE Day to 1,350,000 in March 1948.[17] Thus, even if Soviet figures are accepted at face value, the USSR enjoyed a two to one advantage. However, the real disparity was even greater, especially in infantry forces. Soviet ground troops in 1950 have been estimated at between 2,500,000 and 4,000,000; the U.S. Army at that time was down to 593,000 troops.[18]

Soviet demobilization was extensive. However, large numbers of conventional forces were maintained, especially on the country's western flank. Soviet forces in East Germany and Eastern Europe amounted to approximately thirty divisions, more than half-a-million men. Another 50 to 60 divisions, of a total of 175, were stationed in the Western military districts of the Soviet Union.[19]

Thus, though the Second World War had wreaked terrible havoc and destruction, the USSR was at the war's end the most powerful military force in Europe. Germany, Britain, and France, the Great Powers of the inter-war period, had been physically and economically drained by the war. The rest of Europe was a shambles. As Churchill declared two years after VE Day: "What is Europe now? It is a rubble-heap, a charnel house, a breeding ground of pestilence and hate."[20] For all its losses, the USSR was militarily the strongest nation in Europe. In terms of overall strength, however, the USSR was a lesser power than the United States. This was true on two counts. First, the U.S. had suffered no wartime damage to its economy or its civilian population. In fact, the American economy was booming. By 1944, it was producing 45 percent of the world's total war equipment and munitions, one-and-a-half that of all of the Axis powers combined.[21] Second, and much more important, the United States had in 1945 successfully developed and used atomic weapons.

America's monopoly of atomic weapons must have made a great impression on the Soviet leaders. While they were undoubtedly pleased by the rapid demobilization of American forces after the war and, especially, by their large-scale (though not complete) withdrawal from Europe and Asia,[22] Stalin must still have been seriously concerned about Washington's future political role. A wealthy, robust United States armed with atomic weapons, a country whose political objectives in the uncertain and troubled post-war world were not clear (not even to itself), presented a potential challenge—the only conceivable one—to the interests and political ambitions of the Soviet Union. Prudence suggested that the Kremlin turn quickly to the development of its own atomic weapons arsenal. And Stalin, if nothing else, was prudent.

Thus, though Stalin appeared only mildly concerned when told by President Truman at the Potsdam Conference in July, 1945, that the U.S. had exploded the world's first nuclear bomb,[23] he was clearly determined to break the U.S. atomic monopoly as quickly as possible.[24] The USSR had begun to work on its own nuclear weapons program in 1942 or 1943. However, for good psychological reasons, Stalin publicly ignored the military significance of atomic weapons and stressed the basic importance of conventional military forces.

Throughout most of the Second World War, Stalin emphasized the critical importance of five "permanently operating factors" which, in his judgment, were decisive in time of military conflict: (1) the stability of the homefront, (2) the morale of the armed forces, (3) the quantity and quality of divisions, (4) the armament of the armed forces, and (5) the abilities of the commanders. This formula, for which he was later criticized, completely omitted any reference to nuclear weapons. In fact, Stalin publicly deprecated their role. On September 24, 1946, for example, he declared:

> I do not believe that the atomic bomb is as serious a force as certain politicians are inclined to regard it. . . . They cannot decide the outcome of war since atomic weapons are by no means sufficient for this purpose.[25]

Stalin's public posture clearly was feigned. The Soviet leader, for purposes of diplomacy, sought to stress those areas in which the USSR had the greatest strength—conventional ground forces—and to question the importance of the West's most powerful weapons. By pretending indifference in this way, he sought to deny the United States such advantage as its nuclear superiority might afford. As Stalin observed, atomic weapons "are intended to intimidate the weak-nerved." Not if you ignore them.[26]

Though he publicly downplayed nuclear weaponry, the record indicates that Stalin fully intended to acquire a nuclear capacity for the USSR. A hint of his determination is to be found in his famous "Election Speech" of February 9, 1946. In this address, as will be recalled, Stalin exhorted the war-weary Soviet population to the task of rebuilding the country's ravished economy as quickly as possible. In addition, he noted,

> Special attention will be devoted . . . to the widespread construction of all manner of scientific research institutions that can give science the opportunity to develop its potentialities.
>
> I have no doubt that if we give our scientists proper assistance they will be able *in the near future not only to overtake but to surpass the achievements of science beyond the boundaries of our country.*[27] (Italics added.)

Stalin's promise was fulfilled. As a result of his "special attention," Soviet scientists unlocked the secrets of the atom with surprising speed. The first known Soviet atomic explosion occurred in August, 1949. In September, 1953, slightly less than four years later, the USSR tested its first hydrogen bomb. America's nuclear monopoly had been broken.

When Soviet nuclear weapons were introduced in the early 1950s, they were essentially oriented toward relatively short-range operations. Soviet delivery forces consisted largely of light and medium bombers, best suited to bring nuclear fire power to bear against Europe and bases near the Soviet border, not against the United States. Throughout the Stalin era and into the 1950s, the Kremlin's focus was on European rather than intercontinental targets. Soviet nuclear delivery forces, much as the Soviet ground troops mentioned earlier, were directed against NATO.[28]

Despite Soviet nuclear achievements, the western strategic lead grew enormously in the mid-1950s. During the 1940s, the United States had produced very few atomic weapons. However, the situation changed very dramatically during the Korean War (1950–1953) when American military capabilities were greatly enlarged. The U.S. expanded its nuclear weapons stockpile[29] and, as important, produced and deployed large numbers of long-range B-52 bombers. It was during this period that the Strategic Air Command (SAC) was created. Presumably, Soviet forces were also expanded at this time, but the United States acquired a commanding lead. As one informed analyst has observed:

> In the years 1954–55 the gap between Soviet and U.S. military power was probably wider than it ever had been before or would be again. . . . In those years the United States on very short notice could have destroyed as much of the Soviet industry and population as it willed, secure in the belief that the Soviet retaliation against the United States would have been trifling.[30]

Despite this change in the balance of military forces, the general predisposition in Soviet strategic thinking towards a "Europe-first" orientation continued in the post-Stalin period. The new Khrushchev regime decided not to attempt to overtake the American intercontinental strike force. While greatly expanding its strategic air power, the Soviet government did not, as many in the West then feared, give high priority to developing its long-range bomber forces. Thus, by 1960, the overall bomber strength of Soviet strategic air forces were estimated to be about 1,500 aircraft as compared to 1,800 planes in SAC. However, in terms of long-range bombers, the U.S. maintained at least a three to one margin.[31]

The Soviet decision not to compete with the United States in the production of long-range bombers suggests Moscow's reliance on a "hostage" strategy. The Kremlin leaders probably believed that the U.S. could be deterred from pressing its military advantage and taking action against Soviet interests by making Western Europe hostage for American behavior. In order to carry out this strategy, all Moscow needed was a credible threat of a Soviet nuclear attack against Western Europe. For these purposes, the Kremlin's medium-range BADGER bomber force was adequate.[32]

The Soviet decision also may have been influenced by another factor. The USSR had for several years been attempting to develop long-range missile capabilities. In opting for a medium-range rather than an intercontinental bomber force, Khrushchev may have believed that ballistic missile technology offered a more promising way to overcome American strategic superiority than production of long-range bombers.

In the fall of 1957, the missile investment began to pay off. On August 26th, the Soviet Union tested the first intercontinental ballistic missile. On October 4, Soviet rockets launched the first earth satellite, Sputnik I. These spectacular achievements appeared to have transformed the world balance of forces; the strategic superiority which SAC's long-range bombers had till then afforded the United States seemed to have been nullified. The whole world now appeared exposed to the threat of nuclear-tipped Soviet intercontinental ballistic missiles.

In fact, despite this demonstration of Soviet technological prowess, the strategic balance of forces did not significantly alter. Many in the West, in a fit of pessimism, talked grimly about the military and political implications of the Soviet achievement; others worried aloud about the rapid Soviet deployment of ICBMs which, they claimed, resulted in a "missile gap" to the decided disadvantage of the United States. But the Jeremiahs in Washington (and elsewhere) proved mistaken. To the great surprise of many, Khrushchev failed to convert the USSR's headstart in missile technology into an operational inventory of intercontinental ballistic missiles.

The "missile gap" much like the earlier "bomber gap" proved to be mythical. The only time the USSR may have had more operational ICBMs than the United States was in late 1959 and early 1960; even then, Soviet forces were more than counterbalanced by U.S. B-52 bombers. And in 1961, the United States was certainly producing more ICBMs than the USSR. Though Soviet production had accelerated considerably, the U.S. was producing a vastly superior ICBM force by 1962. By late 1962, at the time of the Cuban missile crisis, the U.S. had at least a three-to-one advantage in strategic weapons.[33] As Table 12 indicates, America's advantage had become massive by late 1964.

Table 12

Strategic missile strengths (late 1964)

	USSR	USA
ICBM Launchers	200	900
Submarine-Launched Ballistic Missiles (SLBM)	120	480
Heavy Bombers	200	600

Source: Wolfe, op. cit., p. 183, fns. 93 and 94.

Why did Khrushchev forego his initial advantage? Why did the Soviet Union fail to convert its startling breakthrough in ballistic missile technology into superiority in actual strategic forces? Though hard evidence regarding this important decision is not available, a number of factors seem to have been involved.

First, Soviet economic growth had slowed considerably during the latter half of the 1950s. The Kremlin leaders were obviously concerned to maintain investment in the civilian sectors of the economy at levels adequate to promote rapid industrial growth. They were also under growing pressure to expand investment in the long-neglected sphere of consumer goods, especially agriculture, and to modernize the Soviet economy (electrify railroad transportation, develop a modern chemicals industry, and more). Furthermore, there was the need to support Moscow's recently initiated foreign aid program. Finally, within the military–space program itself, competition for funds was keen. Soviet space exploration had absorbed considerable resources. Similarly, the research program for a missile defense system was a great burden. Thus, the Soviet decision not to deploy large numbers of ICBMs was made in the context of increasingly straitened economic circumstances.

A second factor was the Soviet leaders' undoubted concern that they not be overtaken by the rapid pace of technological change. They may have decided that, rather than invest heavily in large numbers of relatively primitive, cumbersome, liquid-fueled missiles, it would be more prudent to await the development of a second-generation of missiles which would be more accurate, smaller and solid-fueled. Until such time as a more sophisticated system could be developed, a relatively small force of 75 to 100 "first generation" missiles may have been considered adequate.[34]

The decision not to deploy a large number of ICBMs also involved internal political considerations. On this, as on all questions, Khrushchev framed his policy with an eye to its effect on his relations with his colleagues in the Kremlin. As we shall see in Chapter 6, this particular decision was shaped by the immediate policy objectives of his struggle against a more conservative faction in the Party leadership.[35]

Though Khrushchev decided not to develop a major missile force at this time, one fact should be kept in mind: the Soviet leaders did have the technical means of doing so. That the Soviet leaders chose not to implies that they did not feel especially endangered. Had Khrushchev believed that American strategic superiority posed an active and serious threat to Soviet security, he undoubtedly would have proceeded to develop a major ICBM force, whatever the economic burden. Clearly, he did not. He obviously believed that it was safe to prolong Soviet inferiority in intercontinental forces. The USSR did produce and deploy considerable numbers of medium- and intermediate-range missiles (MRBMs and IRBMs, with respective ranges of 700 and 1,100 miles). These 750 missiles could be targeted only against NATO forces in Europe or American bases along the Soviet border.[36] Khrushchev, obviously, was still relying on a "hostage" strategy.

Soviet strategic forces, therefore, remained inferior to those of the United States. Khrushchev, as Thomas Wolfe has observed, settled for a "second-best strategic posture."[37] In his decisions regarding both long-range heavy bombers and intercontinental missiles, he chose a compromise course. Thus, although he brought about a substantial improvement in Soviet strategic forces, at the end of his tenure in office in 1964 Khrushchev left the Soviet Union inferior to its major adversary in intercontinental delivery systems.[38]

Recent force levels

In the period since Khrushchev's ouster, a basic change has taken place in the East–West strategic balance: the USSR has moved from a position of strategic inferiority to the United States to one of approximate parity. In fact, as Table 13 indicates, the USSR currently has a larger number of land-based intercontinental weapons than has the U. S.

Table 13

Nuclear strike forces (July 1973)

	USSR	USA
ICBMs*	1527	1054
SLBMs*	628	656
MRBMs and IRBMs	600	—
Long-Range Bombers	140	442
Medium-Range Bombers	800	74
Nuclear-Powered Ballistic-Missile Submarines	44	41
Deliverable Nuclear Warheads**(1970)	5662	7502

Source: The Military Balance, 1970–71, 1973–74 (London: The International Institute for Strategic Studies, 1970, 1973). Reprinted by permission.

*Figures for ICBMs and SLBMs indicate the number of delivery vehicles, taking no account of actual or potential MIRV (or MRV) capability of the American Minuteman III ICBMs and Poseidon Ballistic Submarines or the Soviet SS-9 ICBMs.

**On the figures (1970) for nuclear warheads, 6,000 of the U.S. total were then fitted to vehicles designed to reach Soviet territory while only 2,000 of the Soviet warheads were associated with vehicles having a range capable of striking the continental United States.

The first indication that the USSR had decided to accelerate ICBM production appeared in the summer of 1966 when intercontinental missiles began to appear in increasing numbers. Given the lead time of around eighteen months required for their construction, it is probable that the decision to deploy these new ICBMs must have been made in late 1964 or early 1965, shortly before or just after the Brezhnev–Kosygin regime came to power.[39] By October, 1966, the number of ICBM launchers reached about 340; a year later the operational figure was 720, representing a deployment of more than one new launcher a day. As Table 14 indicates, the crossover point in ICBM forces came in 1969 when the USSR reached the U. S. figure of 1,050. By 1972, the Soviets had in place more than 1,500 missiles, or 40 percent more than the U. S. Thus, during the first eight years of the Brezhnev–Kosygin regime, the USSR deployed more than 1,300 ICBMs as compared with a total of 200 during Khrushchev's time in office. Further, the number of missile-launchers in place on Soviet nuclear-powered submarines had grown from 120 to 628.

This transformation in Soviet strategic capability has been dramatic. Until very recently, the Soviet military posture has been substantially inferior to that of the United States. In fact, it was not until sometime in the early or mid-1960s that the USSR acquired a nuclear strike force with what strategists call a survivable, second-strike capability.[40] By 1969, however, the USSR had achieved parity in land-based ICBMs. The significance of this development for world politics was considerable. Soviet

Table 14

Growth of strategic missile strength, 1960–1973 (midyears)

		1960	1961	1962	1963	1964	1965	1966	1967	1968	1969	1970	1971	1972	1973
USA	ICBM	18	63	294	424	834	854	1054	1054	1054	1054	1054	1054	1054	1054
	SLBM	32	96	144	224	416	496	592	656	656	656	656	656	656	656
USSR	ICBM	35	50	75	100	200	270	300	460	800	1050	1300	1510	1527	1527
	SLBM	—	some	some	100	120	120	125	130	130	160	280	440	560	628

ICBM—Intercontinental Ballistic Missile
SLBM—Submarine Launched Ballistic Missile

Source: The Military Balance, 1973–1974, op. cit., p. 71. Reprinted by permission.

acquisition of a major strategic strike force transformed the USSR from an essentially continental military power into a global one. Until the mid-1960s, Soviet military power was vast but not truly worldwide; Soviet forces were generally focused on the area immediately contiguous to the USSR's border regions, especially on Europe. With the acquisition of a vast arsenal of strategic weapons, Soviet power has become truly inter-continental.

Moscow's accomplishments, significant though they are, should not be taken to imply that America's strategic position has remained fixed since 1966, a conclusion which a hasty reading of Table 14 might imply. This is not the case. The American strategic arsenal has been improving in qualitative terms (more accurate guidance systems for missiles, increasingly lighter but more explosive payloads). Most striking, however, has been the American development of the MIRV—the miltiple independently targetable re-entry vehicle. In this area of strategic technology, the United States is well ahead of the USSR. According to a 1972 report of the authoritative International Institute for Strategic Studies, the U. S. has deployed

> some 200 Minuteman 3 ICBM with up to three warheads each and some 160 *Poseidon* SLBM able to carry about 10 warheads each. When *Polaris A3* missiles . . . are also taken into consideration, the smaller American ICBM/SLBM force can now, in theory, deliver approximately 4,300 warheads on about 3,550 . . . separate aiming points. The Soviet Union . . . has not yet tested MIRV and its current ICBM/SLBM force is still capable of threatening a maximum of only about 2,090 separate aiming points. When long-range bombers are also taken into account, the present strategic offensive forces of the United States could, in theory, attack about 5,580 aiming points while their Soviet equivalents could attack only 2,510.[41]

And although it was announced in the summer of 1973 that the USSR had successfully tested the MIRV system, the continued greater sophistication of U.S. strategic forces remains a highly important factor in the nuclear power balance.

Nevertheless, the strategic relationship between the U.S. and the USSR has been altered. The shift in the military balance of forces becomes especially apparent if we take into account other changes in the Soviet defense posture. While not as dramatic as the decision to expand their strategic weapons arsenal, the Kremlin leaders have recently adopted a series of measures geared to improve the mobility and flexibility of Soviet military forces. Starting in about 1964, efforts have been underway to improve the maritime, air and logistic elements within the Soviet military—to improve long-range air transportation, to expand the size and flexibility of Soviet naval forces and to develop amphibious landing capabilities. In addition to enlarging Soviet strategic power, the Kremlin has been attempting to extend the "reach" of its conventional military forces.

In this regard, the most dramatic change has been the striking increase in the activities of the Soviet Navy. Soviet naval forces have traditionally confined their operations to the closed seas around Russia's shores, most notably the Black and Baltic Seas. In the mid-1960s, this situation began to shift when, at the time of the 1964 Cyprus crisis, a modest Soviet naval presence was established in the Mediterranean Sea. However, it was not until additional units were dispatched to the Eastern Mediterranean during the Arab–Israeli War of 1967 that this turn in Soviet policy began to attract attention. The inclusion of a few tank-landing and troop-landing ships carrying black-bereted troops of naval infantry (or marine) forces captured particular notice. Though Soviet naval forces were inadequate to the task of taking on the American Sixth Fleet (and their forces arrived largely after the peak of the crisis), this unprecedented display of amphibious capability clearly demonstrated the Soviet Union's preparedness to intervene in this conflict if necessary.[42]

Since 1967, Soviet naval forces of considerable size (thirty to forty warships, including ten submarines) have been on permanent patrol in the Mediterranean—a striking departure from past Soviet naval practice of hewing to areas along their periphery. The new approach of the Soviet Navy was expressed by Admiral S. E. Gorshkov, head of the Soviet Navy, as early as 1963, when he declared:

> In the past, our ships and naval aviation have operated primarily near our coast . . . concerned mainly with operations and tactical coordination with ground troops. Now . . . we must be prepared through broad offensive operations to deliver crushing strikes against sea and ground targets of the imperialists *on any points on the world's oceans and adjacent territories.*[43] (Italics added.)

The new posture which Admiral Gorshkov suggested has been very much in evidence in recent years. In addition to the establishment of a permanent naval presence in the Mediterranean, which at times has been more numerous than the fifty or more warships of the American Sixth Fleet, Soviet naval forces have for the first time in their history patrolled the Indian Ocean, the Red Sea, and the Persian Gulf. Even the onetime "American Lake," the Caribbean Sea, was intruded upon in 1969 when a squadron of seven Soviet warships sailed into the area and conducted anti-submarine exercises in the Gulf of Mexico.[44]

Though the Soviet presence in the Mediterranean and Caribbean Seas and the Indian Ocean still has not transformed the world's balance of power, it does symbolize a striking Soviet success in breaking out of Russia's traditional realm in the Baltic and Black Seas. The Red Fleet is now out in the warm water. (In April, 1970, in honor of the one hundredth anniversary of Lenin's birth, the largest Soviet exercises in history were held when over two hundred warships were deployed throughout the world.)[45] An oft-proclaimed objective of Tsarist foreign policy (dating back to the time of Peter the Great who apparently had hoped at one time to seize the Island of Madagascar off East Africa and thereby penetrate the Indian Ocean) seems to have been achieved. As the newspaper of the Soviet Defense Ministry, *Krasnaya zvezda (Red Star)*, wrote in 1970, "the age-old dreams of our people have become a reality. The pennants of Soviet ships now flutter in the most remote corners of the seas and oceans."[46]

Much of this naval activity is merely symbolic. So far, Soviet naval squadrons visiting the Caribbean and the Indian Ocean are very much on "show the flag" cruises, merely demonstrating the USSR's ability to ply these distant waters should it desire to do so. However, the Soviet Mediterranean presence is rather more substantial. The Soviet naval forces here have been reinforced by the arrival of new ships, such as the helicopter carriers *Moskva* and *Leningrad,* each capable of carrying thirty to thirty-five helicopters plus several hundred "naval infantrymen" and ocean-going amphibious landing ships; they also have had access to several Arab ports and dockyard facilities in places such as Latakia (Syria), Port Said, Alexandria, Mersa Matruh (Egypt), Hodeida (Yemen), Aden, and Mogadishu and Berbera (Somalia).[47] Though the Soviet Mediterranean fleet still cannot match the U.S. Sixth Fleet—the two American attack carriers with their jet fighters and fighter bombers attached to the Sixth Fleet have more fire power than the Soviet helicopter carriers that are useful mainly for anti-submarine warfare—it is now established as an important force in the region. Thus, in response to Western concern about Soviet naval activity in the Mediterranean area, the USSR declared:

> Soviet ships entered the [Mediterranean] Sea on the strength of the U.S.S.R.'s sovereign right to make free use of this open sea. We have a full right to this from historical, political, economic and geographic points of view. . . . As a Black Sea and, in this sense, a Mediterranean power [the USSR] is closely connected with all problems involving the peoples of this area of Europe, Africa and Asia. It is directly interested in insuring the security of its southern border.[48]

Moscow clearly intends to maintain a permanent naval presence in the area.

In order to support its expanded role, the Brezhnev–Kosygin regime has greatly enlarged the size of the Soviet navy. In addition to the two helicopter carriers, the Soviet fleet has recently acquired a full-size attack carrier, the *Kiev* (with a second under construction), and almost three hundred submarines.[49] Of these, forty-four are nuclear-powered and, like the American *Polaris* and *Poseidon,* are equipped with missiles (twelve to sixteen each) for submerged firing. Apparently, in addition to its traditional role of interdicting the sea communications of potential adversaries, the submarine arm has acquired the new mission of contributing to Soviet strategic power.

There have also been changes in several of the other armed services. As noted earlier, Soviet naval infantrymen are now deployed with the USSR's fleets around the world. These "Black Berets," akin the U. S. Marine Corps, were revived in 1964—having been disbanded in the 1950s—and now number about 17,000.[50] Furthermore, the Soviet air transport facilities—military planes capable of carrying tanks, troops and self-propelled artillery—have been greatly expanded. As Thomas Wolfe has pointed out, the quick seizure of Prague by Soviet airborne troops and the massive air-resupply operation mounted after the June, 1967, war to replenish Egypt's depleted forces graphically demonstrates the extraordinary growth of Soviet airlift capabilities.[51]

The developments described above, when taken together, involve changes in military capabilities without precedent in Russian history. Soviet naval and air forces are now capable of playing a totally new role; they can now project Soviet military power anywhere in the world. As several admirals proudly boasted in speeches marking Soviet Navy Day during the last few years, Soviet sea power has extended its reach "to remote areas of the world's oceans previously considered a zone of supremacy of the imperialist powers." According to *Pravda,* the arrival of the Soviet fleet ended America's "uncontrolled domination of the Mediterranean." Ancient Rome's motto for the Mediterranean, *mare nostrum*—revived by Mussolini and, more recently, by the "American imperialists"—had now, according to Moscow, fallen into oblivion. Henceforth, official naval sources declared, the mission of the Soviet Navy would include "constantly cruising and patrolling whenever required in defense of the state interests of the Soviet Union."[52]

The significance of these developments cannot be overemphasized. As a result of force build-ups in the mid and late 1960s, the USSR has reached a state of rough parity with the United States, including quantitative superiority in long-range nuclear missiles, and an unprecedented mobility based on world-wide naval expansion. This dramatic improvement in military capabilities was accomplished at very great cost. The fact that Soviet strategic capabilities (especially air and naval forces) were, as late as the mid-1950s, considerably smaller than those of the United States indicates that investment in defense-related production in the USSR since then must have been very great indeed. As one analyst has observed, "no other major economy has increased rates for defense expenditures at the rate of the Soviet Union between 1960 and 1965."[53] In purely military terms, however, these monies have been well-spent. In 1963, the USSR had a land army capable of fighting a war in Europe (or in the Far East) and a nuclear force for long-range bombardment with very little, save its traditionally large submarine fleet, in between. This situation has dramatically changed. Today, for the first time since their disastrous defeat at the hands of the Japanese almost seventy years ago, the Russians are experimenting with the use of seapower in waters far removed from their traditional preserves.[54] Furthermore, they have acquired an air transport fleet which affords Soviet strike forces a new flexibility.

What this suggests is that the USSR is no longer merely a large Eurasian power; it now can project its physical presence into distant conflicts around the globe. Moscow's traditional strategic orientation— focusing on Europe and land armies—clearly has been abandoned. In addition, strategic relations between East and West have been transformed. The familiar situation in which the United States could intervene in troubled areas around the globe without fear of being challenged has now most assuredly passed. Today, there are two major powers with world-wide strategic capabilities.

Is the USSR "defense-minded"?

What are the political implications of these shifts in the East–West military balance? The most obvious relates to the changed character of the American strategic position. In earlier periods, American military superiority gave the U.S. a considerable margin of safety. In the view of many, it guaranteed world peace. Now, however, the enormous increase in Soviet strategic capabilities has added a new and possible dangerous dimension to East–West relations. The environment which created the tenuous but stable peace, it is said, has been disturbed and with it the stability of the peace. A forceful presentation of this position has been given by Zbigniew Brzezinski who writes that

> Until now peace was safeguarded through asymmetrical deterrence.
> U.S. self-restraint and one-sided deterrence . . . interacted with the Soviet
> instinct of self-preservation and Moscow's deliberately fostered ambiguity
> and even exaggeration of its own power. That system worked for 20 years.
> It is being replaced by a novel state of symmetrical deterrence in which U.S.
> instinct of self-preservation and rationality interacts with the Soviet instinct
> of self-preservation and rationality . . . in the setting of parity.[55]

The question arises: will the changes in the international environment from "asymmetrical" to "symmetrical" deterrence affect Soviet foreign policy behavior? "Power tempts—not only serves—policy," notes Brzezinski.[56] Will Moscow's newly acquired ability to project the "reach" of its conventional forces to distant shores entice it to use this power?

One's answers to these important questions depends largely on how one reads the basic purposes and security orientation of the Soviet leadership. There are divergent opinions, as one would expect on such an important matter. One school of thought sees the current Soviet build-up largely in terms of what it regards as the USSR's "defensive orientation." In his March, 1969, press conference, for example, President Nixon made the following interesting observation:

> I would also like to point this out—an interesting thing about Soviet military
> and diplomatic history: they have always thought in defensive terms and if
> you read their—not only their political leaders but their military leaders—the
> emphasis is on defense.[57]

The President's interpretation, which must be read as a political statement as well as a personal judgment, reflects a fairly widespread view that the Soviet leaders have a deep-seated traditional preference for defense over offense. Former Defense Secretary Robert McNamara identified himself with this position several years ago when he observed that huge Soviet expenditures on air defense programs in the past are to be explained by the fact that "they have almost a religious conviction on the subject of defense."[58] Clearly, an argument could be made that the recent investment in strategic and conventional military forces is compatible with a defensive orientation. Numerous analysts, including former Secretary McNamara, have suggested that the sixty-seven Anti-Ballistic Missiles (known as the Galosh System) installed around Moscow reflect this defensive "philosophy."[59]

Others take a more pessimistic view and look upon the growth of Soviet military power with considerable alarm. While these analysts may agree that Soviet policy has in the past been defensively oriented, this is seen to be the result of necessity, not desire. The Kremlin's European focus, its great concern with protecting national security, and the generally inward-looking orientation of Soviet policy in past years was the product, it is said, of Soviet weakness rather than will. With the rapid growth of Soviet military forces, such constraints on Kremlin policy have been removed. And, in the view of the most pessimistic, the situation is now becoming quite dangerous. Having achieved approximate equality with the United States, the USSR is said to be striving for actual military supremacy. For example, the editor of the authoritative naval publication, *Jane's Fighting Ships*, has warned that the USSR's naval forces are becoming a "super navy of a super power" whose policy increasingly appears to be one of "show the flag and police the world."[60] The marked shift in the strategic balance, it is argued, will lead the USSR to a more active, if not more aggressive, policy, one in which the Kremlin leaders might well be tempted to undertake a more dangerous range of risks and bolder policies in crisis situations. At the very least, it is argued, with the expansion of its conventional and nuclear strength at "flood tide," the USSR will be a more difficult, less cooperative, if not actually more dangerous adversary in the years ahead.

Making judgments regarding Soviet intentions are, at best, an extremely hazardous undertaking. It is impossible to predict with much accuracy what most countries might do in the future. Numerous factors, both domestic and international, affect how new situations are perceived, alternatives assessed, and policy choices arrived at. While analysis of changes in military capabilities may help define what the USSR can consider attempting to accomplish, comparative force levels by themselves cannot explain very much.

Some light can be shed on our question regarding Soviet "defense-mindedness" if we examine the motives which may have led the Kremlin leaders to undertake this costly military expansion program. From its timing—the original decision was probably approved in late 1964—we can assume that Moscow agreed to this course of action in response to the frustrations laid bare by the Cuban missile crisis. (As Soviet Deputy Foreign Minister V. V. Kuznetsov told an American official shortly after the crisis broke, "Never will we be caught like this again."[61]) Soviet political strategists had long been operating under the weight of American military predominance. Some in Moscow had undoubtedly taken the position that the United States took actions it did not allow the USSR simply because it was stronger. They probably argued that superior strength, not equity, had for many years allowed the U.S. to build military bases close to the Soviet border while denying similar advantages to the Soviet Union.[62] The October, 1962, Cuban crisis undoubtedly helped make their argument convincing. Having been compelled by the United States, under threat of massive nuclear bombardment, to withdraw their missiles from Cuba, the Soviet leaders must have now agreed that continued military weakness was politically intolerable. A decision, thus, was taken to end their inferiority in strategic weapons.

While their experience in the Caribbean convinced the Kremlin authorities of the need to divest themselves of the liability of a continued second-best strategic posture, it also taught that the immobility of Soviet forces was a major handicap. This lesson was brought home even more dramatically by the war in Vietnam. American intervention in Southeast Asia in 1965 provided a startling demonstration of the flexibility of America's military forces. The United States moved 100,000 men 10,000 miles in 100 days with relative ease of transport and supply and without reducing its forces elsewhere in the world. Soviet forces were not mobile at that time. If the Soviet Union had decided to intervene with troops in Vietnam it would have had enormous problems in getting the troops there, landing them, and supporting them once they had arrived.

Thus, as during the missile crisis,[63] the Soviet Union had no way of intervening in Vietnam, far from its main forces in Eastern Europe, short of going straight to nuclear war. To help remedy this situation, Moscow decided that the development of a mobile naval and air transportation system would allow Soviet forces a wider range of military options. The Kremlin thus began to carry out a change in strategic orientation similar to one which had occurred in the United States during the early 1960s; they adopted the strategic doctrine of "flexible response." In fact, they began to use essentially the same language.[64]

Seen from this perspective, the Kremlin's decision to increase the flexibility of Soviet military forces made eminent sense. Ever since the end of World War II, the Soviet leaders had been compelled to sit and watch while the U.S. deployed its military forces around the world with relative impunity. Not only had Washington ringed the USSR with military bases but, relying on an extensive long-range air and naval transport system, amphibious landing capabilities and a world-wide network of staging bases, American force intervened militarily in Berlin (1948), Korea (1950), Lebanon (1958), Vietnam and the Dominican Republic (1965). Had they wanted to, the Kremlin leaders simply did not have the physical wherewithal even to contemplate taking a similar course of action—except, of course, in Eastern Europe. Many in Moscow obviously felt that the time was now ripe to reduce this American advantage. Some probably also argued that the USSR had an obligation to counter what in the mid-1960s was seen as an increasingly aggressive American foreign policy. Highly agitated by the deep U.S. involvement in Vietnam, a number of Soviet leaders apparently became convinced that American military power was being committed to the suppression of "progressive" movements in the underdeveloped world. Flexible military power would allow the Soviet Union directly to challenge such American aggression. As a Yugoslav writer observed, Moscow began to embark upon "a policy of countering the [American] strategy of local and restricted war" by providing itself with the kind of military capability to conduct that "selfsame local and unrestricted war."[65]

While the desire to counter the United States may not have been the Kremlin's original motivation, this rationale has increasingly become a key element in the official Soviet explanation of their new strategic posture. Thus, as Admiral Gorshkov has boasted: "The flag of the Soviet navy now proudly flies over the oceans of the world. Sooner or later, the United States will have to understand it no longer has mastery of the seas."[66] The Soviet presence in the Mediterranean is explained on two grounds: first, in terms of protecting Soviet security interests. The U.S. Sixth Fleet, according to Vice-Admiral Smirnov, is stationed in this area, thousands of miles from American shores,

> in order to control lines of communication passing through the zone of the Black Sea and the Mediterranean Sea, as well as to be prepared to strike at enemy targets from the sea and air with nuclear and conventional weapons, and the Soviet Union and other socialist countries are designated as the principal enemy.
> In these circumstances, the interests of security have demanded that the Soviet Union indefatigably strengthen its capacity.[67]

The presence of Soviet vessels in the Mediterranean serves another "noble lofty aim"—to challenge the "gendarme function" of the Sixth Fleet. The arrival of Soviet naval vessels, suggests Smirnov, disrupts the American ability to intervene in the area; this implies "the loss of the usually unrestricted freedom to engage with impunity in any dark deeds the American imperialists choose." The United States has lost

> the freedom to threaten Mediterranean states that have taken the path of political independence, the freedom to weave nets of military ventures, to support rotten, reactionary regimes with bayonets and to help carry out counter-revolutionary plots and coups—freedoms that have now disappeared into oblivion.[68]

In his view, Soviet naval presence in the Mediterranean helps ensure this.

Thus, the improvement in Soviet capabilities may have induced a change in strategic outlook. In the past, the USSR has been cautious in offering its support to local "progressive" movements and, with the exception of the Middle East, has been very reluctant to commit Soviet troops beyond East Europe and its Far Eastern border areas. However, it now has acquired the kinds of military forces capable of directly challenging

American positions at various points around the globe. The temptation to use them for such purposes will undoubtedly be there. As much was suggested by Soviet Foreign Minister Andrei Gromyko when he declared in 1968: "To paralyze the policy of aggression in any manifestation and in any area of the world—this is the task advanced and solved in practice by our country, together with the other peace-loving states."[69] The option of "containing imperialism" is now an open one.

The very acquisition of strategic mobility has already altered the situation. Even if the USSR adheres to a prudent, low-risk posture, the strategic options available to the United States have changed. Soviet adoption of the strategic doctrine of "multiple military options" and the development of mobile force capabilities must mean that the United States will enjoy less freedom of action in the future. Now Washington will have to think twice about moving its own strategic forces. It is possible to imagine a situation in which both American "Green Berets" and Soviet "Black Berets" are dispatched to an underdeveloped third country in support of opposite sides in a local crisis. No longer alone in its ability to project its physical and military presence, the U.S. will inevitably have to tread more cautiously for fear of stumbling into the Russians.

The Western failure to act at the time of the coup in Libya in September, 1969, may well be evidence of the inhibitory influence of the Soviet naval presence to which Vice-Admiral Smirnov referred. Though the combined British and American forces stationed in Libya far outnumbered and outgunned the small and inexperienced Libyan army, Western troops simply stood by while rebel forces ousted pro-Western King Idris.[70] While numerous factors may explain Western policy, American and British passivity stands in marked contrast to their behavior during earlier Middle East conflicts. For example, in order to stabilize the shaky regimes in Beirut and Amman in 1958, the U.S. Sixth Fleet landed Marines in Lebanon and provided cover for a British landing in Jordan. In 1969, the introduction of a new element onto the scene—the Soviet navy—could only have had a cautionary effect on Western policymakers. Such, indeed, is Moscow's claim. The "socialist community," declared *Radio Moscow,* "by the very fact of its existence," ensured the successful establishment of the new Libyan regime.

Were it not for the socialist states, the imperialist powers could have eliminated this regime in a few hours, just as they have dome more than once in the past. . . . Perhaps there are some who believe that the American Wheelus bases and the British bases in Libya were evacuated because the new regime evoked admiration and appreciation among those who occupied them! . . . No the real reason for what happened . . . was that those foreigners . . . were aware that any military interference in the affairs of the independent Arab state would have invited an immediate and very firm reaction from the Soviet Union. . . .[71]

Soviet spokesmen also contend that "the imperialists" were forced to abandon their plans to seize Arab oil fields during the 1973–1974 oil embargo solely because of the power and benevolent attitude of the

USSR. The increased might of the socialist world, it is claimed, means that "the aggressors are no longer strong enough, . . . no longer dare, as in the past, to impose their will with impunity upon the peoples of the developing countries. . . ."[72]

The salient question remains: Will the Soviet leaders, having achieved parity in strategic weapons after nearly a decade of strenuous effort and sacrifice, now seek to capitalize on these achievements by actively pressing for political advantage and accepting, where necessary, a far wider range of risk? In short, will power tempt policy? Or will a militarily powerful Kremlin leadership, secure as never before in history from external threats, now agree to a more responsible and cooperative role in world affairs?

The evidence on this vital question remains unclear. The Soviet leaders are themselves probably uncertain as to their future course of action. This is true, in part, because they have apparently discovered that it is far more difficult then generally realized to translate military, especially nuclear, power into political power. As Walter Slocombe has observed:

> On the historical record, even nuclear monopoly, much less a first-strike superiority over a lesser nuclear power, does not give its possessor dominating political influence which a comparison of strictly military capabilities would imply. The years of nuclear monopoly and first-strike superiority strongly suggests that nuclear power alone, however great, is no talisman for diplomatic fortune.[73]

The Soviets recognize this point—at least as it concerns the United States. America's failure in Vietnam, they have repeatedly argued, is the result of Washington's refusal to recognize that even the "immense military might of the United States has its limits."[74] It is logical to assume that at least some Soviet leaders may view their own military power in similarly modest terms.

Not only is the relationship of military power and political influence ambiguous, as both Washington and, apparently, Moscow now seem to realize, but political adventurism is not always linked to military strength. Thus, as former Defense Secretary McNamara noted, "it is by no means obvious that the Soviets will pursue policies more risky, or adventuristic, merely because of their growing strategic capability. Indeed, it is a striking historical fact that the most adventuristic Soviet behavior since World War II has come at times of relative Soviet strategic weakness, rather than strength."[75] Increased military strength *might* encourage a more belligerent aggressive policy stance towards the West; thus far, at least, it has not.

The likelihood remains, that a stronger military posture will inevitably make the USSR more difficult to deal with. U.S. strategic superiority in the 1950s and 1960s was an important constraint on Soviet behavior; strategic inferiority obviously set a limit on the risks on which Moscow policymakers could safely run. That constraint has now been reduced and the limit raised. The scope for more assertive action has been increased. Thus, in some future crisis, when the Soviets believe themselves to be in a strong strategic position, they may well prove more recalcitrant, less amenable to compromise, and more unyielding in their demands. Furthermore, in such circumstances, the hard-liners in the Soviet leadership are likely to argue that the time has come to make the U.S. swallow diplomatic defeat much as the USSR was forced to do in 1962. Brzezinski has observed in this connection: "One does not know how the Soviet leaders retroactively interpret the Cuban Missile Crisis, but might they not now speculate that the U.S. would have acted differently if symmetrical deterrence existed."[76] They undoubtedly also speculate about the options, denied them in 1962 because of the existing military balance of forces, which are now open.

The significance of the recent Soviet military build-up is still not easily judged. On the one hand, the USSR has acquired an enormous weapons capability—including vast strategic weapons stockpiles plus a considerably increased capability for global military involvement. In addition, large, well-equipped conventional military forces with considerable tank, tactical aircraft, and missile capabilities are stationed in Eastern Europe and on the border with China—forces whose fire power and state of readiness far surpass those of possible enemies across the border (and seem, especially in Europe, to contradict Moscow's announced policy of détente). To the extent that their newly achieved military capabilities persuade them to think they are militarily the equal of the United States, the Soviet leaders may indeed seek to pursue Soviet interests more vigorously and, at the very least, be tempted to undertake a policy of "containment of American imperialism."

There are trends, however, which point in another, less menacing, direction. There is some evidence that Moscow has come to recognize that military power cannot easily be translated into tangible advantage or usable political strength. Events in the Middle East, especially the ouster of Soviet military advisors from Egypt in 1972—which dramatically revealed how fragile, despite its massive military and economic assistance, Soviet influence in the area actually is—must have helped bring this message home. Further, the Soviet leadership has expressed great concern to avoid taking "rash actions" which might jeopardize Soviet security interests. For example, they have spoken with great apprehension about the dangers of "escalation" inherent in "local wars"; they have expressed fear that even minor conflicts, should they "escalate," might eventually threaten to engulf the Soviet Union itself. Thus, the Kremlin has consistently refused to become directly involved in "wars of liberation" and has at times sought to discourage them. (This conservative policy posture brought the wrath of the Chinese down on the heads of the Soviet leaders.)

Furthermore, it was clearly their recognition of the danger of nuclear confrontation which led the Kremlin leaders to recognize that limits must be placed on their rivalry with the United States and, as part of this recognition, to sign formal agreements in May, 1972, limiting the deployment of offensive and defensive missile systems. Though these documents, resulting from the SALT negotiations, represent only a partial step forward in the direction of arms control,[77] they do indicate a real mutual concern regarding the dangers—and costs—resulting from the unrestricted buildup of strategic weapons.

Soviet intentions thus seem contradictory and ambiguous; there appear to be conflicting tendencies in Soviet policy. Some trends seem to indicate a continuation of "defensive" and generally inward-looking traditions, a desire to avoid conflicts, to work for serious arms limitations and to concentrate resources on serving civilian needs and on enlarging consumer benefits. Others indicate a more belligerent attitude which aspires to a dominant world position for the USSR, to repay the U.S. in kind for its "containment" policies and, generally, to expand the Soviet presence in the Middle East, in South Asia, and elsewhere.

Which posture Moscow will ultimately adopt—a "forward" policy or one sensitive to the dangers of confrontation and the need for mutual accommodation—will depend, of course, on many factors, of which the changing military balance is but one. Future Soviet policy will also be shaped by the opportunities and challenges that arise from a rapidly changing international environment. Here, in particular, the military and diplomatic posture of the United States and China are obviously of signal importance. Policy choices will also be influenced by the particular balance of forces within the domestic Soviet political system—which elements, with what traditions, concerns, and bargaining power, prevail at any given time in the policy process.

Finally, lying at the heart of this question, is the political character and world outlook of the current Soviet regime. The effect of increased strategic power on Soviet behavior will depend, at bottom, on whether the Kremlin leadership feels itself basically threatened by outside powers or, on the whole, secure; whether it finds itself generally satisfied with the present world order or is desirous of fundamental changes; whether it regards itself as basically estranged from the other nations and governments of the world or as sufficiently a part of the current international political system as to share a real interest in working toward accommodation on the very difficult issues that divide them. It is to the examination of these basic political attitudes and values and the impact of the domestic political system on them that the next chapters are addressed.

Notes

[1]As noted earlier, per capita production is still not especially high, especially in consumer goods. According to one study, the USSR in 1970 ranked eighteenth in the world in terms of GNP *per capita*. *World Military Expenditures, 1971* (Washington, D. C.: United States Arms Control and Disarmament Agency, 1972), p. 50.

[2]*The Military Balance, 1973–1974* (London: The International Institute for Strategic Studies, 1973), p. 6; and *Strategic Survey, 1972* (London: The International Institute for Strategic Studies, 1973), p. 3.

[3]The above discussion is based essentially on *The Military Balance, 1972–1973,* (London: The International Institute for Strategic Studies, 1972), pp. 6–8, 72.

[4]Quoted by Louis Fisher, *Russia's Road from Peace to War, Soviet Foreign Relations, 1917–41* (New York: Harper and Row, 1969), p. 4.

[5]See George Fischer, *Soviet Opposition to Stalin* (Cambridge: Harvard University Press, 1952).

[6]See Sorlin, *op. cit.,* p. 184f. Though party militants were the most determined members of the population, they undoubtedly had mixed motives. While many were undoubtedly politically convinced *apparatchiki,* some, especially those who joined the Party for careerist reasons, fought well out of fear as much as out of loyalty. As Sorlin suggests, they had the most to lose for as Party members they faced certain execution at the hands of the Nazis. On the crucial influence of the Communist Party during the siege of Leningrad, see Gouré, *op. cit.*

[7]Full-time students at colleges or other institutions of higher learning are deferred until they graduate or flunk out. Under a 1967 revision of the draft law, a year's active service after graduation is now obligatory.

[8]*The New York Times,* October 22, 1967.

[9]*Ibid.,* February 10, 1964, and Thomas W. Wolfe, "The Military," in Allen Kassof, ed., *Prospects for Soviet Society* (New York: Frederick A. Praeger, Publishers, 1968), p. 136. The above discussion is derived, in part, from Wolfe's article, especially pages 133–136.

[10]*Krasnaya zvezda,* March 27, 1969; quoted in Colette Shulman, ed., *We the Russians* (New York: Praeger, Publishers, 1971), pp. 214–15.

[11]*The Limitations of Strategic Arms,* Part II, pp. 66, 80.

[12]Published in *Oktiabr* (October), No. 9, 1969; reprinted in Shulman, *We the Russians,* p. 203.

[13]For a recent analysis of Soviet problems recruiting an adequate number of qualified officers, see *The New York Times,* March 19, 1973.

[14]As one analyst has written of the functions of the Warsaw Pact, "Militarily it is an administrative headquarters within the Soviet Ministry of Defense designed to rationalize and coordinate East European resources, training and defense policy; it has neither a command function nor a logistic establishment separate from that of the Soviet Armed Forces." Malcolm Mackintosh, *The Evolution of the Warsaw Pact,* Adelphi Papers No. 58 (London: The Institute for Strategic Studies, June, 1969), p. 17.

[15]Figures based on *The Military Balance, 1973–74, op. cit.,* pp. 10–13, 87–92 and *The New York Times,* September 3, 1971.

[16]Thomas W. Wolfe, *Soviet Power and Europe, 1945–1970* (Baltimore: The Johns Hopkins Press, 1970), p. 10, fn. 6. The Soviet figure usually cited in this context is taken from a speech by Khrushchev in 1960. Wolfe suggests that Khrushchev deliberately deflated his figures to demonstrate the USSR's contribution to disarmament in the post-war years. Though precise figures cannot be fixed with any certainty, Wolfe makes a persuasive case for his higher estimate.

[17]John C. Campbell, *The United States in World Affairs, 1948–49* (New York: Harper & Bros., 1949), p. 7.

[18]Wolfe, *loc. cit.* and Russell F. Weigley, *History of the United States Army* (New York: The Macmillan Co., 1967), p. 569.

[19]Wolfe, *op. cit.,* p. 38, fn. 15, 53.

[20]Quoted in Campbell, *op. cit.,* p. 30.

[21]*Keesing's Contemporary Archives,* Vol. V, 1943–1946, p. 7472.

[22]The size of the U.S. military establishment did not substantially increase until the Korean War began in June, 1950.

[23]"On July 24 I casually mentioned to Stalin that we had a new weapon of unusual destructive force. The Russian Premier showed no special interest. All he said was that he was glad to hear it and hoped we would make 'good use of it

against the Japanese.' " Harry S. Truman, *Memoirs, I: Year of Decisions* (Garden City: Doubleday and Co., Inc., 1955), p. 416.

[24]In his recently published memoirs, Marshal Georgi Zhukov indicated that Stalin did in fact appreciate the significance of President Truman's revelation and that the Soviet leader remarked that evening that he was going to tell those in charge of Russia's atomic program "to step things up." Marshal G. K. Zhukov, *Vospominania i razmyshlenia* (Reminiscences and Reflections) (Moscow: *Novosti Press Agency*, 1969), p. 713; cited in Wolfe, *op. cit.*, p. 36, fn. 8.

[25]Quoted in "Changing Military Thought in the Soviet Union," *World Today*, Vol. XIII, No. 12 (December, 1957), p. 520. Much of the discussion of Stalinist military doctrine is based upon this useful article.

[26]*Ibid.* As George Quester has pointed out, this is the logical posture for those nations still without nuclear weapons. "To discourage intimidation, the pain inflicting or terroristic effects of nuclear weapons must also be minimized; one must express scepticism about the physical destruction they cause. . . . By feigning a near-indifference to the sorrow that atomic weapons can cause, one can perhaps deny others the clues they need to press their advantage in crises." See his "On the Identification of Real and Pretended Communist Military Doctrine," *Journal of Conflict Resolution*, Vol. X, No. 2 (June, 1966), p. 173. Mao's slogan, "The atomic bomb is a paper tiger," is of the same piece.

[27]J. V. Stalin, "Election Speech . . ." *op. cit.*, p. 123.

[28]Wolfe, *op. cit.*, pp. 40–41.

[29]Herbert S. Dinerstein, "The Soviet Outlook," in Robert E. Osgood, et. al., *America and the World, From the Truman Doctrine to Vietnam* (Baltimore: The Johns Hopkins Press, 1970), pp. 89, 92.

[30]Herbert S. Dinerstein, *Fifty Years of Soviet Foreign Policy* (Baltimore: The Johns Hopkins Press, 1968), p. 39.

[31]Wolfe, *op. cit.*, pp. 178–84. The fact that the Soviets decided to concentrate on the medium-range BADGER rather than the long-range BISON and BEAR bombers explains why Western predictions of the mid-1950s of a "bomber gap" proved to be a myth.

[32]*Ibid.* Wolfe also suggests that Stalin's concentration of troops in Eastern Europe could have had the same deterrent purpose in view; *i.e.*, by creating the impression that Soviet forces were prepared for rapid advance to the Atlantic, the militarily superior American forces would be restrained. *Ibid.*, p. 46f.

[33]American ICBM production was greatly accelerated by the new Kennedy Administration in 1961. Not only was American production of ICBMs significantly increased—with a still greater deployment scheduled for the coming years—but American missile technology had been rapidly improving. Thus, the newly developed solid-fuel Minuteman missile was beginning to replace older Atlas and Titan ICBMs. For an interesting discussion of the impact of the Kennedy Administration's defense policy on Moscow, see Dinerstein, *Fifty Years of Soviet Foreign Policy*, pp. 46–50.

[34]For an elaboration of this argument, see Wolfe, *op. cit.*, p. 182.

[35]Schwartz, "The Cuban Missile Venture," *op. cit.*, pp. 286–296.

[36]Wolfe, *op. cit.*, pp. 183–84.

[37]*Ibid.*, p. 134.

[38]*Ibid.*, pp. 134–35, 182–84.

[39]Wolfe, *op. cit.*, p. 432. Another source indicates that this decision might have been taken in the last months of the Khrushchev regime. Walter Slocombe, *The Political Implications of Strategic Parity*, Adelphi Papers No. 77 (London: Institute for Strategic Studies May, 1971), p. 5. This does not seem very likely. Khrushchev, as we shall later see, was wedded to a rather different economic–strategic game plan which did not include large-scale spending for defense. This, in fact, helps explain why the military joined in the cabal to oust him in 1964. It is true, however, as Slocombe points out, that research and development work for these new weapons, including the third-generation SS-9s and SS-11s as well

as the Y-class (Polaris-type) submarines, must have been carried out during the Krushchev years.

[40]Slocombe, *op. cit.*, p. 1. The precise date involved is somewhat hazy. Slocombe states that it may have been as early as 1962 or as late as 1966. The significance of this development is clear. It was only then that Soviet strategic forces became large and sufficiently well-protected that they could absorb the heaviest attacks that the U.S. could launch against Soviet nuclear forces and still be able to retaliate and inflict a crippling blow against the United States. Until then, the Soviet claim to be able to deter the U.S. was largely a bluff—*i.e.*, until then the American nuclear forces, in a "preemptive first strike," could have effectively destroyed the Soviet strategic arsenal.

[41]*The Military Balance, 1972–73, op. cit.*, p. 85. While Soviet missiles have larger "throw-weight" capabilities, U.S. planes more than compensate for any advantages gained. Soviet ICBMs and SLBMs could, in theory, carry a payload of 6.5 million pounds as against 3.8 million pounds for the United States. However, U.S. B-52s and FB-111s could carry 33.4 million pounds against some 4.8 million pounds for their Soviet counterparts. *Strategic Survey, 1972, op. cit.*, p. 17.

[42]Wolfe, *op. cit.*, p. 443f. See also Thomas W. Wolfe, "The Soviet Quest for More Globally Mobile Military Power," RAND *Memorandum*, RM-5554-PR, (Santa Monica: The RAND Corporation, December, 1967), p. 10.

[43]Quoted in Martin Edmonds and John Skitt, "Current Soviet Maritime Strategy and NATO," *International Affairs* (London: January, 1969), p. 42.

[44]*The New York Times*, December 13, 1968; July 20, August 21, 1969; October 10, December 24, 1970; March 23, 1971.

[45]*Ibid.*, April 15, 17, and 23, 1970.

[46]Quoted in C. L. Sulzberger, "The Dream of Czar Peter," *The New York Times*, May 7, 1971.

[47]*The New York Times*, February 14, 1968; November 13 and December 24, 1970; and April 9, 1973.

[48]Quoted in *ibid.*, November 11, 1968.

[49]Submarines have always been the main strength of the Soviet Navy. The USSR entered World War II with about 220 submarines, the largest force in the world at that time. Wolfe, *Soviet Power in Europe*, p. 45. On the Kremlin's recent interest in full-size carriers, see *The New York Times* (February 27, 1973 and January 14, 1974).

[50]*The Military Balance, 1973–74, op. cit.*, p. 7; see also Wolfe, *Soviet Power in Europe*, p. 444.

[51]Wolfe. *Soviet Power in Europe*, p. 448.

[52]*Ibid.*, p. 446 and *The New York Times*, November 28, 1968.

[53]Cohn, "General Growth Performance of the Soviet Economy," *Economic Performance . . .* , p. 10. See also Michael Boretsky, "The Growth of Soviet Arms Technology—A Debate," *Survival*, Vol. XIV, No. 4 (July–August, 1972), p. 175. Boretsky makes the seemingly obvious but often disputed point that in order to play "catch up," the Soviet rate of investment in defense industries must have been greater than in the United States in absolute terms and, relatively, a far greater burden on the decidedly smaller Soviet economy.

[54]During the Russo–Japanese War (1904–1905) a Russian naval squadron (commanded by Admiral Rozhdestvensky), sailed from the Baltic Sea for Vladivostok in the Far East. After seven months at sea, and shortly before it was to arrive, it was attacked by a superior and more efficient Japanese force at the Straits of Tsushima (off Korea). Within a few hours, the Russian squadron was wiped out of existence.

[55]Zbigniew Brzezinski, "Peace and Power," *Encounter*, Vol. XXXI, No. 5 (November, 1968), p. 8.

[56]*Ibid.*, p. 3.

[57]"Transcript of President Nixon's Press Conference," *The New York Times*, March 15, 1969.

[58]*Department of Defense Appropriations for 1968*, Hearings Before a Subcommittee on the Committee on Appropriations, House of Representatives, 90th Congress, 2nd Session, Part II. (Washington Government Printing Office, 1967), p. 198.

[59]*Ibid.*

[60]*The Times* (London), July 29, 1971; and the *Los Angeles Times*, July 29, 1971.

[61]John Newhouse, *Cold Dawn The Story of SALT* (New York: Holt, Rinehart and Winston, 1973), p. 68.

[62]This point is well argued, in connection with the U. S. bombing of North Vietnam, by Herbert S. Dinerstein, "The Soviet Outlook," *op. cit.*, pp. 76–77.

[63]The relative inflexibility of the Soviet position was driven home during the Cuban Crisis when, as a result of American pressure, Guinea and Senegal denied Russian planes the right to refuel in Conakry or Dakar, thus preventing Moscow from bypassing the U.S. blockade and reinforcing their exposed installations in Cuba. Robert F. Kennedy, *Thirteen Days* (New York: W. W. Norton and Co., 1969), pp. 122–123.

[64]See Wolfe, *Soviet Power in Europe*, p. 452.

[65]Quoted in Thomas W. Wolfe, "The Soviet Military Since Khrushchev," *Current History*, Fall, 1957, No. 338 (October, 1969), p. 225.

[66]Quoted in *The New York Times*, July 20, 1969.

[67]Vice-Admiral Smirnov, "Soviet Ships in the Mediterranean," *Krasnaya zvezda*, Nov. 12, 1968, p. 3; translated in *CDSP*, Vol. XX, No. 47 (December 11, 1968), p. 7. Translation copyright 1974 by the Current Digest of the Soviet Press; published weekly at The Ohio State University by the American Association for the Advancement of Slavic Studies; reprint by permission.

[68]*Ibid.* Translation copyright 1974 by the Current Digest of the Soviet Press; published weekly at The Ohio State University by the American Association for the Advancement of Slavic Studies; reprint by permission.

[69]"On the International Situation and the Foreign Policy of the Soviet Union," report by Deputy A. A. Gromyko, USSR Minister of Foreign Affairs, *Pravda*, June 28, 1968; translated in *CDSP*, Vol. XX, No. 28 (July 31, 1968), p. 12.

[70]"Libya's Young and Thin Against the Old and Portly," *The Economist*, (Dec. 6, 1969), p. 26.

[71]*Radio Moscow* in Arabic to the Arab World 1530 GMT 31 January 1974; transcribed in Foreign Broadcast Information Service, *Daily Report*, Soviet Union, No. 23, February 1, 1974, p. F6.

[72]*Radio Moscow* in Persian to Iran, 1630 GMT 4 February 1964; *ibid.*, No. 25 February 5, 1974, p. A5. For an interesting analysis of Soviet intervention behavior, see James M. McConnell and Anne M. Kelly, "Superpower Naval Diplomacy and The Indo-Pakistani Crisis" (Arlington, Va.: Center for Naval Analyses), Professional Paper No. 108 (February, 1973), pp. 7–9.

[73]Slocombe, *op. cit.*, p. 2.

[74]G. Arbatov, "Amerikanskaya vneshnaya politika no poroge 70-kh godov [American Foreign Policy on the Threshold of the 70s]," *SShA*, No. 1 (January, 1970), p. 28. In this regard, none other than Henry Kissinger is quoted as follows: "The paradox of contemporary military strength is that a gargantuan increase in power had eroded its relationship to political power . . . in other words . . . power no longer translates automatically into influence."

[75]*Department of Defense Appropriations for 1969*, *op. cit.*, p. 268.

[76]Brzezinski, "Peace and Power," *op. cit.*, p. 8.

[77]A very judicious reading of the SALT agreements can be found in *The Military Balance, 1972–1973*, *op. cit.*, pp. 83–86 and *Strategic Survey, 1972*, *op. cit.*, pp. 14–19.

3

Soviet political beliefs: historical influences and traditions

It is not enough and basically it is not true to say, as so many have said to me, that the Russian people are like people everywhere and only the Government is different.

The people, too, are different. They are different because wholly different social and political conditions have retarded and perverted their development and set them apart from other civilizations.

—Walter Bedell Smith[1]

Nations, in some ways, are like people. While having many things in common, each in important ways is unique. And, as with people, a nation's behavior is often best understood in terms of the psychological attitudes and style which characterize its personality. Whatever its material economic and military circumstances, the beliefs, expectations, interests, self-image, hopes and fears of each nation exercise a profound influence on its policies and behavior.

Though each nation shares some features of its outlook with others, the particular "mix" which constitutes its political personality or character is distinctive. This is quite natural since the forces which shape it—geographic perspectives, anthropological patterns, domestic political requirements, and religious and cultural traditions—are varied and complex. Moreover, the manner in which these forces fashion each nation's political personality reflects its singular historic experiences. This fact, seemingly obvious, is often poorly understood. Many people tend to view other nations as but quaint foreign versions of themselves. We tend to believe, unconsciously, that the assumptions and values of our own society are both natural and universal; other peoples and their leaders are seen to be much like our own. When nearly every political leader wears trousers, notes Robert Conquest, "it seems to be felt that basic cultural differences cannot exist as they would have been understood to do between a turban-clad Sultan and a periwigged Hanoverian king."[2] Other political systems are assumed to share the same norms as we do.

Such, alas, is not the case. People do differ; and, whatever their outward appearance, nations which have inherited very different historical experiences and traditions will not share the same norms or values.

Their unique history has left a distinctive imprint on the memories of the Russian people. As historians have long noted, the people of Soviet Russia share a tradition and history very different, even alien to our own. While this fact is generally understood in the abstract—the exploits of Ivan the Terrible, Peter the Great, and Nicholas the Cudgel have long fascinated Western students—its significance for current political, especially international, behavior is rarely appreciated.

How do the historic experiences of prerevolutionary Russia influence Soviet behavior? The USSR today, after all, is very much different from the Russia of Nicholas II, not to mention the Grand Duchy of Muscovy. And, furthermore, most of Russia's ancient concerns—Sweden, Turkey, Poland, warm water seaports—have been reduced to relatively minor status, while new problems virtually unknown to the tsars—for example, the United States—have emerged. How then does past history influence the present?

The problem of assessing the psycho-historical forces underlying current policies and attitudes is admittedly a difficult one. First of all, the subject itself is extremely elusive. Many of the concepts normally employed—"security," "hostility," "suspiciousness"—are derived from individual psychology and do not lend themselves very easily to an analysis of international political behavior. The Soviet world outlook, furthermore, contains inconsistencies and contradictions the influence of which is difficult to assess. There is, finally, the problem of changeability. Soviet attitudes and values often undergo shifts. Some "core beliefs" in the Soviet *Weltanschauung* may well be disappearing and new, quite different beliefs replacing them.

Difficult though it may be, it is critically important that we attempt to understand the basic pattern and trends in the Soviet world outlook. I stress this point because there is a danger, one into which foreign policy analysts and even statesmen sometimes fall, to think in terms of bloodless abstractions and to use such terms as "vital," "objective," "national" interests. Though political leaders often resort to such rhetoric to cloak their policies with an air of legitimacy, there is no such thing as objective "national interests." Interests are subjective, not objective; they are shaped by changing human judgments and values, not by any objective or eternal requirements of the state. As Fritz Ermath has wisely suggested,

> . . . interests are a function of the self-image of a ruling group, its conception of its role in history and society, and, closely related to this, its conceptions of the probable results of certain alternative future events. Interests are the results of events, ideology, history, geography, a host of amorphous perceptions filtered through the minds of men.[3]

It is with the historical roots of these amorphous conceptions and perceptions—the weight of the inherited traditions of the past on the mind of the current Soviet leadership—that we are now concerned.

The imprint of history

The international behavior of the USSR, as many observers have noted, bears striking resemblance in both content and style to that of its Tsarist predecessors. The reason for this is not too hard to find. However "revolutionary" the outlook of a particular leadership, the traits and values which bundled together make up its political personality cannot escape the cultural roots of the Russian people from whom they have sprung. Much to the dismay of the ideologically inspired, attitudes and habits of mind which harken back to the pre-Petrine culture of old Muscovy continue to surface and occasionally seem to dominate the thinking of those in power in Moscow.

Among the most important of the qualities and traits rooted in history which bear on current Soviet behavior are those associated with Russia's imperial tradition. Over a period of several centuries, Russia's Tsars created one of history's great empires. The size of the empire was truly monumental. From the middle of the fifteenth century, when the Tatar hold on their lands began to crumble, Russia's rulers expanded their control from the 15,000 square miles of which the Duchy of Muscovy was comprised to the 8.5 million square miles over which Nicholas II, the last of the Romanovs, reigned. As a result of its territorial vastness, Russia was viewed with great suspicion by the nations of Europe. For many, Tsarist expansionism, carried out by military conquest, clearly indicated the regime's unlimited ambitions. Friedrich Engels, for example, saw Russia as a nation "dreaming about world supremacy." A similar assessment was made by the acute French observer of nineteenth century Russia, the Marquis de Custine, who saw "world conquest" as the key to Russian history. "An immense ambition," he wrote, "ferments in the hearts of the Russian people. That nation, essentially aggressive . . . dreams of world domination."[4]

Russia's reputation as an expansionist power was especially widespread during the nineteenth century. Deservedly so, for between 1815 and 1914 Russia acquired vast territories in the Caucasus, in Central Asia, and in the Far East. It was not until then that most of present day Soviet Armenia, Azerbaidjan, Turkistan, Kazakhstan, the Amur and Ussuri Provinces and Sakhalin were acquired. Thus, despite the growing social ills from which it was already suffering, nineteenth century Russia's sprawling empire deeply impressed its neighbors. And, though she was at war for much less time than in earlier periods, Russia, as always, kept a larger standing army than any of the other powers.

Russia's military reputation was also enhanced by the active role it played in the preservation of the established monarchical order in Europe. In the 1830s, Polish defiance of Russian authority was harshly suppressed. During the revolutionary unrest in Europe in the late 1840s, Nicholas I again moved thousands of troops, this time to maintain the rights of the Hapsburgs in Rumania and Hungary. As a result of these efforts, Nicholas earned for himself the ignoble title of "Gendarme of Europe."[5] For Engels, as for many other Europeans, Russia's "ceaseless intervention in Western affairs" was designed to "secure it the mastery of Europe." To this end, in his view, it was capable of any ruse. "There was no land grab, no outrage, no repression on the part of Czarism which was not carried out under the pretext of enlightenment, of liberalism, of the liberation of nations." Its purposes remained constant, "the attainment of its own single, never-changing, never-lost-sight-of objective: the domination of the world by Russia. . . ."[6]

Despite the harsh judgment of Engels and others, it would be inaccurate to characterize Tsarist foreign policy as desirous of world dominion in any meaningful sense. The Tsars were indeed aggressive and expansionist, as the numerous small and weak peoples who had fallen victim to Russian rule could testify. Its expansion, however, was not according to any fixed plan or wholly explicit in its intentions. Russia was spurred on ever to enlarge her territory by a complex of motives. While many nineteenth century local Russian officials in Central Asia and the Far East may have shared a vision of Russia's imperial mission, this was not apparently true of the government itself. Russia's military conquest in these areas "was due much more to the enterprise and energy of governors-general and soldiers in outlying areas, who often took the initiative without or even against instructions from St. Petersburg which was too far away and had too poor communications to keep them under effective control." Though often vexed by the complications thus created, the Tsar preferred to accept the lands his ambitious subordinates acquired. Despite the fact that the planting of the Russian flag at the mouth of the Amur River in August 1851 occurred in violation of instructions, Nicholas I declared, "Where the Russian flag has been run up, it must not be hauled down."[7]

Russia's motives for its three centuries of "gathering lands" were varied. The outthrust to the Baltic under Peter the Great reflected Russia's determination to reach the sea. Antagonism toward Poland, which led to the absorption of western Poland by Russia, was religious and cultural as well as political. In Central Asia, the Far East, and the

Caucasus, Russia was spurred on by the quest for a secure frontier, the effort to fill the power vacuum which lay between the Russian border and British India (for fear of being excluded from these regions by the ever-expanding British Empire), the temptations offered by weak and unstable neighbors (the Ottoman Empire, Persia, Afghanistan and China), the desire for economic gain, and the rivalries and ambitions of vainglorious local commanders.[8]

The enormous expansion which occurred between the fifteenth and twentieth centuries was clearly very mixed in its origins, reflecting both "offensive" and "defensive" motives. While there was a streak of Messianic universalism in Russian religious thought, in which Moscow as the "Third Rome" was considered obliged to prepare the way for the salvation of all mankind by spreading the gospel of the Orthodox Church to distant lands, few of its Tsars were thus inspired.[9] In a sense, Russian expansionism was "defensive"—motivated by fear as much as by a desire for glory or profit.

The role of fear as a shaper of Russian policy is not difficult to understand. Throughout most of their history, the Russians have experienced a nearly constant threat of invasion and the danger of war. With no natural boundary on the west (or, until the eighteenth and nineteenth centuries, on the south or east), wide open to incursion by often fierce and hostile neighbors, the peoples of Russia have been compelled for ten centuries to fight off invading armies. From the Golden Horde of Genghis Khan, which in the thirteenth century imposed the "Tatar Yoke," to the Nazi invasion of 1941, Russia has suffered repeated onslaughts. According to one historian, Russia endured 160 foreign invasions during the period of Western Europe's Renaissance (1228–1462), and ten great wars with Sweden and Poland during the seventeenth and eighteenth centuries, the period of the Enlightenment.[10] The nineteenth century witnessed the Napoleonic Wars (which saw the burning of Moscow), the Crimean, and Russo-Turkish Wars; and in the twentieth century came the Russo-Japanese War and World Wars I and II.

These tragic and bitter experiences have had a powerful influence on Russian development. First they helped shape the highly centralized, autocratic character of Tsarist rule. To survive in this hostile environment, the Russians had to organize their lives along quasi-military lines, united and disciplined. The whole society had to be prepared for continuous military defense. To command the men and resources necessary to protect the state, its government had to be in complete control. Thus, while others have faced foreign invaders without themselves adopting despotic methods of rule, the Russians, in the words of Cyril Black, "to a greater extent than most peoples . . . have seen themselves facing a choice of unity under an autocrat or subjugation by a foreign power."[11]

This condition of nearly constant siege laid the basis for the omnipotent Tsarist state. Complete discipline and service to the state—no "society" outside the state—was the price seen as necessary for survival. It also produced, not surprisingly, an idiosyncratic view of the outside world, characterized in large measure by suspicion and fear. The Russians have survived the great trials which confronted them, according to Louis Halle, "only because they learned at an early age to trust no one, to be suspiciously alert, to keep their own counsel, and to substitute guile for superior strength where superior strength was lacking."[12] A history of successive invasions, therefore, produced a "national sense of insecurity." It gave rise, according to George Kennan, to a "neurotic view of world affairs" based on a "traditional and instinctive Russian sense of insecurity." The Russians throughout their history "have dealt principally with fierce hostile neighbors." Given these experiences, "all foreigners are potential enemies."[13]

Proceeding on the assumption that their neighbors were hostile, which they often were, the Russians came to believe that caution and suspicion were the only safe guidelines. It became traditional Russian policy to maintain large armies. Even in the sixteenth century, Muscovite Russia "put into the field great standing armies while the Western powers were still contenting themselves with little companies of mercenaries."[14] As part of their effort to protect the motherland from external dangers, Russia's leaders also stressed continued expansion. "Behind Russia's stubborn expansion," as Kennan has noted, "lies only the age-old sense of insecurity of a sedentary people reared on an exposed plain in the neighborhood of fierce nomadic peoples." In his view, "conceptions of offense and defense are inextricably confused" in Russian history.[15] While much of Russia's expansionism undoubtedly reflected the predilection of its leaders for military adventures (as during the reign of Peter the Great), Russia's wars often reflected the fears and apprehensions of its rulers about the intentions of others.

Given a history of dealing primarily with unfriendly neighbors, Russian diplomacy has been concerned less with cultivating friendly relations with foreign powers than with "impressing an adversary with the terrifying strength of Russian power. . . ."[16] Here, Russia's historical experiences acted to reinforce the traditions of Byzantine diplomacy. (The Byzantine Empire, which Old Muscovy claimed to succeed as the new or "Third" Rome, exerted considerable influence on Russian political as well as religious beliefs. In the view of many historians, Byzantine diplomacy contained "the mainsprings of Russian diplomatic practices."[17]) The ruling circles of Byzantium regarded the state as the highest value in society and protection of the state as the sole purpose of diplomacy. The only measure of judgment in foreign affairs was seen to be power; foreign affairs were generally seen as "power relations subject only to what is known in the *Arthashastra* as the law of the fishes" (where little fish are the natural nourishment of big fish).[18] In Russia, as in Byzantium, diplomacy thus came to be considered "a quasi-military activity. In this contest, negotiation was a strategic device, designed to lead to victory rather than to compromise or mutual understanding."[19]

For the Russians, as for Byzantium, diplomacy could be defined as "the science of managing the Barbarians." And, again like Byzantium,

Russia was particularly sensitive to the areas which bordered on it. "Here," writes Adda Bozeman, "the Byzantine diplomats had the mandate of maintaining the Empire's existing spheres of influence, of coping with the steady pressure of the Barbarian tribes by drawing the new arrivals into the circle of hedge-guarding imperial clients that was meant to serve as an outer line of defense."[20] Kennan reaches much the same conclusion regarding Russia's attitudes toward its neighbors. Writing in 1944 of the problems of reaching a settlement on the Polish question, he observed: "There is no border zone of Russian power. The jealous and intolerant eyes of the Kremlin can distinguish, in the end, only vassals and enemies; and the neighbors of Russia, if they do not wish to be the one, must reconcile themselves to being the other."[21]

The distinctive characteristics usually ascribed to Russian diplomacy—hostility, suspicion, deception, aggressiveness, and xenophobia—can best be understood in terms of Russia's unhappy historical experiences (which themselves had served to reinforce similar traits characteristic of ancient Byzantium). These features, however, were not merely defensive reactions to a hostile environment. They often reflected highly belligerent, even arrogant, cultural and religious beliefs regarding Russia's unique historical mission. Historians have long noted ancient Muscovy's traditional xenophobia, its contempt for the foreign, its distaste for the un-Russian. Inspired by its own sense of virtue and purity, as "the conservatrix of Christ's truth . . . the true image of Christ which had been dimmed in all other religions and all other nations," Russia avoided contacts with impure, tainted foreign infidels. It was long believed, as Dostoevsky observed, that close relations with the rest of Europe "might even exercise a harmful and corrupt influence upon the Russian mind and the Russian *idea;* that it might distort Orthodoxy itself and lead Russia along the path to perdition. . . ."[22] Given such attitudes, Moscow saw little need to engage in diplomatic relations with other nations. Certain of its own superiority, Russia scorned the external world. Foreign missions in Moscow were treated with disdain.

The spirit which underlay this religious and cultural self-conceit is captured in the verses of the eighteenth century Russian poet, Derzhavin, who wrote:

> Hark, hark, O Universe
> To vict'ries beyond human power;
> Listen, O astounded Europe
> To the exploits of these Russians.
> Peoples, know and understand
> Believe ye that with us is God;
> Believe that, aided by His hand,
> A single Russian can defeat
> All your abysmal evil forces,
> Peoples, know this dread Colossus:
> God is with us, so honor ye the Russian.[23]

Historic Russia saw itself as the center of the universe. The world of the non-Orthodox was simply of little matter. Moscow's feeling about foreigners is aptly illustrated by Richard Pipes when he recalls "the symbolic ceremony of washing hands which the Tsar performed after dismissing an embassy, using a discreetly covered pitcher and basin placed for this purpose by his throne."[24] Thus, much like the Byzantine Empire, Moscow claimed a unique position among all Christian nations. As one astute historian has observed, "If Russia was the first land of Christianity, and if orthodox Christianity were the only true Christianity, then Russia was obviously in a class by itself, at least in the society of Christian nations, as the lone protagonist of what is right."[25] As with their Byzantine predecessors, this exalted self-image gave rise to glorification of the state and governmental absolutism on the one hand, and a Messianic kind of imperialism on the other.

These professions of superiority, based in large measure on traditions inherited from Byzantium, introduced a chronic psychological tension between Russia and the nations of non-Orthodox Europe. It produced, initially, arrogance and contempt in Russia's behavior towards the West. Russian negotiating techniques, as the diplomatic historian Gordon Craig has noted, reflected its self-image. The first Russian diplomats who visited the West, it is recounted, behaved like "baptized bears." The diplomatic delegation which Peter the Great led to the West in 1697–1698 literally ruined the house which quartered them in London—curtains, quilts and bedding left in shreds, three hundred windows broken, twenty paintings vandalized, floors irreparably scarred, dozens of chairs smashed. "Damage of this nature," writes Craig,

> could not be attributed wholly to inadvertence or to lack of breeding. Much of it appeared to be a deliberate flouting of Western convention in order to demonstrate Russian superiority.[26]

"This behavior," Craig continues, "accorded with other unpleasing traits of these first embassies: rudeness in matters of protocol, scornful disregard for the laws of the land to which they were accredited, and studied incivilities in their relations with their opposite numbers." Convinced that its own religious and political arrangements far surpassed all others, Russia made for a most uncomfortable and difficult neighbor.

Russia's relations with the West grew increasingly complex in the eighteenth and especially the nineteenth centuries as its leaders became less certain of their superior virtues. In terms of economic development, Russia has lagged seriously behind the nations of Europe throughout most of its history. Confronted by what in contemporary jargon would be called Russia's "economic–technological gap," Peter the Great began his sweeping reform program and enlarged contacts with the West. He hoped thereby to bring backward Russia up to the standards of the eighteenth century—to make Russia a modern military power. Ambitious though his efforts were, neither Peter nor the other "modernizers" of eighteenth and nineteenth century Russia succeeded. And, as the Industrial Revolution spread throughout Europe, the gap between Russia and the West grew even larger.

Western technological superiority was a source of great concern. Sensitive to the military disadvantages which backwardness imposed, Russia's rulers brought in Western experts to modernize Russian industry and improve its arms. For some, Russia's backwardness was a challenge and an inspiration. Isolated for much of its history from the main currents in European life, Russia, they believed, was a semi-Asiatic peasant backwater. To overcome the gap between Russia and the rest of Europe, it was essential in their view to increase Russia's participation in Western political and cultural life.

In contrast to these "Westernizers," the "Slavophiles" sharply attacked Western practices. Embarrassed by the challenge of Europe's materially superior culture, they responded by condemning the political–social–cultural system of the West. Among the Slavophiles, traditional antiforeign attitudes remained deeply rooted. Western ideas and institutions were an anathema in their view. Much like their predecessors in Old Muscovy, they believed that Russia's unique and superior culture must be preserved from outside—Western—influences.

Whether moved by the arrogance of traditional Muscovite messianism or by a sense of their nation's stark backwardness, the Russians viewed the West with considerable ambivalence. Arrogance and conceit blended increasingly with a sense of inferiority and, one suspects, assertions of Russian supremacy often masked the shame produced by a sense of backwardness. Thus we have the rather pathetic attempt to assert the superiority of the *mir*, the traditional Russian communal form of landholding, while the achievements of Western industry and culture were denounced as "vulgar," "stagnant," and "bourgeois."[27] Attitudes toward the West of the Russian intelligentsia of whatever persuasion, Slavophile or Westernizer, were strongly held. However, whether inspired by hatred or envy, they were always somewhat neurotic.

Contemporary resonances

Men make their own history, but they do not make it just as they please; they do not make it under circumstances chosen by themselves, but under circumstances directly encountered, given, and transmitted from the past. The tradition of all the dead generations weighs like a nightmare on the brain of the living.[28]

—*Karl Marx*

Despite Marx's sensitivity to the influence of history, many of his followers claimed to be quite free of the past. According to a recent Soviet textbook, the Bolshevik Revolution in 1917 "gave birth to a totally new foreign policy . . . this could not have failed to change, as indeed it did change, the nature of foreign policy, its objectives, the sources of its strength and influence, and its means and methods."[29]

The uniqueness of Soviet foreign policy was especially stressed by the early Bolshevik leaders. Karl Radek, for example, vigorously denied that Soviet foreign policy in the inter-war period bore any relationship to the policies of its Tsarist predecessors. Unlike the Tsars, he declared, the Communist regime did not seek possession of the Dardanelles or conquest of Port Arthur or Dairen in northern China. Furthermore, "Tsarism or any other bourgeois regime in Russia, would necessarily resume the struggle for the conquest of Poland and the Baltic States. . . . The Soviet regime, on the contrary, is most anxious to establish friendly relations with these countries. . . ."[30]

The Soviet denigration of historical influences reflects, paradoxically, its basic Marxist commitments (based on what can only be viewed as a vulgar reading of Marx). A nation's foreign policy, it is argued, is a direct function of its domestic socio-economic system. "The deep-lying distinction between the economic basis of socialism and that of exploiting societies gives rise to fundamental distinctions in foreign policy," declare Soviet authors.[31] Thus, the foreign policy of a "socialist" USSR is seen as fundamentally different, in objective and method, from that of "exploiting" Tsarist regimes.

Without falling victim to the historicist view that attempts to explain the present wholly in terms of the past, it seems reasonable to conclude that history has indeed weighed heavily, much as Marx said it would, on recent generations. This was particularly obvious during the Stalin era. Less concerned with ideology than Lenin or any of his successors, Stalin often studded his speeches with historical references and openly identified the USSR with the cause of historic Russia. Thus, in his "Catch Up in Ten Years or Be Crushed" speech of 1931, Stalin recounted the continual "beatings" which "Old Russia" suffered—at the hands of the Mongol khans, the Turkish beys, the Swedish feudal lords, the Polish and Lithuanian gentry, the British and French capitalists, the Japanese barons—because of her backwardness.[32] Furthermore, in his famous V-J address marking the end of the war against Japan, Stalin remarked that victory and repossession by the USSR of southern Sakhalin (lost in the Russo–Japanese War) finally removed "the dark stain" of defeat inflicted on prerevolutionary Russia. "For forty years have we, men of the older generation, waited for this day," declared the triumphant Soviet dictator.[33]

The influence of historical experiences and traditions obviously persist. Nowhere can this be seen more clearly than in the Kremlin's abiding commitment to protect Russia's historic lands. During the late 1930s and the 1940s, Stalin launched what was, in effect, a "regathering of the lands" campaign. By the end of the Second World War, Eastern Poland, the Baltic States, Bessarabia, and Southern Sakhalin, territories lost earlier in the twentieth century, were all restored to Russian rule. (Of the territories in which Radek had denied any interest, Stalin established Russian control or predominant influence over all except the Dardanelles.) The only major omission in this campaign was Finland, which still retains the independence from Russian rule it acquired in 1918. Soviet influence in Helsinki, however, is considerable, especially in matters of foreign policy. (There are other small exceptions. Control has not been regained over the Kars district of eastern Turkey, bordering on Soviet Armenia. However, Moscow now does possess territories never before controlled by Russia—Ruthenia, the northern half of East Prussia, and the Kurile Islands.)

Soviet concern for traditional Russian lands can also be seen in its reaction to the Chinese claim that more than 1.5 million square miles of Russian territory were obtained illegally from China. According to Peking, the Treaties of Aigun (1858), Peking (1860) and Ili (1881), by which Russia acquired the territories that today compose the Amur and Maritime Provinces and large parts of Soviet Central Asia were "unequal treaties" which Tsarist regimes forcibly imposed on China. Peking's charges, part of the Sino–Soviet Cold War, are rejected out of hand. And, in repudiating the Chinese claims, the Soviet leaders have clearly reaffirmed their commitment to protect Russia's traditional interests and lands. Thus, in a 1968 speech to the Supreme Soviet, Foreign Minister Gromyko declared:

> Our foreign policy is distinguished and will continue to be distinguished by firmness in upholding the state interests of the Soviet people, in insuring the inviolability of our land's frontiers, our coasts and our airspace, and in safeguarding the dignity of the Soviet flag and the rights and security of Soviet citizens.[34]

Party Secretary Brezhnev clearly endorsed this position when he reminded his listeners at the 24th Party Congress that "We are not foregoing the interests of the Russian state."[35] This obviously nationalist rhetoric must have sounded odd coming from the titular head of the international communist movement; thus, perhaps, his muted language. However, international commitments aside, Brezhnev and the Soviet leadership are very much committed to protecting the territorial integrity of Russia's historic borders.

Solicitude for such obvious national interests as frontier inviolability may seem the natural concern of all political leaders. It was not true, however, for the early Bolsheviks, most of whom were more interested in promoting the triumph of socialism on a world scale than protecting the national interests of Russia. It was in this spirit that, in 1919, the new Soviet regime formally renounced Tsarist conquests of Chinese territory. However, the imperatives of the situation Lenin faced as ruler of a war-weary but beleaguered Soviet Russia increasingly led him away from his internationalist concerns. Needless to add, the USSR never did relinquish control of any of the disputed lands to China.

Clearly committed to the protection of Russia's "national interests," the Soviet leaders, much like their predecessors, are acutely sensitive to the vulnerability of their western border. And, not surprisingly, they have adopted policies toward Eastern Europe similar in purpose—if not in method—to those employed by the Tsars. Russia's rulers, whatever the regime, have sought to protect themselves from potentially dangerous adversaries in Central and Western Europe by creating a buffer zone of states under their influence along Russia's western frontiers. This posture has often been characterized as a policy of defensive expansion—an extension of Soviet power westward motivated more by fear than by lust for conquest. The creation by Stalin of a belt of satellite states in Eastern Europe in the aftermath of the Second World War is very much a part of this tradition, as is the recent Soviet invasion of Czechoslovakia. Anxiety regarding the future of Russian influence in Eastern Europe led Brezhnev in 1968—much as it had Nicholas I in 1831 regarding Poland—to adopt a policy of military intervention.

The evidence of continuity in foreign policy can also be seen in Russia's rather distinctive self-image. Firm in their conviction regarding the "scientific" validity of the doctrines of Marx and Lenin, the Soviet leaders share old Russia's pretensions regarding the universal validity of official—then Orthodox, now Communist—faith. Like the rulers of Old Muscovy, they tend to see themselves as the bearers of a unique message and the center of a new, higher civilization. Now as in the past, Moscow proclaims itself an example to all peoples.

These beliefs, rooted in history and buttressed by ideology, give rise to a number of striking personality traits. First, ideological exclusiveness always breeds xenophobia. Evidence of this abhorrence of foreign values is still, sad to say, very much present. Thus, like their Muscovite ancestors, the Soviet leaders seem to share a profound lack of interest in the non-Russian. While Soviet diplomats work hard at learning what goes on beyond their frontiers, George Kennan writes, they seem to share something of the "boredom and distaste which the life of the Western countries, in particular, seems always to have aroused in Russians traveling abroad." Western achievements, he notes, were invariably taken for granted "as something entirely meaningless or directly wearisome and distasteful—a form of useless good order that induced emptiness of the spirit and homesickness."[36] This indifference to things foreign persists. When Stalin's daughter, Svetlana, sought a passport to go to India, high-ranking member of the Secretariat of the Soviet Communist Party Mikhail Suslov seemed puzzled. Why, he wanted to know, did she want to go? "What is it that attracts you abroad? Why, my family and I never go abroad, and don't even feel like going. It is not interesting!"[37]

Suslov's disinterest in things foreign reflects the traditional Russian conception of itself as the center of the universe. Inspired by the faith that Russia, and Russia alone, is the bearer of Communism's (or Christ's) teachings, that their system is superior to all other systems, life abroad is simply of no concern. Such attitudes also contribute to what Louis Fischer has referred to as Russian national megalomania. One explanation for Moscow's continuous concern about "capitalist encirclement" during the inter-war period, he wrote, "was the conviction that the USSR was the navel of the universe. . . . [And] if Soviet Russia was the center of the world, she was easily encircled."[38] Much the same megalomaniacal strain underlies Moscow's anxieties regarding "Western anti-Soviet campaigns." This was particularly apparent at the time of the fiftieth anniversary celebrations of the Bolshevik revolution. In the Soviet view, the numerous conferences and seminars held in 1967 in leading American universities (including Harvard, Columbia, and Princeton) on the February and October Revolutions of 1917 were nothing less than instruments of a vast propaganda effort orchestrated by highly placed U.S. government officials to defame the USSR.[39] The community of Western scholars concerned with Russian affairs, no less than official representatives of "bourgeois" governments, are often identified as servants of anti-Soviet policies laid down by Western imperialist ruling circles.

Relations between Russians and foreigners are continually troubled by what amounts to morbid suspiciousness. The foreigner and his ideas are viewed warily. Hundreds of articles continue to appear in the press warning Soviet writers and artists and Soviet young people against the blandishments of foreign, especially Western, culture. They are cautioned against prostituting themselves before "false idols"—from Western literary techniques and musical forms to hair and dance styles. Foreigners within the Soviet Union are viewed with great suspicion. It is an axiom in Soviet political circles, writes Svetlana, that "every foreigner in the USSR is a potential spy; more than one sharp eye must therefore be kept on him, and he must never be trusted."[40] If not actually as agents of foreign intelligence, foreigners are regarded, at the least, as bearers of alien thoughts. To prevent "the harmful and corrupt influence on the Russian mind" which Dostoevsky feared, the Soviet government has traditionally sought to keep its citizens from establishing close relations with foreigners. Even the exchange of information between Soviet and foreign scientists is restricted. In the view of the Soviet nuclear physicist, Andrei Sakharov, such policies reflect the regime's deeply held fears regarding the "penetration of hostile ideology."[41]

Suspicion and apprehension of foreigners, fear of intimate contacts, secretiveness, obsession with espionage, and hypersensitivity to foreign criticism are all character traits the Soviet regime shares with its Tsarist predecessors. On occasion, traces of the studied contempt which early Russian diplomats showed their foreign colleagues also reveal themselves. Thus it was when Karl Radek deliberately insulted and blew pipe smoke in the face of the chief German negotiator at the Brest–Litovsk talks, General von Hoffman, in 1918.[42] So it was again when Khrushchev and the whole Soviet delegation pounded their shoes at the United Nation's General Assembly in 1960. Such behavior, to be fair, is unusual. The comportment of Soviet representatives abroad in recent decades has generally adhered to the more civilized standards of normal diplomatic practice. (And, it has been reported that Khrushchev's U.N. behavior caused considerable embarrassment among Party leaders in Moscow.) Nevertheless, a residue of anti-foreign sentiment remains embedded in the Russian political culture. Thus, in explanation of the persistently poor service in Soviet hotels, an official Intourist representative revealingly observed: "We have been educated that to serve foreigners was a humiliating job."[43]

Such anti-foreign attitudes are to some degree contradicted by the intense interest, especially on the popular level, in things Western, from literature and science to jazz and fashions. These attitudes are shared by numerous Soviet officials who relish the opportunity to travel in Western Europe and the United States and often display an acute (sometimes excessive) sensitivity to foreign opinion. At the same time, the regime condemns the use of foreign words and concepts in Russian speech as "the weeds of barbarism."[44]

Soviet relations toward the West, in particular, are marked by much the same ambivalence and tension as those of prerevolutionary Russia, and for much the same reasons. On the one hand, the West is resented; on the other, in terms of its technological accomplishments, it is greatly admired. In the hope of stimulating Soviet economic performance, the Kremlin has been urging Soviet industry since the 1930s to "catch up" with the advanced capitalist nations. Typical of such efforts was the speech made in 1939 by Party leader Molotov when he told the 18th Party Congress that "the biggest economic task of the USSR," was

> to catch up with and overtake . . . economically the most developed capitalist countries of Europe and the United States of America. . . . Then and only then will the significance of the new era in the development of the USSR unfold itself, the era of transition from a socialist to a communist society.[45]

Since the end of World War II, attention has been focused on the United States. Thus, in May, 1957, Khrushchev launched a campaign to catch up with the United States in the production of milk, butter and meat by 1970. In 1960, he also added consumer commodities including textiles and footwear.

"Catching up with America" is a revealing slogan. For the Russian people, the United States is very much the standard of comparison, the land which has achieved the material prosperity to which they aspire.[46] In setting forth this not-too-distant goal of 1970 to achieve something approximating American living standards, Khrushchev clearly hoped to inspire Soviet workers and farmers to ever greater efforts. More important, for our purposes, was his second objective—to disprove Western claims that the Soviet economy was inferior to those of the capitalist nations. The longer Western superiority was maintained, he undoubtedly felt, the less impressive the achievements of Soviet socialism would appear. Furthermore, fulfillment of these goals would help disprove Western critics who argued that the USSR neglected the needs of its citizens. In addition, Khrushchev was also very much aware that a nation's reputation for economic achievement could have political ramifications. The United States' economy, he noted, "by its volume and productivity acts on the psychology of literally the entire Western world."[47] By improving Soviet living standards, "the minds of undecided peoples" around the world would be strongly influenced. Then, he declared in 1960, "we will enter the open seas in which no comparisons with capitalism will anchor us."[48]

Although Khrushchev himself had quietly abandoned his 1970 target date—he undoubtedly knew it to be unrealistic from the very outset—his successors are also very much concerned to "catch up" with America, especially in modern industrial technology. In a speech before the Supreme Soviet (parliament) in November, 1971, Premier Aleksei N. Kosygin declared that "By 1975, total industrial and agricultural output of the USSR will exceed the present production level of the United States."[49] Kosygin, much like Khrushchev, seeks to prove that the Soviet system is, at the very least, the equal of the capitalist West. An editorial in *Pravda* spells out the Kremlin's concerns in clear terms:

> For many decades bourgeois propaganda has alleged that socialism is a system under which personal freedom and initiative are suppressed, where the material welfare of man is sacrificed to the state, etc. It would be wrong to deny that substantial masses of the people in the West are still [held in] thrall to these ideas. They can be refuted only by practical arguments. That is why such tremendous revolutionizing importance attaches to the measures of the Communist Parties of the socialist countries in creating an efficient economy, raising the well-being and cultural level of the working people and developing socialist democracy.

Thus, in order to help improve the reputation of the USSR "among the working people" of the world—including those within the Soviet Union itself—the Kremlin leaders now proclaim that their "internationalist duty" consists, first and foremost, in the "successful construction of socialism and communism in the socialist countries."[50]

We shall return to this rather striking interpretation of the USSR's "supreme internationalist duty" in Chapter Four. For the moment, let us focus on Moscow's continued obsession about closing the economic gap with the West. Russia's historical inferiority complex apparently still weighs heavily on the minds of its leaders and imposes a psychological burden which only "catching up with America" can remove. If the USSR can in fact "overtake and surpass" the United States, the Soviet leaders will have overcome Russia's traditional legacy of backwardness. This helps explain the extraordinary pride which the Kremlin obviously took in early Soviet space accomplishments. The launching of Sputnik I in 1957 and the space flight of Yuri Gagarin in 1961 symbolized, for her leaders and her people, the end of old Russia and the emergence of a new, modern, advanced Soviet society. Soviet space accomplishments, however, have not been sustained. Could these efforts be renewed and United States successfully overtaken, the historical legacy of backwardness would be done away with for good.

"Catching up with America," therefore, represents the Kremlin's struggle with Russia's past. The struggle is deeply rooted. It sometimes manifests itself in rather strange ways. Stalin's daughter recounts, for example, the telling response of Lazar Kaganovich, long-time Politburo member, to the visit of the internationally renowned violinist, Yehudi Menuhin, to Moscow. During a performance of Bach's "Concerto for Two

Violins," in which Menuhin was accompanied by the great Soviet violinist, David Oistrakh, Kaganovich turned to Svetlana and winked: "See how *our* boy is beating the American." "To him," Svetlana notes, "it was a contest, a kind of horse race."[51]

The persistence of American supremacy troubles even Russians who are critical of the current regime. Dissident nuclear physicist Andrei Sakharov notes, for example, that the gap between the U. S. and the USSR regarding the use of computers in the civilian economy "is so wide that it is impossible to measure it." Further, in other advanced fields, "no one feels the importance of our role is growing."

> On the contrary. At the end of the 1950s our country was the first to launch a Sputnik and a man into space. But at the end of the 1960s we lost our lead, and the first men to land on the moon were American.

Thus, he laments, "Rather than catching up with America, we are falling even farther behind."[52]

Concern regarding continued American superiority has had important domestic ramifications. The apprehension which the Soviet leaders have expressed about an economic slowdown in the USSR suggests one economist, "is due not to what occurred in the USSR but what occurred in the U.S."

> If the U. S. had followed the historical path of decline foreseen by Marxian theory, the recent slowdown in the Soviet growth rate may have been regarded as a normal phenomenon in a successful maturing socialist society. If there were no U.S., there would be no great economic reform in the USSR today, and no new search for a better form of socialist economic organization.[53]

Recent Soviet efforts to improve economic performance therefore, are in some degree motivated by the Kremlin's concern to "catch up."

Self-conscious of their own inferiority, the Soviet leaders are willing, as was Peter the Great, to borrow Western technology. Thus, Party leader Brezhnev reported to a meeting of the CPSU Central Committee that "an activization of mutually beneficial economic relations" between the USSR and the United States, Japan and other Western industrial countries "and the use of new potentialities along this line will promote peace and is in accordance with the interests of our people."[54] With the assistance of Western science and technology, Soviet economic backwardness, it is hoped, will be overcome.

The Soviet effort to "catch up with America" resembles, in some ways, a classic diplomatic rivalry. Much as imperial Germany sought to replace England as the leading world power in the early twentieth century, so the USSR is striving "to overtake and surpass" the United States. And, much like Avis, Moscow "tries harder." What makes this competition abnormally tense, however, is the Soviet conviction of their own superior virtues. The leaders of the USSR claim to represent a politico-socio-economic system which is, in every way, more advanced than that of the capitalist West. However, since their actual economic performance still is not commensurate with these pretensions, relations with their capitalist "betters" in the United States has often been marked by a special resentment. While willing to import Western technology, Western culture is scorned and reviled. Commenting on his 1959 visit to the United States, Khrushchev observed that "capitalism isn't just an unjust economic system. It is a way of life that leads to a corruption of important values."[55] Embarrassed by American economic productivity, Moscow feels it necessary to assert its moral and spiritual superiority.

Very much like its Tsarist predecessors, the Soviet regime is saddled with two basically inconsistent attitudes towards the outside world. While it has, since its inception, felt itself to be the harbinger of a new, progressive, morally superior, socio-economic order, the Kremlin leaders have been very much aware of the hollowness of their claim. It is the tension produced by the gap between self-image and reality which lies at the root of its neurotic attitude toward the West. Moscow's secretiveness, its hypersensitivity to criticism or even to close observation are explained by this inferiority complex. (The USSR's hostility to American Sovietology can also be understood in these terms. Criticism of "the bourgeois falsifiers of history," especially American writings on the Soviet Union, is a minor industry within the Soviet publishing enterprise.) This also explains the extreme sensitivity displayed by the Soviet Union to the numerous American bases on its borders. These installations serve as a physical reminder of Soviet military inferiority and vulnerability.

The reverse is also true. While hypersensitive to any action or situation which might call into question their claim to Great Power status, the Soviet leaders have always responded with unusual warmth to those who have recognized their accomplishments. Presidents Franklin D. Roosevelt and John F. Kennedy, for example, occupy a special place in the Soviet pantheon of bourgeois political leaders—FDR for recognizing the USSR diplomatically in 1933, after several previous administrations had been unwilling to do so, and President Kennedy for the "realism" with which he is said to have approached Soviet–American relations in 1963.*

*In his American University speech of June 10, 1963, President Kennedy called for an American reassessment of its attitude toward the USSR (he actually warned both the U.S. and the USSR against adhering to a "distorted and desperate view" of the other); he noted, with compassion, past sufferings of the Soviet people and stressed the Great Power and responsibility of the USSR. This posture, which seemed to recognize Soviet contributions and pay tribute to their achievements—and even hinted that the United States may in the past have had a distorted view of the USSR—had tremendous psychological impact on Moscow. More than any of his recent predecessors, Kennedy, in his last year in office, seemed to treat the Soviet Union as fully the equal of the United States. The Partial Test-Ban Treaty and other agreements of that year seemed to confirm this posture. Having accorded Moscow recognition of its achievements and treatment commensurate with that of an equal, the President was accorded the high reputation of a "realist."

Given these attitudes, the recent growth in Soviet military power is a source of deep psychological satisfaction to the Kremlin leaders. While the USSR has long claimed the right to Great Power status,[56] Soviet strategic weapons capabilities now allow the Kremlin to assert this role with increasing confidence. Thus, Foreign Minister Gromyko proclaimed in 1968 that the scope of Soviet power and its broad-ranging diplomatic activities gives the USSR "special" responsibilities and obligations, especially in preserving world peace. As he declared:

> The Soviet people do not have to beg for the right to have a say in settling any question involving the maintenance of international peace, freedom and independence of the peoples, and their own country's broad interests.
> This right is ours by virtue of the Soviet Union's position as a great power.[57]

Having acquired great military strength, the men in the Kremlin are now insisting upon their right to "have a say" regarding "any question" they consider important. In line with this view, the Foreign Minister has declared that "the Soviet Union, which as a major world power has extensive international ties, cannot take a passive attitude toward events that may be territorially remote but affect our security and the security of our friends."[58] This position, he suggests, has been generally recognized by the international community for, "during any urgent situation, however remote it may appear from our country, the Soviet Union's reactions are awaited in every capital in the world."[59]

Thus, from a nation long a pariah in the international community—because of its backwardness, its harsh autocracy and, more recently, its revolutionary ideology—Russia is now claiming recognition of its status as a world power. "An important index of success in foreign policy," declared Party leader Brezhnev in 1970, "is the prestige of the state and the extent of its influence on the course of world affairs." On both counts, he proudly observed, the Soviet leadership has "worthily represented their people in the world arena."[60]

Especially pleasing in this regard, was former President Richard Nixon's state visit to the Soviet Union in May, 1972. The visit itself was symbolic acknowledgment by the leading Western power of the "special role" being played in world affairs by the USSR. As Soviet President Nikolai V. Podgorny declared when toasting President Nixon, "this is the first official visit by a President of the United States of America in the history of relations between our countries. This alone makes your visit . . . a momentous event."[61] Even more gratifying, however, were the texts of the agreements signed in Moscow according to which President Nixon explicitly recognized the "special responsibility" of the USSR (along with the United States) for preserving world peace and controlling international tensions. Thus, to the obvious delight of the Kremlin leaders, the Soviet Union was now viewed by the United States as its equal.[62] Indeed, for a few exhilarating days, Moscow seemed to have become the center of the world. *Moscow Radio* reported with great pride on the activities of the International Press Center in Moscow during the summit conference—570 newsmen representing over 50 newspapers were accredited, 2,705 pages of information and over 300 photographs were transmitted. "Within five days," reported the Soviet news agency TASS, "the newsmen bought 9,600 cups of coffee. . . . These are mere details. The main thing is that the International Press Center in Moscow during several days was the center of the most important world news."[63] After years of trying, Moscow had become, if only briefly, "the navel of the universe."*

Conclusions

The Kremlin leaders are undoubtedly gratified by mounting evidence of the USSR's growing international prestige. They currently do enjoy a reputation in world affairs such that, as Soviet writers have long claimed, important decisions cannot be made without their participation. What are the implications of these developments for the historic Russian attitudes toward the outside world? What influence will such achievements exert on the inherited traditions of the past—expansionism, suspiciousness, a neurotic ambivalence toward the West—as they affect the attitudes and behavior of the current Soviet leadership?

A number of interpretations are conceivable. Let me mention just two. The USSR's greatly enhanced military power and prestige may tend to encourage a policy of increased assertiveness and even aggressiveness toward the outside world. A stronger Kremlin may become a more arrogant Kremlin, one which actively seeks to pursue all the rights and privileges of superpower status. The Soviet leaders may well believe that it is now their turn to enjoy the power and prestige so long refused their country. As a high ranking Soviet U.N. official has written, "The erstwhile Soviet Republic has evolved into the USSR, now an undisputed world power which, having been denied this status during the inter-war period, not unnaturally insists on claiming and exercising its conventional attributes."[64] Thus, although the international environment is much too dangerous to pursue their objectives recklessly, there are undoubtedly men in (or near) the Party top leadership who would want to use the newly enlarged Red Fleet much as Britain used the Royal Navy—to project their power and influence around the globe.

*To see how far the Soviet leaders have come, especially in their own eyes, such remarks should be compared with those made by Nikita Khrushchev regarding his initial visit to the United States in 1959. To be greeted by President Eisenhower at National Airport in Washington, recalled Khrushchev, "made me feel immensely proud; it even shook me up a bit. . . . Here was the United States of America, the greatest capitalist power in the world, bestowing honor on the representative of our socialist homeland—a country which, in the eyes of capitalist America, had always been unworthy or, worse, infected with some sort of plague." (From *Khrushchev Remembers: The Last Testament* (Little, Brown), quoted by Stephen S. Rosenfeld, "Khrushchev and Summit Patterns," *The Washington Post*, June 28, 1974.

In the Chinese view, at least, this is what the Soviet leadership is currently attempting. According to Peking, Moscow is actively pursuing expansionist objectives, particularly in the Middle East. In order to rationalize their sizable naval deployment in the Mediterranean Sea, the Chinese note, the Kremlin has claimed that developments in this area involve Soviet security interests. The USSR has asserted that since it is a "major power in the Black Sea, it is also a major power in the Mediterranean Sea." Such pronouncements, declare the Chinese, are based on "gangster logic." To put it plainly, the 'borders' and 'security' alleged by the Soviet Government mean that wherever it attempts to commit aggression and expansion will become its 'borders' and be where its 'security' is threatened. . . ."

Peking takes an equally cynical view of Moscow's claim to world power status.

> In order to expand in all parts of the world, the Soviet Government has even gone so far as to advocate cosmopolitanism and shouted that the USSR is a "major world power"; so long as "it involves our security or that of our friends" the Soviet Government "will not remain passive," no matter how distant the "geographic location" may be. This is an out-and-out theory of aggression and expansion . . . which has nothing to do with "border security."[65]

What Moscow desires, according to the Chinese, is not merely world power status but "world hegemony." Thus, when Party leader Brezhnev declares that the Soviet Union is a "mighty socialist power occupying an enormous territory in Europe and Asia," that this places a "special responsibility" on Soviet foreign policy and that "we do not shy away from this responsibility,"[66] the Peking leadership does not consider such declarations especially comforting. "What the Soviet leaders of today are frantically seeking is the establishment . . . of a great empire controlling the whole Eurasian continent."[67]

The USSR's recent achievements, therefore, may tend to reinforce Russia's historic sense of hostility toward the outside world, and lead to a more assertive policy, one which will now strive for a decisive shift in the world balance of forces. Convinced of their own superiority—a conviction strengthened by their vast military power—the Kremlin leaders may be anxious to flex their new muscles. Thus, in the years ahead they may probe for ways to expand Soviet influence around the world, to weaken the positions of their major rivals, China and the United States, and to inhibit their freedom of action in South Asia, Europe, the Middle East, and other parts of the world.

Such an interpretation is certainly arguable. In the view of many (in the West as well as in China), an increasingly powerful USSR still tied to a neurotic view of world affairs might well be a growing source of danger to the international community. However, another interpretation seems possible. It is conceivable that Moscow's new international situation may, eventually have precisely the reverse effect; it may tend to encourage a less belligerent, less assertive and less expansionist policy posture.

The *Weltanschauung* of previous Kremlin leaders was largely a function of two major characteristics of Russia's international situation; a near-permanent threat of invasion and danger of war, and an historic sense of inferiority before a technologically more advanced Western culture. On both counts, important changes have recently taken place in Russia's international situation, changes which eventually may produce significant modifications in Russia's traditional world outlook. The Soviet security environment, as we have seen, has dramatically improved. Protected by powerful armed forces and an enormous weapons arsenal, the USSR is not likely again to become the hapless victim of foreign invasion. The Kremlin leaders' knowledge of this fact—and no one knows it better than they—cannot but affect their psychological attitudes. This increased sense of physical security, it seems reasonable to argue, will tend to reduce Soviet anxieties about the outside world. It also might, over time, exert a moderating influence on some of the historic traits—suspiciousness, nervous aggressiveness, xenophobia—which have made the USSR so difficult to deal with in the past.

A more secure Soviet leadership has already become a somewhat more relaxed Soviet leadership, one whose relations with former enemies and current rivals—especially West Germany and the United States—are far better than at any time since the end of World War II. Apprehensions regarding the danger of war have clearly not disappeared; fear of China (along with internal economic considerations) undoubtedly inspired Moscow's policy of détente with the West. Nevertheless, it seems fair to conclude that the Soviet authorities look upon the threat of foreign aggression with less anxiety than had any of their predecessors.

While the Kremlin's sense of physical security has been improved, Russia's national sense of inferiority has been reduced. Many national governments, observes Charles Yost, suffer from "aggravated inferiority complexes." Regimes so afflicted, he writes, are "enormously sensitive, . . . inflamed by the merest suggestion of patronage or criticism, imagining threats or dangers where none exist, indulging in verbal bluster to mask their fears and weakness. . . ."[68] Yost's observations could easily be applied to explain much in Russian and Soviet history. It is open to question, however, whether this pattern still persists.

To the extent such judgments can be accurately gauged, Russia seems to have overcome its historic sense of inferiority. In fact, as we have seen, Russia's traditional status-anxiety no longer has much basis in reality. In place of Old Russia's self-image as a backward, second-rate power, one somehow deserving of a minor role in world affairs, the USSR's very considerable economic and military accomplishments now justify her claims to Great Power status. Furthermore, Western willingness to recognize the USSR's Great Power role has helped reassure the Kremlin authorities of the legitimacy of their place in world affairs. Such reassurance, regarding both security and reputation, has already given rise to an increasingly sophisticated and self-confident Soviet diplomacy. It may, in time, nurture a spirit of reasonableness and cooperation.

What this interpretation attempts to suggest is that Soviet foreign policy is not static but evolutionary. Though many of its roots are to be found in Russian history, traditional habits of mind and values, it can be argued, are slowly being modified. Changes in the USSR's historical situation are working to destroy the psychological conditions on which the traditional world view was built. To the extent that they existed in the past, Russia's inferiority, backwardness, and vulnerability to external attack have all been significantly diminished. In a new international environment, the Kremlin's historic self-image is undoubtedly undergoing change. Traditional attitudes and beliefs, having little basis in fact, are gradually losing their influence.

This attempt to probe the psychological basis of Soviet foreign policy is obviously highly speculative. (Such analyses are undoubtedly what George Kennan had in mind when he suggested that the study of Soviet behavior meant grappling with "the unfirm substance of the imponderables."[69]) Nevertheless, it seems reasonable to suggest that while past history continues to press "on the brain of the living" as Marx said it would, its relative weight is slowly being diminished.

Notes

[1]Walter Bedell Smith, "Introduction," *Journey for Our Time, The Journals of the Marquis de Custine* (New York: Pellegrini and Cudahy, 1951), p. 8.

[2]Testimony of Robert Conquest, *International Negotiations*. Hearings before the Subcommittee on National Security and International Operations of the Committee on Government Operations, U.S. Senate, 91st Congress, First Session, Part I (Washington: Government Printing Office, 1970), p. 2.

[3]Fritz Ermath, *Internationalism, Security, and Legitimacy: The Challenge to Soviet Interests in East Europe, 1964–1968*, RAND Memorandum RM-5909-PR, (Santa Monica: The RAND Corporation, March, 1969), pp. 145–146.

[4]Quoted in George F. Kennan, *The Marquis de Custine and His Russia in 1839* (Princeton: Princeton University Press, 1971), pp. 87–89.

[5]Much of this discussion is based on G. H. Bolsover, "Aspects of Russian Foreign Policy, 1815–1914," in Richard Pares and A. J. P. Taylor, eds., *Essays Presented to Sir Lewis Namier* (London: Macmillan and Co., Ltd., 1956).

[6]Friedrich Engels, "The Foreign Policy of Russian Tsarism," reprinted in Robert A. Goldwin, *et al.*, eds., *Readings in Russian Foreign Policy* (New York: Oxford University Press, 1959), pp. 74, 79.

[7]See Bolsover, *op. cit.*, p. 322.

[8]See *ibid.*, and Philip E. Mosely, "Aspects of Russian Expansion," in his *The Kremlin and World Politics* (New York: Vintage Books, 1960), pp. 42–66.

[9]The essence of this belief can be found in the writings of Nineteenth Century Slavophiles. See, for example, Dostoevsky's *The Diary of a Writer*, excerpts of which are set forth in *Readings in Russian Foreign Policy, op. cit.*, pp. 18–24.

[10]Bertram D. Wolfe, *Three Who Made a Revolution* (New York: The Dial Press, 1948), p. 19.

[11]*The Limitation of Strategic Arms*. Part I, p. 6.

[12]Louis J. Halle, *The Cold War As History* (New York: Harper and Row, 1967), p. 13.

[13]George F. Kennan, *Memoirs, 1925–1950* (Boston: Atlantic, Little, Brown and Co., 1967), pp. 549–560.

[14]Wolfe, *Three Who Made a Revolution*, p. 20.

[15]Kennan, *Memoirs, op. cit.*, pp. 533, 551.

[16]*Ibid.*, p. 560.

[17]Adda B. Bozeman, *Politics and Culture in International History* (Princeton: Princeton University Press, 1960), p. 325.

[18]*Ibid.*, p. 496. *The Arthashastra* is an ancient Indian guide to the pursuit of political power. Compiled by Kautilya, it is in many ways the predecessor to Machiavelli's famous *The Prince*.

[19]*Ibid.*

[20]*Ibid.*, p. 328.

[21]Kennan, *Memoirs, op. cit.*, p. 209.

[22]Dostoevsky, *op. cit.*, p. 18.

[23]Quoted in Abram Tertz (Andrei Sinyavsky), "On Socialist Realism," *Dissent*, Vol. VII, No. 1 (Winter, 1960), p. 57. Reprinted by permission.

[24]Richard Pipes, "Russia's Mission, America's Destiny, The Premises of U. S. and Soviet Foreign Policy," *Encounter*, Vol XXXV, No. 4 (October, 1970), pp. 3–4.

[25]Bozeman, *op. cit.*, p. 355.

[26]Gordon A. Craig, "Techniques of Negotiation," in Ivo J. Lederer, ed., *Russian Foreign Policy* (New Haven: Yale University Press, 1962), p. 354.

[27]For an elaboration of these themes, see Robert F. Byrnes, "Attitudes towards the West," in *Russian Foreign Policy, op. cit.*, pp. 109–141. A similar cultural and psychological antagonism developed between Rome and Byzantium centuries earlier. Here, however, the roles were reversed as the West felt culturally backward before the rich, ornate, splendid spectacle that was Byzantium. Feeling self-conscious about their cultural inferiority to the East, Rome "often affected to despise Byzantine culture as a display of sodden luxury." Bozeman, *op. cit.*, pp. 302–303.

[28]Karl Marx, *The 18th Brumaire of Louis Napoleon*, in Karl Marx and Friedrich Engels, *Selected Works*, Vol. I (Moscow: Foreign Languages Publishing House, 1951), p. 225.

[29]B. Ponomaryov, A. Gromyko and V. Khvostov, eds., *History of Soviet Foreign Policy, 1917–1945* (Moscow: Progress Publishers, 1969), p. 9.

[30]Karl Radek, "The Bases of Soviet Foreign Policy," reprinted in Philip E. Mosely, ed., *The Soviet Union, 1922–1962: A Foreign Affairs Reader* (New York: Frederick A. Praeger, Publisher, 1963), pp. 101–102.

[31]*History of Soviet Foreign Policy, 1917–1945, op. cit.*, p. 10.

[32]Stalin, *op. cit.*, p. 455.

[33]I. V. Stalin, *Sochineniia [Works]*, Vol. 2 (1941–1945), Robert H. McNeal, ed. (Stanford: The Hoover Institution, 1967), p. 214.

[34]"On the International Situation and the Foreign Policy of the Soviet Union." Reported by Deputy A. A. Gromyko, *op. cit.*, p. 16. Translation copyright 1974 by the Current Digest of the Soviet Press; published weekly at The Ohio State University by the American Association for the Advancement of Slavic Studies; reprint by permission.

[35]"Report of the C.P.S.U. Central Committee to the 24th Congress of the Communist Party of the Soviet Union." Report by Comrade L. I. Brezhnev, General Secretary of the Central Committee, *Pravda*, March 3, 1971; translated *CDSP*, Vol. XXIII, No. 12 (April 20, 1971), p. 7.

[36]George F. Kennan, "A Note on Russian Foreign Policy," *Encounter*, Vol. XXXVI, No. 2 (February, 1971), p. 54.

[37]Svetlana Alliluyeva, *Only One Year* (New York: Harper & Row, 1969), p.

48. Particularly revealing here is the fact that Suslov has for many years been responsible for the CPSU's international activities.

[38]Fischer, op. cit., p. 222.

[39]See, for example, "On Provocations 'At the Highest Level,'" Pravda, May 27, 1967, p. 3.

[40]Alliluyeva, op. cit., p. 24.

[41]"Letter of A. D. Sakharov, V. F. Turchin and R. A. Medvedev to the Leaders of the (Communist) Party and (Soviet) Government," March 19, 1970; reprinted in The Limitation of Strategic Arms, Part II, pp. 112–113. So obsessive is official suspiciousness that, according to an eminent Soviet biochemist, the rules for the issuance of passports for Soviet citizens to go abroad is a state secret. Furthermore, as he found by careful observation, every single letter going into or out of the Soviet Union is secretly read by a special government bureau (which he compares favorably with the Black Office established for similar purposes by Alexander I). These extraordinary findings appear in Zhores A. Medvedev, The Medvedev Papers (New York: St. Martin's Press, 1971).

[42]George F. Kennan, Russia and the West under Lenin and Stalin (Boston: Atlantic-Little, Brown & Co., 1960), p. 42.

[43]The New York Times, October 17, 1969.

[44]The New York Times, February 20, 1974; see also "For a Deeper Study of Social Processes," Pravda, May 27, 1973, p. 2; translated in CDSP, Vol. XXV, No. 21 (June 20, 1973), p. 22.

[45]Quoted in Gregory Grossman, "Communism in a Hurry: The 'Time Factor' in Soviet Economics," Problems of Communism, Vol. VIII, No. 3 (May–June, 1959), p. 2.

[46]It is striking, in this regard, to read Alexander Blok's prerevolutionary poem, "New America" (1913), in which a "world dark with factory chimneys" was foreseen with great anticipation for the area beyond the "water-full river" (Volga). See Ladis K. D. Kristof, "The Geopolitical Image of the Fatherland: The Case of Russia," Western Political Quarterly, Vol. XX, No. 4 (December, 1967), pp. 952–953.

[47]Quoted in Nancy Nimitz, "The Agricultural Scene: The Lean Years," Problems of Communism, Vol. XIV, No. 3 (May–June, 1965), p. 14.

[48]Quoted in Imogene Erro, "'Catching Up and Outstripping': An Appraisal," ibid., Vol. X, No. 4 (July–August, 1961), p. 24.

[49]The New York Times, November 25, 1971.

[50]The text of this important editorial, "The Supreme Internationalist Duty of a Socialist Country," Pravda, October 27, 1965, pp. 3–4, is translated in CDSP, Vol. XVII, No. 43 (November 17, 1965), pp. 6–9. Translation copyright 1974 by the Current Digest of the Soviet Press; published weekly at The Ohio State University by the American Association for the Advancement of Slavic Studies; reprint by permission.

[51]Alliluyeva, op. cit., p. 411.

[52]"Letter of A. D. Sakharov, [et al.]," op. cit., p. 112.

[53]Testimony of Joseph Berliner, The Military Budget and National Economic Priorities, Part III, "The Economic Basis of the Russian Military Challenge to the United States," Hearings Before the Subcommittee on Economy in Government of the Joint Economic Committee, Congress of the United States, 91st Congress, 1st Session (Washington: Government Printing Office, 1969), p. 906.

[54]The New York Times, April 30, 1973.

[55]Quoted in Peter H. Juviler and Henry W. Morton, eds., Soviet Policy-Making (Frederick A. Praeger, Publisher, 1967), p. 17.

[56]Even back in the 1930s, Izvestia was writing about the major role then being played by the Kremlin in world affairs. "The USSR," it declared, "thanks to

its size, its social structure, and the rate of its development, is a tremendous force." Quoted in Fischer, *op. cit.*, p. 223.

[57]"On the International Situation and the Foreign Policy of the Soviet Union" Report by Deputy A. A. Gromyko, *op. cit.*, p. 16. Translation copyright 1974 by the Current Digest of the Soviet Press; published weekly at The Ohio State University by the American Association for the Advancement of Slavic Studies; reprint by permission.

[58]"Questions of the International Situation and the Foreign Policy of the Soviet Union," Report by Deputy A. A. Gromyko, U.S.S.R. Minister of Foreign Affairs, *Pravda*, July 11, 1969; translated in *CDSP*, Vol. XXI, No. 28 (August 6, 1969), p. 4.

[59]"On the International Situation and the Foreign Policy of the Soviet Union," Report by Deputy A. A. Gromyko, *op. cit.*, p. 16.

[60]Leonid I. Brezhnev, "Creatively Accomplish New Tasks of Communist Construction," *Pravda*, June 13, 1970; translated in *CDSP*, Vol. XXII, No. 25 (July 21, 1970), p. 11.

[61]*The New York Times*, May 23, 1972.

[62]See especially the "Basic Principles of Mutual Relations" and the Joint Communique signed by President Nixon and Communist Party leader Brezhnev at the end of the state visit. In *ibid.*, May 30, 1972. Special joint responsibility was also implied regarding other matters including disarmament, the Middle East and, in general, promoting international cooperation. Moscow's claim to equality was further bolstered by the 1973 Summit, especially by the joint U.S.–U.S.S.R. agreement on the prevention of nuclear war. According to one Soviet commentator, U.S. acceptance of the policy of peaceful coexistence which this agreement symbolized was based on the fact that Washington had been "forced . . . to recognize once and for all, the viability, full equality and invincibility of the socialist system. . . . This is a very great gain for socialism. . . ." M. Kudrin, "An Important Step Toward Strengthening Peace." *International Affairs*, No. 10 (1973), pp. 10–11.

[63]*Radio Moscow* (TASS International Service in English), May 29, 1972.

[64]Evgeny Chossudovsky, "Genoa Revisited: Russia and Coexistence," *Foreign Affairs*, Vol. 50, No. 3 (April, 1972), p. 568.

[65]"Refute the Soviet Revisionist Gangster Theory," Radio Peking Domestic Service, December 15, 1971; reprinted in "Chinese Comment on Soviet Foreign Policy," *International Negotiations*, Subcommittee on National Security and International Operations, Committee on Government Operations, U.S. Senate (Washington, D.C.: Government Printing Office, 1972), p. 3.

[66]Brezhnev, "Creatively Accomplish New Tasks. . . ," *op. cit.*, p. 12.

[67]From Remarks Before the Security Council by Ambassador Huang Hua, Permanent Representative of the PRC to the UN, December 5–6, 1971, "Chinese Comment on Soviet Foreign Policy," *op. cit.*, p. 2.

[68]Charles Yost, *The Insecurity of Nations* (New York: Frederick A. Praeger, 1968), p. 66.

[69]Kennan, *Memoirs, op. cit.*, p. 499.

4

Soviet political beliefs: ideological influences

. . . The ideas of economists and political philosophers, both when they are right and when they are wrong, are more powerful than is commonly understood. Indeed the world is ruled by little else. Practical men, who believe themselves to be quite exempt from any intellectual influences, are usually the slaves of some defunct economist. Madmen in authority, who hear voices in the air, are distilling their frenzy from some academic scribbler of a few years back. I am sure that the power of vested interests is vastly exaggerated compared with the gradual encroachment of ideas. Not, indeed, immediately, but after a certain interval; for in the field of economics and political philosophy there are not many who are influenced by new theories after they are twenty-five or thirty years of age, so that the ideas which civil servants and politicians and even agitators apply to current events are not likely to be the newest. But, soon or late, it is ideas, not vested interests, which are dangerous for good or evil.

—John Maynard Keynes[1]

When we examine the foreign policy objectives of the Soviet leaders, their priorities seem very similar to those of other national leaders. The Soviet government seeks to achieve self-preservation, security, prosperity, and prestige. However, the manner in which such goals are defined and the mode by which they are satisfied are determined in considerable measure by historically rooted attitudes and values. Thus, the requirements of "security" are shaped by the expectation of external danger, an expectation deeply affected by Russia's historical experiences. The Kremlin's world outlook, its perceptions, and its expectations are also shaped by the distinctive Soviet political system. The Russian people *are* different. So is their pattern of government.

One of the most important ways in which the government of the USSR is "different" lies in the rather unusual psychological foundations on which all Communist regimes rest. A Communist political system is, by self-definition, an "ideocracy." The leaders of such regimes base their claim to loyalty and obedience neither on ancient traditions (these were ostentatiously cast aside in the USSR at the time of the Communist seizure of power in 1917) nor on democratic elections. (Though elections are regularly held, they serve to mobilize the populace in support of the regime's policies, not to legitimize its rule.) Communist revolutions create a system of Party rule that derives its authority from the Party leaders' self-appointed role as the sole correct interpreters and executives of "the laws of history" as revealed by Marx and Lenin. Ideology, therefore, justifies the power of the political elite and the existing system.

Of the numerous uncertainties surrounding the foreign policy of the USSR, few have caused greater confusion than the relationship of ideology to foreign policy. If we take them at their own word, we must begin by believing that the Soviet leaders are Marxist–Leninist. Does this really matter? Does official doctrine actually shape Soviet policy or is it mere scholastic ideology whose only real function is to provide the slogans which decorate public buildings and Party posters? Rhetoric aside, do the Soviet leaders today really take seriously the writings of Marx, who lived in the pre-automobile and pre-airplane era, or those of Lenin, who died before the advent of television, nuclear weapons, intercontinental missiles and computers? Do the Communist doctrines based on their teachings actually serve as a guide to action, as it is claimed, or are they merely used to rationalize policies undertaken for more prosaic reasons? One's response to these important questions has profound policy implications. Before we seek to answer them, a broad survey of Communist political thought as it relates to foreign policy is very much in order.

Communist doctrine on foreign policy

We shall begin our assessment of the influence of ideology on behavior by examining Soviet foreign policy from the perspective of the Soviet leaders themselves. One of the first things we find upon entering their intellectual framework is that the foreign policy of the USSR is "scientifically correct" in the view of the Soviet leaders. This notion, rather strange to the Western ear, derives from their fundamental philosophical commitment to "scientific socialism"—to the view that the march of history proceeds not "as a wild whirl of senseless deeds of violence," to quote Engels, but according to basic laws which Marx is said to have discovered. Awareness of these laws, it is claimed, gives Soviet foreign policy its "scientific character." "The scientific basis of socialist foreign policy," writes one Soviet analyst, "is expressed above all in the fact that it is formed and implemented in accordance with the objective laws of social development determining the course of world history including the leading tendencies in the development of international relations."[2]

The "objective laws" on which Soviet policy is said to be based relate, of course, to Marx's materialist conception of history and especially to his analysis of capitalism. From 1917 until this day, the makers of Soviet foreign policy have proclaimed that the defining feature of the current stage of historical development is the inexorable collapse of the capitalist system and its replacement by socialism. "Capitalism," notes a recent Soviet handbook, "once all-powerful, is falling into decay. Socialism, which was once only a dream of happiness . . . has now become a reality in a substantial part of the globe.[3] "Rent by deep and acute contradictions," "world capitalism" is on its way out. Nothing it can do will save it. "The moribund capitalist system will never be able to alter the inexorable march of history. . . . It is ripe for proletarian socialist revolutions for we are living in the historic epoch of man's transition from capitalism to socialism."[4]

It is the Soviet view that the world is undergoing a historic revolutionary transformation in which capitalism is being replaced by a new and superior system—socialism. A new world is aborning. Knowledge of this fact, it is claimed, gives Soviet foreign policy great advantages. Awareness of the basic "laws of social development" underlying this revolutionary process give Soviet diplomacy "the possibility not only of understanding the current tendencies of international life but also of permitting the desirable collaboration with the march of events."[5] Bourgeois diplomacy, by contrast, does not have these possibilities. "By its very nature the foreign policy of a bourgeois state cannot be scientific because it runs counter to the basic requirements of socio-economic development and social development as a whole."[6] That is to say, it ignores the revolutionary character of contemporary international life. As a result, its policies are "based on downright empiricism . . . pragmatism," and "are largely only a reaction to situation arising in the world."[7] Bourgeois statesmen cannot "collaborate" with objective laws of which they are ignorant.

The international class struggle

Within this "scientific" framework, a number of principles can be derived. Essential to the Soviet view of foreign policy is its class character. "There is no such thing," says Soviet Foreign Minister Andrei Gromyko, "as foreign policy in general, a policy that fails to include or reflect the interests of definite classes and their ideologies."[8] Thus, in the view of the

Soviet leaders, "the socialist character" of the USSR's social and political system endows its international behavior with a number of distinctive qualities. First, and most important, its "socialist character" is said to link the Soviet regime with the cause of peace. "From the hour of its establishment, socialism and peace were inseparable." Socialist Russia, furthermore, was bound to follow "genuinely democratic standards of international intercourse" such as respect for the integrity and sovereignty of all nations, noninterference in the internal affairs of all states and peoples, and equality of all nations. So the Soviet Union is said to be committed to the principle of the "peaceful coexistence of states with different social systems."[9]

The Soviets see the "peaceful, democratic, nonaggressive" character of their foreign policy as the direct result of the popular character of their regime. According to Kremlin sources, the Bolshevik Revolution gave rise to the first truly democratic regime in history, one in which the country is ruled by and in the interests of all the people. As a result, the basis for a truly different foreign policy was created. As one Soviet text has stated, "the Great October Socialist Revolution . . . gave birth to a totally new foreign policy that served not the exploiters but the working people, the working class, which came to power and championed the interests of the entire nation." Thus, in contrast to the policies of the "exploiters," the "motive force" of Soviet foreign policy is seen to be

the desire of the working people, standing at the helm of the state, to create the most favorable conditions for building the new, more just and free society. The objective of the socialist economy is to satisfy the steadily growing material and cultural requirements of the people. War hinders the attainment of this objective.[10]

Thus, the "peace-loving" character of Soviet foreign policy is seen to be not a question of expediency or tactics, "not a transient thing, but a permanent, indispensable characteristic . . . one determined by the existence of a socialist system."[11] The basic objectives of a "socialist system"—developing the economy and culture—could only be damaged by war. Perhaps, ask two Soviet analysts, there are factors in the USSR which create a personal interest in war? Their answer, not surprisingly, is "No." Such factors are "alien to the Soviet way of life . . . In the Soviet Socialist society there are no classes or groups of the population that derive profits from war orders or the arms drive. With the disappearance of the *capitalist class*, there disappears the profit incentive to wage war."[12] It is not simply the "disappearance of the profit incentive to wage war" that is said to ensure the peaceful character of socialist foreign policy but the fact that under socialism, true democracy is established. "It is the people," declared Khrushchev in 1959, "who determine the destinies of the socialist states."

The socialist states are ruled by the working people themselves. . . . And people of labor cannot want war. For to them war spells grief and tears, death, devastation and misery. Ordinary people have no need for war.[13]

Its class character, therefore, explains the peaceful orientation of socialist foreign policy. ". . . the inner laws of socialist society make the socialist states an irreconcilable adversary of aggression and conquest, of encroachment on peace, on the security and independence of nations. Socialist foreign policy aims to curb aggressors and insure peace and the independence of peoples."[14] Under capitalism the situation is necessarily very different. Though the bourgeoisie always seeks to mask their objectives by talking in terms of "national interests," such concerns are invariably nothing more than a distorted reflection of their class interests. "What bourgeois governments present as 'national state interests' is usually a very far cry from genuine national interests and . . . prove to be merely the class interests of these governments themselves and of the monopoly-capital groups they represent."[15] These interests lead inexorably to a policy of aggression. "In capitalist society," it is said,

> . . . the driving force behind foreign policy is the desire of the ruling class to consolidate the exploiting system and expand the sphere of exploitation by seizing markets, strategic positions, and foreign territory, by subjugating other peoples. By virtue of its social nature, capitalist foreign policy is one of expansion and aggression, of preparing and starting wars of aggrandisement, of creating military blocks and furthering the arms race.[16]

Thus, in the Soviet view, the "inner laws" of socialism direct its policymakers to pursue a peaceful, democratic foreign policy while capitalism's "ruling class" is impelled by its own internal dynamics to follow a path of aggression, expansion, and exploitation. Conflict between the two is seen as inexorable. In fact, the struggle between socialism and capitalism, "the main contradiction of our time," is now largely in terms of foreign policy. This represents a major shift in the focus of Marxian theory. While Marx saw the movement of history and the collapse of capitalism resulting from a succession of class conflicts *within* industrially developed nations, contemporary Soviet analysis projects this struggle onto the world stage. Marx's class conflict has been internationalized.

This focus on the international features of the class struggle is largely the contribution of Lenin. In his famous *Imperialism, the Highest State of Capitalism* (1916), Lenin sought to bring Marxian theory up to date. He argued that the basic contradiction which Marx found in capitalist society—that between the bourgeoisie and the proletariat—had been substantially modified when in the latter part of the nineteenth century the advanced capitalist nations turned to a policy of colonial exploitation. Lenin argued that in light of the very substantial profits exacted from their colonial possessions, the ruling bourgeoisie in England, France, and Germany could allow fatter wage packets to their workers. As a result, the proletariat experienced a rise in living standards; not surprisingly, their "revolutionary consciousness" sagged.

Though domestic class conflict was seen to diminish, Lenin argued that it had not disappeared. In his view, interclass rivalry between the proletariat and the bourgeoisie was now transplanted onto the world scene as imperialist exploitation gave rise to the enslavement of whole colonial territories. Imperialism, in his view, also led to intercapitalist military competition and ultimately to war. Thus, though revolutionary activity may have diminished in the industrial nations, it was on the rise in the backward countries. And, furthermore, the likelihood of war greatly increased.

In sum, argued Lenin, the main front in the struggle against capitalism was now international. Revolutionary uprisings in the colonies against imperialist rule would severely damage the industrial economies dependent on them; the gigantic bloodbaths produced by imperialist politico-military rivalries would cause domestic unrest; the imperialist system and ultimately capitalism itself would be destroyed.

The Bolshevik victory in 1917 and the successful establishment of a Communist regime in Russia gave further impetus to the "internationalization" of the class struggle begun by Lenin. Regarding their Party as the chief protector and organizer of the "world revolutionary movement" and "the peoples fighting for liberation from imperialism," the leaders of the USSR have, from the very outset, viewed themselves as the surrogate for Marx's proletariat. The class conflict is now writ large: the USSR, the vanguard of all revolutionary forces, has replaced the "proletariat"; the leading capitalist nation (Great Britain, in the inter-war period, the United States, since 1945), replaces the "bourgeoisie." Thus, as a Soviet author recently noted, "the foreign policy of socialist states is fundamentally opposed to that of capitalist states as a result of the opposition between the positions and interests of the proletariat and the bourgeoisie. . . ."[17] While Marx saw the basic contradiction of modern society as that between the proletariat and the bourgeoisie, contemporary Soviet authorities see the class struggle in terms of the contradiction between the two opposing social systems—"socialism" and "monopoly capitalism." The focus of struggle thus shifts from the domestic to the international class struggle, from the proletariat and the bourgeoisie to "socialism" (led by the USSR) and "capitalism" (led by the United States).

These ideological formulations and the Marxist assumptions on which they rest have important implications for the Soviet leaders' image of the outside world and their relations to it. The Marxist–Leninist perspective is clearly based on the assumption of intense political conflict between "dying capitalism" and "emerging socialism." While "the final liberation of mankind from capitalist exploitation" is seen to be a "foregone conclusion,"[18] the international class struggle is viewed as both bitter and of long duration. Much as the proletariat is embroiled in mortal combat with the bourgeoisie, so the forces of socialism are engaged in a life and death struggle with capitalism. The international political world, it is thus assumed, is torn by a mortal struggle in which there is only one fundamental question, *kto-kogo?* or "who [will destroy] whom?"

The inherently aggressive character of modern capitalism makes the world a dangerous place. This is especially true for the Soviet Union for which the capitalists are said to bear an irreconcilable and fundamental hatred. The early Soviet leaders believed with Lenin that bourgeois capitalism "detested Bolshevism with all its heart and soul."[19] Much the same apprehension regarding the basic intentions of capitalism was expressed recently by a leading Soviet official. "The entire course of social development," declared Marshal Grechko, the Soviet Defense Minister, "shows that imperialism has sought and will continue to seek to crush socialism by force of arms. . . ."[20] Unlike the peaceful intentions with which all Soviet policies and purposes are identified, "international imperialism" led by the U.S. is assumed to be (indeed must be) profoundly and basically hostile.

Statements of this sort emanating from a military official are not to be taken at face value. More often than not, they seem to reflect an effort to win larger defense budgets, or at least to win acclaim for the heroic efforts of the Soviet armed forces in protecting the motherland from so dangerous a foe. Yet, in virtually all Soviet writings, the profoundly anti-Soviet attitudes and intentions of the capitalist West are assumed. According to the Central Committee "Theses" adopted in commemoration of the one hundreth anniversary of Lenin's birth, for example, "the principle goal of imperialist strategy" is said to be "the destruction of socialism," the " 'replaying' of the historic battles of the twentieth century, achieving revenge, toppling socialism from the heights of world influence," a goal which, needless to say, "is unattainable."[21]

Capitalist hostility toward socialism is, in a sense, assumed. Socialism, after all, is the sworn enemy of capitalism, its "gravedigger." That the bourgeoisie adopts a hostile stance toward their would-be destroyers is understandable. Thus, according to a recent Soviet analysis, the struggle between the two camps—the socialist and the capitalist—is not "a simple 'confrontation' of the two systems."

> Today, the socialist community not only confronts world imperialism, but by *the very fact of its existence,* by all its socialist activity and its active foreign policy provides the objective premises for the successful completion of the struggle of revolutionary liberation movements, and accelerates social development on the road of progress.[22]

The "very existence" of the socialist community led by the USSR endangers the capitalist world. Little wonder, then, that "imperialism still dreams of a historical revenge against socialism."[23]

The Soviet leaders thus adhere to a dogma which pictures the outside world as hostile and menacing. In addition, from the same ideological assumptions regarding the corrupt nature of capitalism, they regard the governments of Western nations as "basically devoid of any virtue or integrity." Well before the 1917 revolution, the Bolshevik movement had concluded that the political systems found in the West were illegitimate, that their people owed them no loyalty, and that "these governments were doomed by inexorable social forces to eventual destruction. . . . In the Bolshevik view," notes George Kennan, "the Western governments were without exception predatory, reprehensible, devoid of redeeming features and deserving of overthrow. Those who manned them were seen fit subjects for removal from power, disfranchisement and punishment."[24]

In a fundamental sense, all non-Communist regimes are considered illegitimate. Representing the basic interests of the minority ruling classes, Western governments do not truly represent "the people." Furthermore, they are the *last* representatives of minority rule. As Marx and Lenin taught, capitalism is on its way out. Existing political arrangements in the West are regarded therefore, as temporary; the rule of the bourgeois capitalist system is seen as disintegrating. As Khrushchev remarked after a 1963 successful space landing, "We shall give the capitalist world no peace, since it has to go."[25]

The Western world is not only degenerating, it is also collapsing. The tide of history, much as Marx and Lenin predicted, is clearly moving in the direction of socialism. As Communist Party Secretary Suslov declared in 1969, the establishment of the USSR inaugurated a profound revolutionary political transformation which "radically altered our planet's social makeup." To prove his point, the following statistics were cited:[26]

Table 15

Nations	Territory		Population (estimate)	
	Millions of sq. kms.	Pct. of world total	Millions	Pct. of world total
Beginning of 1919				
I. Entire world:	135.8	100.0	1,777.0	100.0
(1) Socialist cos.	21.7	16.0	138.0	7.8
(2) Other cos.	114.1	84.0	1,639.0	92.2
II. Big imperialist powers and their colonies	60.3	44.4	855.0	48.1
III. All colonies and semi-colonies	97.8	72.0	1,235.0	69.4
Beginning of 1969				
I. Entire world:	135.8	100.0	3,520.0	100.0
(1) Socialist cos.	35.2	25.9	1,210.0	34.4
(2) Other cos.	100.6	74.1	2,310.0	65.6
II. Big imperialist powers and their colonies	12.3	9.0	539.2	15.3
III. All colonies and semi-colonies	5.0	3.7	36.3	1.0
IV. Former colonial, semi-colonial countries which became sovereign states after 1919 (excluding socialist states)	79.1	58.2	1,616.0	45.9

While the USSR is embroiled in a titanic struggle with capitalism, there is little doubt of the eventual outcome. As Khrushchev declared in 1959, "We Communists believe that the idea of Communism will ultimately be victorious throughout the world. . . ."[27] And the figures cited by Suslov were meant to demonstrate that this belief was being realized. The world is seen to be undergoing a fundamental reconstruction along socialist lines.

Complete victory, however, is still far off. And while socialist foreign policy is based on "the Leninist principles of the struggle for peace and socialism and against the forces of aggression," Party Secretary Brezhnev reminds his listeners that "the aggressors have not stopped being aggressors. The enemies of the freedom and independence of the peoples have not turned into meek lambs and good fairies."[28] Furthermore, notes Suslov, imperialism's "strength and possibilities" should not be underestimated. It has at its disposal "a great military machine and considerable economic potential."[29] Though eventual victory is certain, the international class struggle will rage for some time to come.

Proletarian internationalism

Soviet foreign policy is viewed by its makers within the context of a historic revolutionary struggle. Until such time as ultimate victory occurs, relations with the "capitalist states" are endowed with a special tension befitting relations with class enemies. Soviet relations with their class brethren in the "socialist" states, their allies in the great revolutionary struggle, are viewed very differently. They are based, not on conflict and struggle, but on "the close bonds of international proletarian solidarity." The basic position on relations among socialist states was well expressed by Nikolai Bukharin, the famous Bolshevik theoretician. Writing in the American journal, *Foreign Affairs*, Burkharin argued that "there is no clash of real interests between proletarian states whatsoever; on the contrary, their real interest is in maximum cooperation." In fact, notes Bukharin, bonds among proletarian states are such that "after a certain stage of development . . . tendencies will be revealed—tendencies toward a state union of proletarian republics." Given such strong common interests and ties, their relations will be very peaceful.

> With the further flowering of proletarian states throughout the entire world war will become unnecessary. War will be impossible in a system of unified Communist society, where there are no classes and even—*horribile dictu*—no coercive state power nor armies. This society will really "turn swords into ploughshares" and release gigantic masses of energy for national creative work for the benefit of all mankind.

A world of socialist states, according to Bukharin, would be a world without war.[30]

Consistent with their class analysis, Soviet writers hold the view that there is a natural harmony of interests among the forces united under the banner of socialism. Founded on the bedrock of common class interests and goals, "a new, heretofore unknown type" of "socialist international relations is said to have appeared." The bourgeoisie built up its system "with fire and sword. Armed conquest and various forms of coercion were its chief means." By contrast, relations within the socialist world are "highlighted by genuine equality, mutual respect of independence and sovereignty, and by fraternal mutual assistance and cooperation."[31]

Close relations among socialist states is also to be understood in the broader context of "the historic revolutionary struggle." It is assumed that the forces of socialism are the main agent in the struggle against capitalism, that the final victory of "the world revolution" will be made possible "by the struggle of the working class, by the activities of its parties and international organizations."[32] To hasten the day of final victory, the paramount task of all revolutionary forces is to join ranks. "Workers of all countries, unite," proclaim Marx and Engels in *The Communist Manifesto*. International unity of the working class is seen as "an objective necessity . . . a necessity engendered by the common social position and class aims of the workers of different countries and by the impossibility of achieving these aims without mutual assistance and support."[33] Ultimate victory—the triumph of socialist world revolution—is seen as possible only on a world-wide scale and on the basis of an international alliance of the working class.

This principle of proletarian internationalism was a matter of some urgency for Lenin. As a recent Soviet text has put it, "With the establishment of Soviet power in Russia, the international policy of the proletariat became a *state* policy for the first time in history."[34] For the Bolsheviks, the question then became the critical one: How would the world's first proletarian state fulfill its obligations under the principle of "international proletarian solidarity"? Initially, Lenin had few doubts; he argued that the only course for a successful revolution was a policy of "revolutionary war." When socialism was successfully established in one or two countries he predicted in 1915, "The victorious proletariat . . . would rise up against the rest of the capitalist world, attracting to itself the oppressed classes of other countries, provoking among them a revolt against the capitalists, appearing if necessary with armed forces against the exploiting classes and states."[35]

At the outset, proletarian internationalism thus included the notion of "revolutionary war." Adherence to its revolutionary obligations, as they were defined by Lenin, implied that the new proletarian regime in Russia would prepare for the triumph of socialism everywhere by inciting revolutions against the rest of the capitalist world, reinforcing such actions by armed force if necessary.

Lenin's commitment to the policy of revolutionary war proved short lived. During the peace negotiations at Brest–Litovsk in early 1918 which took the newly established Bolshevik regime out of the First World War, a number of Lenin's closest colleagues strongly urged that Soviet forces attack Germany with all their strength. A victory by the Russian proletariat, it was thought, would light the torch of revolution in Germany and all of Europe. War would help spark the revolutionary conflagration. Lenin, however, rejected this proposal. Given the newness of the Soviet government, the fragility of its power, and the domestic chaos then prevailing in Russia, he believed such a policy would be suicidal. For him, the primary obligation was to retain power. While still very much convinced that world revolution was generally imminent, at the moment he considered it "a fairy tale." "I quite understand children liking beautiful fairy tales, but I ask: Is it seemly for a serious revolutionary to believe in fairy tales?" To promote the cause of world revolution, he asserted, it was first necessary to preserve the Soviet state. A disgraceful peace, such as that offered by Germany which surrendered territory to secure the survival of Soviet power, was infinitely preferable "to dying in a beautiful pose, sword in hand."[36]

The Brest–Litovsk crisis brought to a head the unresolved dilemma which has confronted the Soviet regime from its very birth, the dilemma of a regime which aspires to act simultaneously as an integral part of the world revolutionary movement (in fact, as its driving force) and as the sovereign power of a state in a system of states. At times, the two roles seemed to pull in different directions. When they did, Lenin invariably saw his obligations best fulfilled in working to protect the interests of the Soviet state. Thus, in the summer of 1919, when the Communist regime established in Hungary by Bela Kun showed signs of collapsing, Lenin chose not to attempt a salvage operation. Deeply involved in its own Civil War, Moscow still felt itself too weak to risk sending military support and a brother revolutionary regime was left to founder.

How did Lenin overcome this dichotomy between proletarian internationalism and *raison d'etat*? The main point to be understood is that the Bolshevik leaders saw no dichotomy. In their view the Russian revolution and the world revolution were one and the same, the former being the harbinger of the latter, and its spark. Thus, when he urged acceptance of Germany's demands at Brest–Litovsk, Lenin did so convinced that such action would best preserve the fragile base of the world revolutionary movement. He wanted to protect the "socialist fatherland," not "holy Mother Russia." As he wrote in January, 1918,

> The moment a Socialist regime triumphs in any one country, questions must be decided . . . exclusively from the point of view of the conditions which make for the development and consolidation of the Socialist revolution which has already begun.
> In other words, the underlying principle of our tactics must not be, which of the two imperialisms it is more profitable to aid at this juncture, but rather, how can the Socialist revolution be most surely and reliably ensured the possibility of consolidating itself, or, at least, of maintaining itself in one country until it is joined by other countries.[37]

Lenin's assumption that the interests of the Soviet regime were identical to that of the world revolution were not totally implausible. It is hard to think how the revolutionary cause would have benefited had the Bolsheviks been crushed. There was considerable truth in the Party Manifesto which asserted that "there could be no greater blow now to the cause of socialism than the collapse of Soviet power in Russia."[38] Lenin's two essential aims—world revolution and national security—were not inconsistent. As E. H. Carr has observed, "World revolution was the sole guarantee of national security; but national security was also a condition of the successful promotion of world revolution."[39] While Lenin still felt that revolution in Europe, especially Germany, was essential to secure the survival of the Bolshevik Revolution (and it was full expectation that revolution in Germany would be forthcoming that Lenin even attempted revolution in Russia), he also sensed that the survival of the Bolshevik regime was essential if the world revolution were ever to occur.

Lenin thus pursued a cautionary approach toward the notion of "revolutionary war." The one major exception occurred in 1920 when, for a brief moment, he saw the possibility of creating a Soviet Poland. Riding the crest of a Red Army victory during the Russo-Polish War, he believed that the Polish people would rise up giving their support to the Soviet armies seeking to liberate them from bourgeois rule. This attempt to collaborate with the march of events failed. The Soviet threat to Warsaw served as a catalyst to unite the Polish people. The advancing Red Army was thrown back. As Lenin later recognized, the Poles saw the Soviet troops not as "brother liberators but foes." Revolutionary consciousness thus went down to defeat before the force of Polish nationalism.[40]

Though Lenin was reluctant to jeopardize the socialist beachhead in Russia for the sake of an ephemeral world revolution, he did attempt to arouse the working class of Western Europe under the banner of world revolution. This was especially true in the first decades of Bolshevik rule. Soviet Russia was, from the very outset, a weak power; its economy was in chaos, its military strength could not be compared to that of any major power, it had no major allies. Feeling isolated and threatened, the Kremlin sought to mobilize support from potential revolutionary allies among the workers of Europe. To achieve his dual purposes—to encourage world revolution and to protect national security—Lenin helped set up a major organizational and propaganda campaign focused on the European labor movement. Playing on the considerable sympathy for what was considered by many in Europe as "the great socialist experiment in collective ownership and control," Moscow won support for its position during the Russo-Polish War. "Hands off Russia" campaigns which sought to prevent the forwarding of war materials to Poland developed in Czechoslovakia, the free city of Danzig (the most important port for Polish traffic) and especially in England. The British trade unions, most notably the dockworkers, strenuously objected to and obstructed the shipment of munitions to be used against the new Soviet Republic."[41]

Moscow's most conspicuous attempt to mobilize the forces of proletarian internationalism came in 1919 with the creation of the Third or Communist International (Comintern). Lenin saw the Bolshevik Revolution in terms of a general revolutionary upsurge. He thus viewed himself as both head of the world's first Communist state and, as a result, the leader of the world-wide revolutionary movement. He took both roles very seriously. Thus, just six weeks after it had been established, the Soviet government allocated two million rubles "for the needs of the international revolutionary movement." In Lenin's view, "The struggle against war and imperialism can be brought to a successful conclusion only if waged on an international scale."[42] To further the world revolution, he put Soviet gold and diplomacy to work as Bolshevik officials took the lead in establishing the Comintern.*

While it is easy to exaggerate Moscow's revolutionary activities, as many at that time tended to do, the rhetoric of world revolution and the noisy activities of the Comintern turned many a hair in the West. Fear of the "red menace" was widespread, especially in the unstable economic and political conditions of post-World War I Europe.[43] With its willingness to dispense " 'technical assistance' in revolution-making"[44] financial and political support (and, in some cases, notably in China, even military assistance) to revolutionary movements—and to organize, encourage the formation, and help direct the activities of Communist Parties around the world, Soviet involvement in the Comintern was a startling innovation in international relations. History has seen occasional instances of officially organized subversion of one government by another. However, the scope of Soviet governmental involvement in such activities was unique. The United States, notes Adam Ulam, sheltered Irish revolutionaries while Britain and France gave asylum to opponents of the regimes in Russia and Italy "but in no case was the government of the place of refuge directly and publicly connected with those activities and in no case was the given revolutionary organization of such a universal character as the Third International."[45]

Despite the sense of dread which the Comintern evoked, this "general staff of the world revolution" was not a very effective revolutionary catalyst. Efforts to incite "more Octobers" simply failed. Nevertheless, Moscow's concern for the activities of the Comintern remained. For the Bolsheviks, revolutions elsewhere (Germany, it was generally felt, was the most likely place) were seen not merely as desirable; they were absolutely essential. In fact, Lenin seriously doubted whether the victorious revolution in Russia could survive without support from abroad. He initially shared Trotsky's view that "either the Russian Revolution will create a revolutionary movement in Europe or the European powers will destroy the Russian Revolution."[46] To help organize and encourage the revolutionary conflagration which the October Revolution was meant to

---

*Such excursions in revolution-making are largely forgotten by contemporary Soviet historians. Placing great stress on "peaceful coexistence," recent analyses of Soviet foreign policy completely overlook Moscow's support of local Communist parties and revolutionary activities during these early years. The Comintern is never mentioned in discussions of the early history of Soviet foreign policy, nor is the fact that the two million rubles just mentioned were allocated by the Soviet *government* "for the needs of the revolutionary international movement" and were put "at the disposal of the foreign representatives of the Commissariat for Foreign Affairs," *i.e.*, for Soviet embassies abroad. Though this was official government policy, such activities do not jibe with the current "peaceful coexistence" theme. Hence they are consigned to the "memory hole." As Orwell wrote in *1984*, "Who controls the present controls the past."

start, Moscow became the chief mainstay of the Comintern—its main inspiration, strategist, and financial supporter.

The failure of the Comintern to promote the revolutionary cause soon began to create problems. The expected world proletarian revolution did not occur. Such revolutionary uprisings as did take place, in Germany and Hungary, were easily put down. Failure led to disenchantment, and belief in the imminence of revolution began to wane; the attention of the Bolshevik leaders concentrated on the survival of the Soviet regime. As the only successful proletarian revolution, the Soviet Republic became the "base" of the world revolution. As such, it became the focus of all attention—to be defended and strengthened "until the time for revolution was again ripe."

This argument, a logical extension of Lenin's position at Brest–Litovsk, was the heart of Stalin's famous doctrine of "socialism in one country." All energies and activity were concentrated on promoting the interests of the USSR. All Soviet policies became, *ipso facto*, in the interests of world revolution. Much as the Bolshevik Party under Lenin had become the sole custodian of the Russian revolutionary ideal, so the USSR under Stalin became the sole protector of world revolution. Under these circumstances, the Comintern was reduced from an agency of international revolution to an instrument of Soviet foreign policy. The concept of proletarian internationalism became indistinguishable from Soviet patriotism and lost all meaning.[47]

Stalin was not only demonstrating a lack of faith in world revolution but his total lack of any interest in events outside of Soviet Russia. Unlike Lenin, Stalin was not very much of an internationalist. He was interested in strengthening Soviet security and maximizing Soviet political influence. Thus, in concentrating on "socialism in one country," Stalin made a virtue out of what was a necessity for Lenin. To the extent that the Comintern was useful in this enterprise, Stalin was willing to exploit its rather elaborate internal political apparatus in the worldwide network of local Communist Parties. The Comintern continued to function throughout the 1920s and 1930s—convening its vast international congresses in the worldwide network of Moscow, and publishing its "revolutionary" declarations and journals exhorting Communists around the world to strengthen their loyalty to the Soviet Union—but its activities were not taken very seriously. When by 1943 the Comintern no longer suited the purposes of the USSR, it was simply abandoned. The loss was not grave because proletarian internationalism was a nonissue for Stalin.[48]

The relevance of doctrine

As all students of Soviet affairs quickly discover, the Kremlin rulers speak in an ideologically garnished rhetoric, lacing their pronouncements and analyses with exhaustive references to Marx and Lenin. The important question remains whether this behavior reveals very much, if anything, about the content of Soviet policy. Does ideology help shape policy alternatives and choices or are doctrinal references merely lip-service to an essentially defunct revolutionary tradition? Do the Soviet leaders actually believe, for example, in the collapse of capitalism and the final victory of Communism? Do they regard the existing state system as temporary? Is war between socialism and capitalism still regarded as inevitable? More concretely, to the extent they are believed, how do the doctrines described previously affect Soviet policy toward Washington? Or Peking? Or Warsaw? How do they influence the Soviet position on arms control? How does their commitment to proletarian internationalism influence policy toward "the forces of socialism" beyond the Soviet borders? How does it affect Soviet policy toward the revolutionary nationalist leaders of the Middle East? Of Africa?

There has long been a strong presumption shared by many analysts that official adherence to Communist doctrine exerts an important influence on Soviet foreign policy behavior. Moscow's constant reliance on revolutionary rhetoric has been thought to reflect the highly ideological content of Soviet political thought and the commitment of the Kremlin authorities to the revolutionary objectives of Marxism–Leninism. Ideology, it is argued, reinforces history. The world outlook of the Soviet leaders—who seem to share an abiding hostility toward the capitalist West, an abhorrence and suspicion of foreign values and influences, cultural self-conceit, tendencies toward messianic expansionism, and an acute sense of insecurity—reflects habits of mind characteristic of previous rulers of Russia. Resting on the foundations of historically rooted perceptions and beliefs, the doctrines of Marxism–Leninism are thought to be securely ensconced in the Soviet *Weltanschauung*.

Despite these views, there is considerable evidence that such ideological constructs as the international class struggle, proletarian internationalism, and their several derivatives are of little actual significance in the formulation (not to mention the day-to day conduct) of Soviet foreign policy. Soviet leaders speak in the language of Marxism–Leninism and make continual reference to revolutionary traditions. Their use of such rhetoric, however, is largely applicable to domestic rather than foreign policy considerations. (We shall return to this point in the next chapter.) The hard substance of Soviet policy, however, is largely unaffected by such doctrinal considerations. While Party Secretary Brezhnev, on his 1971 visit to France, showed his solidarity with the French proletariat by visiting the automobile workers at the Renault plant outside of Paris, and Prime Minister Kosygin talked with Canadian dockworkers during a trip to North America, the real purposes of these Soviet visits were the negotiations with French President Pompidou and Canadian Prime Minister Trudeau. Policy is based on interests, not sentiment. This is particularly true of the nonromantic, highly pragmatic regime currently occupying the Kremlin.

Soviet foreign policy has indeed been "secularized," and to a very considerable degree; to the extent that revolutionary doctrine was ever influential (and some would doubt that this was ever true),[49] it has become increasingly less so with the passage of time. The evidence of "secularization"—of policy based not on revolutionary doctrine but on the more traditional considerations of power and prestige—is substantial. Changes in Soviet attitudes toward diplomatic relations with the bourgeois nations of the world provide a striking example of this phenomenon.

For the early Bolsheviks, the existing state system into which the Soviet Republic was born was seen to be only temporary; it was shortly to be swept away by the world-wide revolutionary movement of which the October Revolution was the initial spark. In keeping with this expectation, Leon Trotsky, upon becoming the first Soviet Foreign Minister, made his famous comment: "I will issue a few revolutionary proclamations to the peoples of the world, and then shut up shop."[50] However, when Soviet Foreign Minister Andrei Gromyko can boast that the USSR "maintains and develops diplomatic relations with 103 states," and is "a member of all major international organizations" (which are said to number "about 400"),[51] it is obvious that the current Soviet leaders are concerned and involved with the existing international order to a degree the early Bolsheviks could hardly have dreamed.

Soviet foreign policy has undergone a progressive de-ideologization; the revolutionary goals have been largely replaced by such traditional norms of international behavior as security, economic well-being, national pride and prestige. Though their rhetoric remains heavily ideological, the Soviet leaders have long abandoned Lenin's dream that the international system could be overthrown by world-wide socialist revolution. The final victory of Communism in the whole world is only "very dimly seen," notes Raymond Garthoff—"not even seen, really, but assumed. How do the Communist leaders visualize the final push, the final fall of the powerful advanced countries? They do not. They believe in it, but they do not have a clear image of how or when the advanced countries would fall."[52]

The Kremlin's faith in the ultimate victory of Communism around the world was poignantly if not very concretely expressed by Khrushchev, when, in an aside from the prepared text of a 1962 speech, he declared:

> This victory will come. It will, it will. No prayers, alms or bribes will help the capitalists—and they do offer bribes. It is a question of time. We have patience. One must be patient and wait—and not only be patient and wait. Our work, the construction of communism, is like yeast used to raise leaven. . . . You and I, our Communist Party, the fraternal Communist parties, and our practical construction of communism are the yeast of the whole world for, so to speak, insuring the victory of communism.[53]

Thus, rather than "provoking" or "inciting" revolution, or pursuing "revolutionary war," the Soviet Union has become "patient"; it seeks to promote the victory of Communism by practical example.

To be fair, the Soviet leaders have always held that the world revolution is a drawn-out process, which would pass through many phases, during which periods of flood tide and ebb tide would alternate.

However, though they continue to assert that "the world capitalist system as a whole is ripe for social revolution,"[54] the policy implications derived from this traditional formulation are strikingly nonrevolutionary. Insofar as the final victory of Communism is foreseen, its achievement is best ensured by strengthening and developing the USSR, "the major edifice of the new world . . . the prototype of the new society of the future of all mankind."[55] (And, as discussed in Chapter Three, the current Soviet leadership is quite open in its commitment to defend the "state" and "national interests" of the USSR: to protect its frontiers, sovereignty, and "the dignity of the Soviet flag.") The requirements of socialist foreign policy are thus virtually indistinguishable from those of Soviet patriotism. Furthermore, the traditional Communist assumptions regarding an implacably hostile international environment has been revised. The notion of the USSR as a nation under siege which persisted throughout the Stalin period has been considerably modified. The principle of *kto-kogo*, which was so basic to the Leninist and Stalinist world view, has given way to the doctrine of "peaceful coexistence."

Peaceful coexistence

The new formula, set forth by Khrushchev in the mid-1950s, de-emphasized the international class struggle—the doctrine of mortal combat between the two main socio-political systems. The policy and expectation of unrestrained political hostility and tension were replaced by the need for greater tolerance and even some degree of cooperation. As Khrushchev declared at the 20th Congress of the CPSU in 1956, "The simultaneous existence of two opposed world economic systems, capitalist and socialist, developing according to different laws and in opposite directions, has become an irrefutable fact."[56] Obviously, the decline of capitalism is not considered imminent. "Soviet economists," writes one official, "have long cast aside former ideas of an automatic collapse or shrinkage of capitalism. On the contrary, they appreciate its ability to develop productive forces and control, to some extent, its cyclical movements. . . ."[57]

The basic thrust of the new doctrine can best be illustrated by quoting Soviet sources themselves. Though, at the 24th Communist Party Congress (1971), General Secretary Brezhnev condemned "American imperialism" for endeavoring "to play the role of a kind of protector of the international system of exploitation and oppression," he went on to stress that Soviet foreign policy is aimed "at the maintenance of normal and, where the situation permits, good relations with states belonging to another social system. As in the past," he declared, "we have consistently upheld the Leninist principle of the peaceful coexistence of states regardless of their social systems."[58]

Modification of traditional views regarding an implacably hostile international environment is the result of two important changes in Soviet thinking. The first relates to the Soviet self-image. The USSR's acquisition, in the early and mid-1950s, of powerful strategic weapons greatly enhanced Soviet self-confidence. This is true on two grounds. First of all, national security—as never before in Russian history—is protected. Moscow is no longer weak and defenseless in the face of a hostile world of powerful aggressive neighbors. The belief that, whatever its intentions, imperialism "can no longer destroy the socialist world by force of arms,"[59] has undoubtedly acted to reduce Soviet apprehensions about imperialism. Even though, according to Khrushchev, the bourgeoisie remained "blinded by hatred of our country . . . and for our communist ideas," and "wish to destroy us,"[60] they now clearly are less able to do so. Furthermore, Moscow's acquisition of intercontinental missiles gave the Kremlin's morale a particularly great boost. In the Soviet view, the acquisition of these new weapons created a completely new strategic situation in which the USSR *for the first time* had weapons capable of threatening the security of its major adversary, the United States. The startled and anxious American reaction to the launching of Sputnik in 1957 bore vivid testimony to the fact that Soviet possession of these new weapons had a "sobering" effect on thinking in Washington.

The leaders of American imperialism, or at least some of them (the "sober, realistic," and "responsible" ones), are now less belligerent, less aggressive, and interested in negotiations. Responding to this new "correlation of forces," they too have sought limited agreements to prevent nuclear war. It was now possible, as perhaps never before, to negotiate with the emissaries of capitalism. Thus, in referring to Khrushchev's dinner in New York in 1959, *Izvestia* editor (and Khrushchev's son-in-law) Alexei Adzhubei noted that while some of the 2,000 businessmen present "had cold looks in their eyes," and some "showed malice," the eyes of others revealed "good will—because there are people there, too, who appreciate that we are all living on the same planet. . . ." The Soviet Union must deal with these men, Adzhubei declared, because they "are the people who run the greatest capitalist state in the world; we must talk to them. . . ."[61]

Given this marked improvement in the Soviet power position and the simultaneously increased disposition of American leaders to treat the USSR with respect, the prospect of longer-term coexistence became a possibility. Moreover, there is a sense in which "peaceful coexistence" becomes a necessity. Earlier Soviet leaders viewed relations with the West as basically hostile; they saw war as a constant possibility. Furthermore, war was considered to be "the midwife of revolution." As the Soviet Ambassador to France declared in 1935, "Why should war frighten us? Soviet Russia emerged from the last war. Soviet Europe will emerge from the next."[62] The extension of Communist rule to virtually all of Eastern Europe after World War II seemed to have confirmed this prediction. The development of nuclear weaponry, however, forced Moscow to alter its thinking. Realizing that major nuclear war could very well endanger the survival of the USSR, the Soviet leaders now admit the necessity of avoiding war completely. The notion of war as a "midwife" of revolution is rejected. Declaring now that "Marxist–Leninist theory has never held that war constitutes a source or prerequisite, necessary for the emergence of revolutions," the authoritative Party journal *Kommunist* asserted that "the question of the relation of war and revolution has assumed a different character in our times." Given the enormous power of weapons of mass destructions, a world war

> ... would cause the complete destruction of the main centers of civilization and the annihilation of whole peoples. It would bring untold suffering to all mankind. Only madmen would want such a catastrophe to happen. ... The working-class does not think of creating a Communist civilization on the ruins of the centers of world cultures, on desolated territories contaminated by thermonuclear fallout, which would be the inevitable consequences of such a war. ... It is, therefore, obvious that a contemporary nuclear war, however one looks at it, can in no way be a factor that would accelerate the revolution and bring nearer the victory of socialism. Quite the contrary, such a war would throw mankind, the revolutionary workers' movement through-out the world, and the construction of socialism and Communism back for many decades.[63]

War is now feared as too dangerous; the belief that revolution and war are often interconnected, a derivative of the Leninist theory of revolution, is now abandoned.[64]

Moscow's realization that the USSR might well not survive a nuclear war and, as Khrushchev declared in 1963, that "no one knows in what plight the survivors [of a world thermonuclear war] would find themselves—even whether they would not envy the dead,"[65] led to the abandonment of yet another tenet of classical Bolshevik theory. In his thesis on *Imperialism*, Lenin had argued that war was an inevitable product of the internal rivalries and tensions of the capitalist system. At the 20th Party Congress in 1956, Khrushchev modified this classical Leninist principle. Admitting that the forces making for war still persist and that "as long as capitalism survives in the world, the reactionary forces representing the interest of the capitalist monopolies will continue their drive toward military gambles and aggression," Khrushchev now stressed that the "peace forces" led by the "world of socialism" possessed "formidable means to prevent the imperialists from unleashing war. . . . " War, therefore, "is not fatalistically inevitable."[66]

Reacting to the exigencies of the new weapons environment, the Soviet leadership under Khrushchev abandoned classical Bolshevik notions which linked war with both capitalism and revolution. These doctrines, whose implications were now considered too dangerous, were relegated to the pre-atomic era. The concept of peaceful coexistence was also redefined. To the extent that Lenin referred to coexistence, it was always in the context of a temporary interlude between the outbreaks of war, a sort of breathing space during which the Soviet Union should seek to strengthen itself for the inevitable conflicts with hostile capitalist powers. Under Stalin, this same view prevailed. After Stalin died, the approach was basically revised. Coexistence under Khrushchev, notes Herbert Dinerstein, was no longer merely an interlude of relaxation of conflict . . . now the greatest socialist power and the greatest capitalist power had a common interest that stretched into the indefinite future. It meant that the struggle between the capitalist and the communist world was limited by a common desire to survive.[67]

Thus, coexistence is no longer merely a temporary strategy based on expediency; it now becomes, in Brezhnev's words, "a Leninist principle" of Soviet foreign policy. What makes this doctrinal shift possible is the specter of nuclear devastation. The underlying assumption of the earlier concept of peaceful coexistence was that relations between socialism and capitalism were basically a "zero-sum" game in which the gains of one side were always at the expense of the other. The adversaries, it was assumed, had no basic interests in common. Now, however, both sides share at least one objective—survival. As an authoritative Soviet writer has observed: "There is no rational option open to mankind; the alternative [to peaceful coexistence] is recurring and possibly catastrophic deteriorations of world relations."[68] Thus, while relations between the two systems are still considered basically antagonistic, their conflicts are now "kept within certain bounds and stabilized short of war by deliberate cooperative efforts on the part of the competitors themselves."[69] The international civil war—signifying a world of unrestrained hostility, rising tension and drift toward war—has thus been replaced by the nonviolent competition and limited cooperation of peaceful coexistence.

Moscow's willingness to adopt a peaceful coexistence strategy is the product, paradoxically, of both an increased sense of security and a heightened sense of insecurity. The Soviet leaders during the inter-war period, feared annihilation. Given their relative power weakness and assumptions regarding the basic anti-Soviet purposes of imperialism, they saw world politics as mortal combat—*kto-kogo*. With the growth of Soviet military power the threat of external danger became less compelling. Soviet security and its ability to "deal with" the West grew accordingly. At the same time, the external environment was growing more dangerous. Developments in weapons technology threatened to get out of hand. Some sort of limited relations with the other nuclear powers was required; Moscow's internal sense of confidence now made it possible to contemplate such undertakings.

Recent Soviet leaders thus have a more temperate view of the international environment than did their predecessors. Their commitment to the doctrines of international class struggle has clearly been modified to favor a less belligerent posture. With the development of massive thermonuclear weapons stockpiles, the Soviet stake in the survival of the existing international order clearly has grown. This is particularly evident in light of the USSR's own considerable economic achievements. "Gone are the days," notes a source close to Moscow, "when the working men . . . had . . . nothing to lose but their chains."[70] Awareness of the jeopardy in which their own accomplishments would be put by such an eventuality, the Soviet leaders have assiduously sought to avoid nuclear war.

Foreign policy doctrine, then, has been influenced by changes in the world environment. Experience or, as a Soviet analyst might put it, "life itself" has compelled the Kremlin to modify traditional Party teachings regarding relations with the outside world. The role of doctrine in any situation, it should also be noted, is shaped by the fact that the "scientific principles" of Marxism–Leninism are subject to interpretations. For example, while some in the leadership (especially among the military and the police) stress the vigilance aspect of the peaceful coexistence policy, others have been more concerned with the urgency of expanding Soviet foreign economic ties. Thus, the particular doctrinal interpretation that wins leadership endorsement at any given time strongly affects policymaking.

Given the changeability of doctrine and its openness to multiple interpretations, what is one to make of the persistence of hostile commentary regarding the capitalist states? Though the need for some degree of cooperation is admitted, the Kremlin still exudes bellicosity and invective when referring to capitalism. The basic legitimacy of non-Communist regimes is still not accepted. In the Soviet view, no "capitalist government" has a moral right to exist. Ultimately, they will all be replaced by regimes truly representing the "working people."

It is in this context that Khrushchev made his famous remark, "We will bury you." In a later statement, Khrushchev explained that he did not mean that the Soviet Union would physically bury the U.S. "When we say that communism will bury capitalism, this does not mean, of course, that the Soviet people, the Communists of the Soviet Union, will inter capitalists of this or that country." What is meant is that Communism will win everywhere in the world. "Such is the teaching of life, of history; a more progressive social system inevitably comes to replace a system which is outliving itself, a progressive system buries a moribund one."[71] For Khrushchev, "we will bury you," meant "we will outlive you and dance at your funeral."

It was Khrushchev's view that even the mainstay of captalism, the United States, was slowly dying.

> We believe that in America, too, mighty forces will grow. . . . These progressive forces which are growing within the American people itself will ultimately win. In place of capitalism, which reigns in America today, the American people will themselves establish a new social system, and this system will be communism.[72]

A similar view was expressed by Brezhnev in 1968 when he declared that the United States was a land of "violence . . . terror" and "political gangsterism." It is a "rotten, degrading, decaying society. . . . Yes," he boasted, "it is true. Monopolist America is decaying. But inevitably it will be replaced by another America, an America of the working people."[73] Recent Soviet leaders have not substantially changed their basic view of the United States and of the capitalist world in general. Early Bolshevism's convictions regarding the basic corruption of its capitalist adversaries seem to persist down to the present.

The impact of such attitudes on policy is difficult to judge. As we shall see in the next chapter, this "negative image of America" performs an important domestic political function; therefore, it may be disseminated essentially for internal political consumption. Nevertheless, historical evidence indicates that such views have had considerable influence, especially on Soviet relations with the West. As Barrington Moore has written:

> The Marxist–Leninist tradition has made it very difficult to reach a *modus vivendi* with the Soviets. . . . A belief in the inherently aggressive tendencies of modern capitalism obviously excludes any agreement except an armed truce of undetermined duration. Likewise, the acceptance of Leninist theory makes it almost impossible to believe in the friendly intentions of American leaders. . . .[74]

Moore's judgments of twenty years ago still appear valid today. Even with the shared need for cooperation to ensure survival in a nuclear environment, the basic capitalist–socialist struggle is still considered "the main contradiction of our time." In the words of the architect of "peaceful coexistence," Nikita Khrushchev, "No treaties or agreements between states can overcome the radical confrontation between the two social systems."[75]

Peaceful coexistence, then, does not imply a reconciliation between two irreconcilable social systems. Though the Soviet leaders have accepted the necessity of prolonged coexistence with capitalism, they still regard conflict between the two systems, even in carefully limited forms, as enduring and inevitable. "In that sense," writes Richard Lowenthal,

> while their approval of "peaceful coexistence" is intended to exclude nuclear war, their rejection of "ideological coexistence" is meant to exclude a true reconciliation just as decisively. Neither Armageddon nor a reconciliation between the opposing systems, but indefinite conflict in limited and controlled forms remain their vision of the future.[76]

Thus, although war between "capitalism" and "socialism" may no longer be thought of as inevitable, political conflict and rivalry clearly still is.

Though Soviet hostility toward the Western capitalist world is by now a well-established tradition, there are indications that even such firmly implanted attitudes may be changing. In this regard, the Soviet –American agreement on "The Basic Principles of Mutual Relations" signed in Moscow in May, 1972, is especially revealing. According to the terms agreed to by President Nixon and Party Secretary Brezhnev, both sides promise to "avoid military confrontations," to "exercise restraint in their mutual relations," to "negotiate and settle differences by peaceful means . . . to limit armaments," and, generally, to increase international cooperation and help promote world peace. The Kremlin leaders also accepted the principle that "differences in ideology and in the social systems of the United States and the Soviet Union are not obstacles to the development of normal relations. . . ."[77] Moscow's endorsement of these "Basic Principles" may be symptomatic of important shifts in the Soviet outlook toward the West. It suggests that though an adversary relationship between the two superpowers still exists, that relationship is to be conducted by written mutual agreement according to moderate rules designed to keep disagreements within narrow bounds well short of open conflict.

Such commitments, to be sure, are only formal promises which can easily be broken; moreover, they fall far short of providing an overall solution to the basic ideological conflict between the two countries. Nevertheless, the Soviet and American governments have codified the rules of the game of peaceful coexistence. In so doing, they seem to have agreed that, despite their rivalries, they share a common interest in stabilizing and improving their relations.

The *modus vivendi* with the USSR which, as Moore noted, has proven so elusive, may now be evolving if not actually at hand. Traditional expectations of mortal combat between socialism and capitalism have given way to far more benign prospects. As Brezhnev declared in a speech made during his visit to West Germany in 1973, "our course is not toward isolating our country from the outside world. On the contrary, we proceed from the assumption that it will develop under conditions of growing cooperation with the outside world, and not only with socialist countries at that, but in considerable measure with the states of the opposite social system as well."[78] The anti-capitalist, anti-Western bias of Communist doctrine and Russian history seems to be waning. The Commander-in Chief of the capitalist world's greatest power has twice been received by the Joint Chiefs of Staff of the world revolutionary movement in their headquarters, agreements have been signed, champagne toasts have been exchanged, and according to an official Soviet spokesman, "all sides are winners."[79] The Kremlin leaders, it is true, still employ the rhetoric of the international class struggle. In so doing, however, they seem to be chanting an old revolutionary melody which may remind them of the struggles and sacrifices of their youth but reveals little about their current purposes. (It was very much this spirit that moved a Kremlin leader to tell the American Ambassador in Moscow that the Cuban revolution made the Soviets feel young again.[80])

Nevertheless, a healthy degree of skepticism regarding Soviet attitudes remains appropriate. Even though the changed international strategic environment has evoked some measure of cooperation between the superpowers, Soviet behavior during the October, 1973, Yom Kippur war gives clear ground for continued wariness. Despite the fact that the USSR had signed (during the 1973 summit meetings in Washington) an "Agreement on the Prevention of Nuclear War" with the United States in which both sides promised "to act in such a manner as to prevent the development of situations capable of causing a dangerous exacerbation of their relations,"[81] the Kremlin did nothing to alert the United States regarding the imminence of war in late September and early October when its Arab partners were preparing their attack. Initially, when the Egyptian forces were doing well, it refused to cooperate in arranging a cease-fire; and it encouraged other Arab states to join the struggle against Israel. In addition, vast arms shipments were sent to the Arabs, thereby complicating the termination of hostilities. Finally, the Soviets threatened direct intervention—to which the U.S. responded with a world-wide military alert. While Moscow backed away from unilateral intervention and thereby avoided a direct collision with the United States, "it was an adversary response that kept the peace that day—U.S. response to the threat of Soviet intervention and Soviet fear of military confrontation."[82]

Soviet behavior, however, was not totally negative. The Kremlin's restraint at the key point in the crisis—when the U.S. armed forces were alerted—can be seen as an effort to contain the confrontation with the United States. Furthermore, Moscow played a positive role in arranging cease-fire agreements which brought the conflict to an end and in helping set the stage for Egyptian–Israeli political negotiations that began in Geneva in early 1974. (These were the first such talks between the two major Middle Eastern adversaries.) Though détente has survived this brief but sharp clash, Soviet behavior during the Yom Kippur war is not reassuring. Despite regular summit conferences and numerous agreements and contacts, we do not seem to have progressed very far from the communication techniques of the Cold War—threats, troop movements, and alerts.[83] While a *modus vivendi* with the USSR may be evolving, clear evidence is still hard to come by. Détente, thus far at least, does not seem to have significantly modified the sometimes harsh methods by which the political competition between the two superpowers has long been waged.

Soviet internationalism

Soviet teachings regarding "proletarian internationalism" have, similarly, been forced to adapt to unexpected historical developments. Relations among "proletarian states" have not taken the course predicted by Bukharin; the essentially supportive and cooperative ties which were assumed to distinguish relations among the socialist states have not developed at all well. In fact, Moscow's experience with its ideological partners has been such that it may be seriously questioned whether the Kremlin still regards as desirable its long-held objective, "the complete triumph of socialism around the world."

It was generally assumed during the inter-war years that the spread of Communism automatically benefitted the interests of the USSR. Recent experience has jarred this assumption. Since 1945, one Communist country for a time became a military ally of the West (Yugoslavia, through her membership in the Balkan Pact), another (Rumania) undertook extensive diplomatic and economic ties with the West, a third (Albania) compelled the USSR to vacate a naval base and severed diplomatic relations, while a fourth (China) has on several occasions shed Soviet blood in major border incidents. Recounting these developments, Adam Ulam comments:

> ... few of the non-Communist neighbors of the Soviet Union would, or could have dared to, display the kind of defiance she has encountered, at times, at the hands of fellow Communists. This must have led to a considerable reassessment of the earlier assumption that the spread of Communism represents, so to speak, so much more money in the bank for the USSR.[84]

These developments must have also led to a reevaluation of the notion that relations among socialist states are of a "new, heretofore unknown type." The spectacle of open conflict between armies of two countries both fighting under the red flag (as on the Sino-Soviet border in 1969) must call into serious question the doctrine that nations sharing common ideologies and economic and political systems should have similar —or, at the least, friendly—foreign policies.

Moscow's frustrations at the hands of its Communist partners has been matched by the failure of another potential revolutionary ally, "the national liberation movement." The so-called progressive or leftist forces in the less developed countries of Asia and Africa were seen as sympathetic to the USSR on two counts: first, they were considered to be important allies in Moscow's global struggle against Western imperialism. The new states' struggles for independence, noted Soviet officials, "shake the big imperialist powers' domination." Second, it was hoped that some of the newly independent states would establish Soviet-oriented Communist or pro-Communist regimes.

Much to the Kremlin's disappointment—and to the surprise of many frightened souls in the West—"the national liberation movement" did not live up to expectations. While many were outspokenly independent and highly critical of their former colonial masters, the leaders of the new states of the Third World were slow to join forces with the USSR. Having just achieved independence, the new nationalist regimes preferred to avoid any political entanglements which might jeopardize their newly won freedom. "Socialism" did not take root in the less developed countries, at least not Moscow's version of "scientific socialism." The often radical, anti-imperialist leaders who assumed power in these areas proved largely unimpressed with Marxism–Leninism. (Of the ninety-odd nations of the Third World, just four—China, North Korea, North Vietnam and Cuba—have established Communist governments.) Many, especially in the Middle East, actively persecuted the local Communist organizations in their countries.

Thus, to Moscow's great dismay, a close relationship between the USSR and "the national liberation movement" never developed. Even where prospects seemed especially favorable and a large amount of economic and military assistance was transferred to assist potential supporters, radical leftist regimes in Egypt, Indonesia, Ghana, and elsewhere in the underdeveloped countries have proved both inadequate as socialists and undependable as allies. In light of their unhappy experience, Soviet interest in the "revolutionary forces" of the Third World has sharply diminished. In fact, to the degree that the USSR is concerned about the less developed areas of the world—which is a debatable proposition—the political coloration of a particular regime is generally of little matter. Moscow's long-standing interest in India, the single largest recipient of Soviet economic aid outside the Communist world, has little to do with the "progressiveness" of the government in New Delhi. The inherent importance of India to future developments in South Asia and, especially, to relations with China has been sufficient to stimulate and sustain Soviet interest.[85]

Given Moscow's disenchantment with the fruits of "socialist internationalism" and its loss of faith in the potential benefits of "world revolution," the USSR today is very cautious in its relations with the "international revolutionary movement." As discussed earlier, Bolshevism's original commitment to support revolutionary activities abroad was not especially profound. The refusal of history to conform to his predictions persuaded Lenin that his first revolutionary obligation lay in protecting Soviet power, not in chasing the phantom of world revolution. For Lenin, as later for Stalin, the operative slogan became: "What is good for the Soviet Union is good for the World Revolution." Lenin's reluctance to resort to "revolutionary war" has given way to even greater circumspection in the nuclear era. Continuing to affirm Moscow's "genuine internationalism," Soviet spokesmen often boast of the USSR's "moral, political and economic support, and, if necessary, support in the form of arms as well."[86] However, as the Soviet leadership has warned, the promise of arms

... does not mean the principle of military support should be irrationally made absolute. *In the age of atomic weapons, calls to settle scores with imperialism by the military might of the Socialist countries are extremely reckless.*[87] (Italics added.)

Assistance in support of revolutionary forces outside the USSR which might result in military clashes with the West are to be shunned.

Recent history offers many examples of the Kremlin's refusal to act "recklessly." Fearful that "adventurist" policies might provoke escalating military conflicts, especially in areas where the United States has commitments and interests, the Soviet leaders have sought to avoid violent confrontations. Therefore, Moscow has downgraded the importance of guerrilla activity in both the Middle East and Latin America. Violence-prone groups, such as the Palestinian Popular Front led by George Habbash, have been sharply condemned, as has the strategy of subversion and violence endorsed by Fidel Castro at the Tri-Continental Congress in Havana in 1966. Furthermore, during the Jordanian civil war (September, 1970), the Soviet Ambassador in Damascus advised the Syrian government to withdraw its troops from Jordan (where they had intervened in support of the Palestinian insurgents) lest they precipitate an American military intervention.

Soviet caution has not been without its costs. It was Moscow's refusal to make new, sophisticated weapons available to Egypt which prompted the expulsion, in July, 1972, of fifteen to twenty thousand Soviet military advisors from the UAR. The Soviet leaders apparently believed that the delivery of such weaponry would have increased the likelihood of armed conflict again breaking out in the Middle East. To avoid a renewal of the Arab–Israeli war and the danger of a Soviet –American confrontation—that the former entailed risk of the latter was borne out in 1973—the Kremlin ignored Cairo's requests for new equipment. According to Egyptian President Anwar el-Sadat, Moscow's refusal only revealed its "excessive and exaggerated caution."[88]

The most striking illustration of Moscow's revolutionary restraint came in connection with the Vietnam War. Just five weeks before his scheduled visit to the USSR (which began on May 22, 1972), President Nixon ordered the bombing of the North Vietnamese capital of Hanoi and the major port of Haiphong. The American initiative, taken in response to a North Vietnamese "massive invasion" of South Vietnam, must have come as a great shock to the Kremlin. Four Soviet ships were said to have been hit during the raid on Haiphong and on May 9, less than two weeks before the Moscow summit was to begin, the United States began mining North Vietnamese harbors (for the first time in the war). To the surprise of many, the Soviet reaction was quite mild. Though official sources "wrathfully condemned . . . these provocative actions" and warned that this "new escalation" aggravated "the international situation," Moscow did nothing in public which might have interfered with the summit conference which went ahead as planned.

Clearly, the Kremlin's first priority was the ongoing Soviet–American rapprochement; the requirements of Soviet foreign policy were seen as more compelling than those of proletarian internationalism. Much was at stake. The Nixon visit involved important prestige factors. It also provided an opportunity to conclude negotiations on a host of important issues, including strategic arms, Soviet–American trade, space cooperation and scientific exchanges. It was also bound up with other elements of the Kremlin policy, especially Soviet relations with West Germany. Given the great importance of the Moscow summit to the general Soviet policy of improving relations with the West, the Soviet authorities did nothing more than protest the American "barbaric bombings."[89]

Hanoi, needless to say, was particularly upset by Soviet policy. On May 21, the day before President Nixon was scheduled to arrive in Moscow, the North Vietnamese Army newspaper accused the Kremlin of showing weakness and of having put its own "national interests against the interests of the world revolution."[90] Obviously stung by such charges, the Kremlin responded sharply. "At times it is said," wrote a ranking Party official, "that in reply to one or another 'tough action' by imperialism the socialist countries and primarily the Soviet Union, should likewise harden their position." The argument urging a "tough" response to the American military initiative, made presumably by Hanoi and possibly by ranking

Soviet leaders, was explicitly rejected. "Socialist policy never derived its strength from primitive, stereotyped patterns, and least of all from imitation of devices and methods employed by the class enemy. . . ." Furthermore, Moscow warned that

> . . . any tendency to be guided by considerations of the moment (for emotional or other reasons), to confine oneself to the interests of the present day while ignoring long-term perspective, has never led to anything good. On the contrary, *such an approach . . . is fraught with danger to the basic interests of all the peoples of the world* which no revolutionary must ever lose sight of; *it is fraught with danger to the building of the new society, the future of the liberation struggle.*[91] (Italics added.)

What the Kremlin authorities were saying was that, however understandable such a response might be, "tough actions" which might endanger the summit meeting must be avoided. This did not imply that the USSR was shirking its international duty. Not at all. It is assumed, after all, that "the building of the new society" in the USSR corresponds to the fundamental interests of the peoples of the world. Given that an improvement in political relations and expansion of trade with the United States is expected to make a significant contribution to the Soviet economy, there could be no question that going ahead with the scheduled conference was consistent with Moscow's socialist obligations.

Thus, though official Soviet spokesmen persistently swear devotion to the principles of "socialist internationalism," they obviously view such commitments through the prism of Soviet national interests. As Kremlin authorities declared in 1965, "the best way to fulfill our internationalist duty to the working people of the entire world is the successful construction of socialism and communism" in the USSR; according to the official Communist Party newspaper, this is the Kremlin's "chief contribution to the development of the world revolutionary movement."[92] Insofar as the Nixon visit was seen as contributing to the internal progress of the Soviet Union, ensuring its success becomes a truly revolutionary policy.

Such cynical manipulation of doctrine leads inevitably to the conclusion that Marxism–Leninism does not determine Soviet policies but functions merely to rationalize decisions made by the Soviet government on other grounds. It is the view of the Kremlin that all Soviet policies are by definition "Marxist" irrespective of their content. Therefore, ideology is less a fountainhead of policy than a system of propaganda. If this be true, is it not fair to conclude that, whatever their ideological pretensions, the Soviet leaders are basically power politicians seeking to further the interests of their country? That they are, in short, more in the tradition of Peter the Great than of Karl Marx?

The weight of evidence seems conclusive. Although still wedded to a revolutionary doctrine, the Soviet authorities see their international responsibilities in largely traditional terms. As long-standing Marxists, they still believe in the ultimate transformation of the world along socialist lines; however, the emphasis is on the word ultimate, for the

Kremlin leaders no longer (if, indeed, they ever really did) view the successful accomplishment of this transformation as a major policy objective. In the words of Vernon V. Aspaturian, Soviet ideology "has been transformed from a vehicle legitimizing world revolution into one legitimizing Communist rule in Russia; instead of raising the standard of revolution abroad, Moscow emphasizes raising the standard of living at home in the name of ideology."[93]

The foreign policy of the USSR, then, is not the policy of revolutionary power, but it is the foreign policy of a Great Power, one deeply involved in a world-wide rivalry with the United States. "Power and influence rather than ideology" characterize American and Soviet policy toward the poor nations. ". . . In the collection of motives which seem to be at work, the sense of contest is uppermost. . . ."[94] The same can be said of Soviet foreign policy generally. The focus today is on national interest, traditionally conceived; on power, security, and prestige, especially in relation to its Great Power rivalry with the United States.

Ideological residues

What then, if anything, is left for ideology to explain? Can we conclude, official Soviet assertions to the contrary notwithstanding, that Marxism–Leninism plays no part in shaping Soviet behavior? Not quite. Communist political ideology is crucially important in maintaining Soviet internal cohesion, a fact that, as we shall see in the next chapter, has especially important implications for relations among Communist states. More generally, Party doctrine continues to affect both the style of Soviet diplomacy and the intellectual framework through which Soviet leaders perceive the outside world.

The influence of doctrine on Soviet diplomatic style is easily seen. All students of the USSR are initially struck (and sometimes captivated by) the distinctively military character of Soviet public affairs. Almost every metaphor in Communist political thought comes from military life. The terms strategy and tactics, vanguard, cadres, reserves, advances, retreats, assaults, and maneuvers are all common to Soviet public discourse. The Communist Party, notes Francis Randall, "fights on various 'fronts'—industrial, agricultural, educational—as well as military. Its history is a succession of 'victories' and 'defeats'—mostly the former. It proceeds according to an overall 'strategy' drawn up by the leadership, but each overall strategic plan allows for different 'tactics' in different 'sectors.' . . ."[95]

This distinctive rhetorical style reflects the extraordinary combativeness of Soviet political ideology. The whole structure of Marxism–Leninism, its *kto-kogo* ("who [will destroy] whom") character, imparts a militancy and suspiciousness to Soviet diplomatic rhetoric. Though the USSR today seems more committed than ever before to the survival of the international political system, traces of its traditional contempt for capitalism and for capitalism's purposes and institutions continue to color

Soviet public attitudes and pronouncements. Khrushchev's famous "We will bury you" remark is a case in point.

The persistence of combative Bolshevik rhetoric has had serious political consequences in the past. It has been observed, for example, that "the stated policy of supporting revolutionary movements, although not vigorously pursued for long periods, has served to increase the insecurity of other nations and in turn to make them more antagonistic to the Soviet Union."[96] Fear of the "red menace" of Bolshevism in the late 1930s tended to blind many in the West (especially in Britain) to the dangers which Hitler posed for Europe. Anguish regarding Moscow's revolutionary purposes was so intense that Hitler's loudly proclaimed anti-Bolshevik stance helped convince some Western leaders that it was possible—even necessary!—to work out a political arrangement with Nazi Germany.[97] Such reasoning led directly to the Munich agreement with Hitler and, shortly afterward, to World War II.

In the more recent period, a case can be made that the hardening in Soviet–American relations which took place after World War II was largely a product of Soviet bellicosity. "Responding to the rhetoric of Soviet ideologues, perceiving Soviet [postwar] expansion as revolutionary and unlimited in intent, . . . the United States," notes Marshall Shulman, "blurred the issue between the actions of the Soviet state and the 'threat of international communism.' " Overreacting to the aggressive and belligerent style of postwar Soviet diplomacy, Washington became obsessed with the Communist menace and "anticommunism became a central dogma of American purpose abroad."[98] The American reaction—the creation of a powerful politico-military coalition (NATO)—to what it saw as a direct challenge to its security can perhaps best be understood in terms of what Charles Yost has called "the law of disproportionate response to miscalculated challenges." However, such miscalculation as may have occurred and the disproportion of the American response was in no small measure a result of Soviet diplomatic belligerence.

The rhetorical aggressiveness of the Kremlin has reflected Soviet insecurity in the face of assumed Western superiority and animosity. The strategy of verbal bluster was designed to mask the regime's fears; it was also geared to deter the stronger Western nations, especially the United States, from launching an attack. Similar uncertainty about their security has made the Soviet leaders, from the very outset, inordinately sensitive about appearing weak before others.

During the early 1920s, for example, Foreign Minister Chicherin suggested that Soviet leaders with important government posts (primarily Lenin and Trotsky) should resign from their positions on the Executive Committee of the Communist International (Comintern). This step, he suggested, would remove any direct connection between the diplomatic activities of the Soviet state and the revolutionary activities of the Comintern. Therefore, the work of the Soviet Foreign Office in conducting diplomatic relations with the capitalist world would be less difficult. Lenin refused. Should they resign, he wrote Chicherin, this would only create an impression of Soviet weakness, of knuckling under to Western pressure. In these circumstances, it was impossible to agree to this request. Thus, for Lenin, "excessive timidity or apologetic airs about the connections of world Communism with Russia would have been an acknowledgment of [the country's actual] weakness and an invitation to further demands and even armed aggression."[99]

Given the Soviet regime's industrial and military weakness in the 1920s, Lenin's apprehensions regarding the appearance of weakness, while perhaps excessive, may not have been completely unreasonable. Such apprehensions, however, continue to this very day. This has been most striking in the Soviet approach to disarmament negotiations. "It has often been the case," observes Marshall Shulman, "that the Soviet Union will take elaborate pains to conceal its anxieties [on matters of disarmament] for fear that it may confer a bargaining advantage upon its adversary." When, after a long delay, the Kremlin agreed to enter talks on strategic arms limitations (SALT), Soviet representatives pressed Washington for an immediate response. This created an impression that the USSR badly wanted talks, even more than the U.S. Soviet representatives then reversed course and became so casual about the SALT talks that many concluded that they had lost all interest in the negotiations. Thus, much as Stalin reacted with indifference upon hearing about the successful atomic explosion at Alamogordo in July, 1945, so the current Soviet leaders, suggests Shulman, have been especially anxious "not to give an impression of Soviet concern lest the United States be encouraged to take diplomatic advantage" of an overly interested USSR.[100]

Such concerns about appearing "weak" or "overly anxious" reflect more than just a healthy suspicion of ambitious adversaries. They seem to indicate Moscow's continued dread of a hostile external universe. (This can also be seen in the Kremlin's passion for secrecy as expressed in its adamant refusal to accept on-site inspection to monitor a ban on underground nuclear testing. Such arrangements, it is argued, would be simply a cover for espionage activities against the USSR.) The classical Soviet apprehension of the outside world—deeply imbedded in Russian history and reinforced by Communist ideology—lives on.

Another feature of Soviet diplomatic style—one quite different from the acute insecurity which has so long bedeviled Russia's leaders—is its universalistic pretensions. According to official Party sources, the rulers of the Kremlin speak for all of mankind. In the words of a recent Soviet handbook on diplomacy, "The goals of the foreign policy of the Soviet Union express the vital interests not only of the peoples of the socialist countries but of all peoples on earth."[101] Underlying this view is the Kremlin's assumption that the Russian Revolution of 1917 opened a new chapter in human history and that, as the lineal descendents of the original Bolsheviks, the Soviet leaders today are the bearers of a new civilization. "Does not the record of the fifty years of development of the Soviet state," asks a recent Soviet writer, "prove that . . . the Soviet people by their labor, great victories and enormous sacrifices have blazed the trail to a new life for all the people of the world?"[102] Having inaugurated the march to a new and glorious future, the Soviet Communist Party, in the words of an earlier writer, Andrei Platonov, "is humanity's honor guard."[103]

Such beliefs are seriously held and, on past occasions, they have led to policy blunders. Assuming that the working people of the world saw Soviet Russia as their protector, Lenin decided in 1920 to send the Red Army across Russia's western border to try to create a Soviet Poland. But the Polish people regarded the Soviet troops as alien Russian invaders, not as "brother liberators," and defeated them at the gates of Warsaw. Soviet calculations at the outset of the Russo–Finnish War (1939–1940) were based on similar fantasies. The *TASS* (Soviet press agency) correspondent in Helsinki in November, 1939, reported the Finnish workers on the verge of revolution, Finnish soldiers deserting in large numbers, and massive popular resentment against the Finnish government. While such reports apparently were read in Finland with considerable amusement, it is highly likely that the content of Soviet diplomatic dispatches were quite similar. "The result was," notes one author, "that the Soviet leaders apparently were led to believe that the Finnish 'masses' were ready to receive the Red Army with flowers and banners."[104] Needless to say, they did not.

This was not merely a matter of faulty reporting. The Soviets simply assumed that the workers in other countries were pro-Soviet. Not only the Communist Party rank-and file but also the Soviet leaders apparently were shocked to discover that the Finns were united in their determination to resist. The impact of this discrepancy between expectation and reality can be seen in the statement made at the time by the Secretary of the Executive Committee of the Communist International. "The war with Finland," he noted,

> is the expression of the failure of twenty-five years of effort on the part of the Communist Parties, of the Communist International. . . . For a long time we have worked to make fighting against the Soviet Union, the first socialist country, impossible. Until now we believed that people would refuse to fight us.
> But it is not so. In Finland even women have taken part in the battle. . . .[105]

Despite the experience of history and the slowness of the people of the world to rush to the Soviet banner, such universalist pretensions continue to find expression in Moscow. The Soviet leaders have always asserted that the people (or, at least, the working people) would always support the USSR—even against their own countries.[106] They have continued to imply what a British Communist once baldly stated: "the Soviet Union is not a foreign power for the workers and the common people."[107]

What sense can be made of such claims? Moscow's attempt to wrap itself in the mantle of virtue is obviously, at least in part, a political ploy. If the USSR can successfully claim to speak for the people of the world and can identify "bourgeois governments" as defenders of narrow, selfish class interests, the USSR becomes morally superior and, therefore, deserving of support. The claim to universally valid policies and objectives, then, is a stratagem to win the political allegiance of "the people" of the world and of the enlightened progressive governments in the newly emergent countries. Thus, despite serious disenchantment with such elements, Moscow continues to insist that the interests of the revolutionary nationalist regimes in the Third World and those of the Soviet Union are one and the same. Repetition of this theme is obviously put forth in the effort to persuade radical leaders in the less-developed countries of the wisdom of maintaining close relations with the USSR, their disinterested and ever-faithful protector.*

This ploy can also be used to neutralize criticism of the USSR. If the principle can be established that the interests of the USSR and those of "the people" are identical, and that Soviet policy is peace-loving, any claim against the Soviet government and its policies or any thwarting of its will is by definition anti-popular—reactionary—and a threat to the peace. This view was well expressed by a French Communist Party official who noted that "all liberation movements, all battles for social liberation, national independence and peace" receive the all-out support of the Soviet Union. "This is precisely the reason why anti-Sovietism, whatever its form and whatever its origins, is a crime and against the interests of the working class and the peoples."[109] Or, as a Soviet author wrote, "to resort to anti-Soviet slogans . . . is to expose oneself in public as an enemy of peace, democracy, and social progress."[110] Any questioning of Soviet policy is tantamount to giving aid to the class enemy.

It would be a mistake, however, to view such claims as merely part of a scheme designed to gain political advantage. Though they may well serve partisan ends, these beliefs reflect genuine convictions. This argument seems especially convincing when one recalls that such attitudes are not new in Russian history. The rulers of Old Muscovy also had proclaimed themselves as the center of a new and better civilization. Thus the smugness and self-righteousness still found in Soviet diplomacy, much like their combativeness and obsessive suspiciousness, represents the legacy of the past—historical and ideological—from which the current generation of Soviet leaders are not yet free.

Though foreign policy seems to have been modified under the pressure of changing international conditions, with many major doctrinal principles abandoned, the style and mental attitudes which underlie the new policies still often take older forms. This may well be a case of cultural lag. Traditional Russian and Soviet habits of mind and expression

---

*This maneuver was well understood by Marx. As he wrote in *The German Ideology*, "each new class which puts itself in the place of the one ruling before it, is compelled, simply in order to achieve its aims, to represent its interests as the common interest of all members of society, *i.e.*, employing an ideal formula, to give its ideas the form of universality and to represent them as the only rational and universally valid ones."[108]

seem to change more slowly than does actual policy. ("Culture," Alfred Meyer has astutely suggested, "is that which lags."[111]) However, more than "mere" cultural lag is involved. The Kremlin leaders are indeed sincere when they proclaim that only a socialist regime can represent the real interests of the people, that (as the official press constantly reiterates) Soviet foreign policy is guided by principles "conforming to the basic interests of the overwhelming majority of mankind." It is, to be sure, unlikely that Soviet policymakers assume any longer that foreign labor movements are loyal to the USSR; they are now too well-informed about the outside world to believe in such fantasies. Nevertheless, the Kremlin rulers remain convinced of the moral superiority of socialism and, especially, of Soviet policies over those of modern capitalism. Indeed, as we shall see, they must. The Soviet authorities are persuaded, furthermore, that they have important international as well as national interests and responsibilities. Given our previous discussion, these commitments seem rather hollow. They are not. Internationalism, as Bernard Morris has suggested, may well be the "crucial bond of the communist movement."[112] Though the Chinese derisively refer to them as "the new tsars," the members of the Soviet Politburo perceive of the USSR as "the fatherland of socialism" and the center of the international revolutionary movement, with all the honor and moral virtue which their Marxist view of history bestows on such a role.

Adherence to the doctrines of Marxism–Leninism affects Soviet behavior in yet another way: it provides the Party leadership with a conceptual framework for organizing their understanding of international relations. Communist ideology supplies the Soviet authorities with intellectual categories that shape their perceptions of world affairs. For example, Soviet political doctrine tends to concentrate the attention of Soviet policymakers on the internal aspects of world politics. Marxism places great stress on the overriding importance of domestic socio-economic factors; as Marx himself suggested in *The Communist Manifesto*, the conflict of social classes is the ultimate determinant of all historical evolution. Thus, to the Soviet leaders, the main actors in world affairs are not sovereign states with distinctive historical and power interests, but conflicting classes whose policies, domestic and foreign, are shaped by domestic economic and social struggles. The ultimate determinant of international politics, therefore, is the struggle of antagonistic class interests and not, as bourgeois analysts would have it, the conflict among states having different "national interests."

The distinctiveness of the Soviet world outlook may best be understood by comparing it with the traditional American approach to diplomacy. One astute analysis views the difference as follows:

—Americans consider tensions in international relations abnormal, and yearn to see them resolved as quickly as possible. We tend to believe that good will is a principal ingredient for their resolution, and that our good will is beyond question. We assume that if tensions persist, it is proof that our adversary is implacably hostile to us. The application of these attitudes to relations with the Soviet Union has led us to excessive and unjustified optimism during periods of détente, and to uncritical acceptance of inevitable and unbounded hostility during periods of tension.

—The USSR tends to view external relations as the inevitable corollary of conflicting social systems. Soviet diplomacy therefore is prepared to accept international tension as normal, and, too often, to view negotiations with the United States as a form of harsh competition from which only one side can possibly gain advantage. In the past, this attitude has often tempted the Soviets to treat the occasional improvements in our relations as a transitory opportunity to achieve narrow tactical advantage. It has led the Soviets to consider the intervening periods of hostility as inevitable, and the causes of that hostility beyond resolution.[113]

Put somewhat differently, the Soviet leaders assume conflict, classes, change, and violence to be part of the natural condition of international diplomacy. The American view focuses on world politics as a matter of legal diplomatic maneuvering between sovereign states; it tends to be preoccupied with the *status quo*, not change, and tends to believe in a natural harmony of interests among nations and the feasibility of compromise.[114]

Moscow's concern with internal political dynamics and its assumptions regarding the inevitability of tension and violence are more in tune with the strife-torn history of international relations in the twentieth century than the generally formal and legalistic American outlook. The Marxist–Leninist world view, however, is constrained by its own rigidities. While sensitive to socio-economic factors, the high priests of Soviet political doctrine have been blind to the powerful force of nationalism in international relations. This has been particularly true regarding relations among Communist states. When first the Yugoslav, then the Chinese and Albanian, and more recently the Rumanian and Czechoslovak government leaders opposed Soviet policies, the Kremlin was caught unaware. The principles of Marxism–Leninism simply did not allow for disagreements among socialist nations. The Soviet rulers have never successfully explained, in doctrinal terms, the origins and nature of their disputes with other Communist regimes. In all instances, conflicts have been accounted for in personal terms; they are always the fault of "revisionist" leaders such as Tito, Mao, and Dubcek who somehow captured power in their respective countries and distorted the "true" socialist character of their regimes.

It is difficult to say whether this ostensibly more dynamic and more "scientific" conceptual framework has helped or hindered the USSR's international performance. In the Communist world, it has clearly been an obstacle to understanding. The Kremlin today persists in stating that Communist China, though temporarily hostile, does not have interests fundamentally antagonistic to those of the USSR; whereas Capitalist America, with whom relations have improved, is a danger in the long run because of the nature of her system. Such perspectives are not "operational": policy toward China is not based on doctrine which, in this case, would only be a source of confusion.

It is also remarkable that, for all its concern with tension and struggle and its consistent identification with forces of "revolution" and "national liberation," the USSR has fared so poorly in the Third World where conflict and violence are everyday facts of life. Although the Soviet rulers have devoted very considerable thought, energy, and effort to exploiting the collapse of imperialism—an event predicted by Lenin as early as 1916—only a scattered few ex-colonies have created Communist regimes. In fact, as Moscow has discovered, the expenditure of considerable resources is rarely sufficient to convert anti-imperialist sentiments and movements into Soviet political allies. Soviet experience in Egypt, Indonesia, Ghana, the Sudan, and China has demonstrated that arms and economic assistance do not create durable political influence.

And so, though they think and speak in terms of "revolution" and "class struggle," the Kremlin leaders—to their own undoubted amazement—have found the political forces of the twentieth century recalcitrant and difficult to harness to their purposes.

Notes

[1]John Maynard Keynes, *The General Theory of Employment, Interest and Money* (New York: Harcourt, Brace and World, 1964), pp. 383–384.

[2]N. Kapchenko, "The Scientific Principles of Socialist Foreign Policy," *International Affairs*, No. 5 (May, 1970), p. 42.

[3]B.N. Ponomaryov, et al., eds. *World Revolutionary Movement of the Working Class* (Moscow: Progress Publishers, 1967), p. 11.

[4]*Soviet Foreign Policy, op. cit.*, p. 36.

[5] E. V. Tarle, "The Methods of Bourgeois Diplomacy," *Istoriya Diplomatii* (History of Diplomacy), Moscow, 1945, Vol. III, p. 764; cited in Max Beloff, *The Foreign Policy of Soviet Russia*, Vol. II, 1936–1941 (London: Oxford University Press, 1949), p. 394.

[6]Kapchenko, *op. cit.*, pp. 41–42.

[7]*Ibid.*, p. 42.

[8]Gromyko, "On the International Situation. . . ," *op. cit.*, p. 15.

[9]*Soviet Foreign Policy, op. cit.*, pp. 17–19.

[10]*History of Soviet Foreign Policy, op. cit.*, p. 9–11.

[11]V. M. Khvostov and L. N. Kutakov, "The Foreign Policy of the Union of Soviet Socialist Republics," in Joseph E. Black and Kenneth W. Thompson, eds. *Foreign Policies in a World of Change* (New York: Harper and Row, Publishers, 1963), p. 224.

[12]*Ibid.* (Italics added).

[13]Nikita S. Khrushchev, "On Peaceful Coexistence," reprinted in *The Soviet Union—1922–1962: A Foreign Affairs Reader, op. cit.*, p. 401.

[14]*History of Soviet Foreign Policy, op. cit.*, p. 11.

[15]V. Gantman, "Class Nature of Present-Day International Relations," *International Affairs*, No. 9 (September, 1969), p. 56.

[16]*History of Soviet Foreign Policy, op. cit.*, p. 10.

[17]D. Tomashevsky, "Some Questions of International Relations Research in Light of Lenin's Teachings," *International Affairs*, No. 6 (June, 1970), p. 75.

[18]*World Revolutionary Movement of the Working Class, op. cit.*, p. 112.

[19]Edmund Demaitre, "The Origins of National Communism," *Studies in Comparative Communism*, Vol. II, No. 1 (January 1, 1969), p. 14.

[20]"The Homeland's Invincible Shield," *Pravda*, February 24, 1971; translated in *CDSP*, Vol. XXIII, No. 8 (March 23, 1971), p. 4.

[21]"Toward the 100th Anniversary of the Birth of Vladimir Ilych Lenin," Theses of the Central Committee of the Communist Party of the Soviet Union, *Pravda* and *Izvestia*, December 23, 1969; translated in *CDSP*, Vol. XXIII, No. 2, (February 11, 1970), p. 9.

[22]Sh. Sanakoyev, "Socialist Foreign Policy and Human Progress," *International Affairs*, No. 5 (May, 1970), pp. 21–22. (Italics added.)

[23]*Ibid.*, p. 22.

[24]George F. Kennan, "The Russian Revolution—Fifty Years After: Its Nature and Consequences," *Foreign Affairs*, Vol. XLVI, No. 1 (October, 1967), p. 16.

[25]Quoted in Mose L. Harvey, "Pre-eminence in Space: Still a Critical National Issue?", *Orbis*, Vol. XXII, No. 4 (Winter, 1969), pp. 978–979.

[26]M. Suslov, "Leninism and the Revolutionary Transformation of the World," *Kommunist*, No. 15 (October, 1969), p. 36.

[27]Khrushchev, "On Peaceful Coexistence," *op. cit.*, p. 403.

[28]L. I. Brezhnev, "Fifty Years of Soviet Armenia," *Pravda*, November 30, 1970) translated *CDSP*, Vol. XXII, No. 48 (December 29, 1970), pp. 4, 3.

[29]Suslov, *op. cit.*, p. 41.

[30]N. Bukharin, "Imperialism and Communism," reprinted in *The Soviet Union—1922–1962: A Foreign Affairs Reader, op. cit.*, pp. 151–152.

[31]*Soviet Foreign Policy, op. cit.*, p. 48.

[32]*World Revolutionary Movement of the Working Class, op. cit.*, p. 111.

[33]*Ibid.*, p. 21.

[34]*Ibid.*, p. 18.

[35]Quoted in Frederic S. Burin, "The Communist Doctrine of the Inevitability of War," *American Political Science Review*, Vol. LVII, No. 2 (June, 1963), p. 337. The argument that Soviet attitudes toward the capitalist West were largely conditioned by the experience of Western intervention in the Russian Civil War (1918–1921) is patently untrue. As this *1915* declaration by Lenin indicated, hostility toward the West was obviously deeply rooted in Bolshevik political thought well before the October Revolution.

[36]Quoted in Merle Fainsod, *How Russia Is Ruled* (Cambridge: Harvard University Press, 1954), p. 90.

[37]Jane Degras, ed., *Soviet Documents on Foreign Policy*, (London: Royal Institute of International Affairs, 1951), Vol. I, 1917–1924, p. 36.

[38]Quoted in E. H. Carr, *The Bolshevik Revolution, 1917–1923*, Vol. III (New York: The Macmillan Company, 1953), p. 56.

[39]*Ibid.*, p. 57.

[40]See Louis Fischer, *The Soviets in World Affairs 1917–1921*, Vol. I (Princeton University Press, 1951), pp. 259–275.

[41]*Ibid.*, p. 265. It is ironic in this regard that Ernest Bevin, later one of Britain's most vigorously anti-Communist labor leaders, declared amidst loud cheers to a dockers' conference in May, 1920, "I am not going to ask the dockers to put a gun in [a] ship to carry on this wicked venture." Quoted in Steven R. Graubard, *British Labour and the Russian Revolution, 1917–24* (Cambridge: Harvard University Press, 1956), p. 92.

[42]*Soviet Documents on Foreign Policy, op. cit.*, Vol. I, p. 22. Ten months later, the Soviet government declared it "the primary duty of the workers and peasants of Russia . . . to prepare active military assistance and food supplies for the working classes of Germany and Austria–Hungary . . . for the social revolution." *Ibid.*, p. 112.

[43]Adam Ulam notes that while there was little actual fear of Soviet power in the 1920s, there was considerable apprehension of Bolshevik ideology. "As a state," he notes, "Soviet Russia lay prostrate. . . ." However, Western statesmen

were greatly afraid of "the example of Russian Communism stirring up social trouble in their own countries. . . ." Thus, he concludes "Russia was the locus of an infection sapping the strength of Europe, not a threat herself." Ulam, *op. cit.*, p. 98.

[44]John H. Kautsky, "Myth, Self-Fulfilling Prophecy, and Symbolic Reassurance in the East–West Conflict," *Communism and the Politics of Development* (New York: John Wiley & Sons, 1968), p. 129.

[45]Ulam, *op. cit.*, p. 130.

[46]Quoted in Demaitre, *op. cit.*, p. 2.

[47]For an excellent discussion of this wrench in international perspective, see Bernard S. Morris, *International Communism and American Policy* (New York: Atherton Press, 1968), pp. 27–38.

[48]The best single-volume treatment of the Comintern is still Franz Borkenau's 1939 survey, *World Communism*, republished in 1962 by the University of Michigan Press, Ann Arbor.

[49]Once Lenin compromised at Brest–Litovsk, according to some, all pretensions toward a "revolutionary foreign policy" were abandoned. In this view, it is a straight line from Brest–Litovsk to Soviet patriotism.

[50]Leon Trotsky, *My Life* (London, 1930), p. 293; quoted in Robert M. Slusser, "The Role of the Foreign Ministry," Lederer, ed., *Russian Foreign Policy, op. cit.*, p. 212.

[51]Gromyko, "On the International Situation. . . ." *op. cit.*, p. 16.

[52]Raymond L. Garthoff, "The Advanced Countries," in Cyril E. Black and Thomas P. Thornton, eds., *Communism and Revolution* (Princeton: University Press, 1964), p. 406.

[53]N. S. Khrushchev, *Radio Moscow* (March 16, 1962); quoted in *ibid.*, pp. 406–407.

[54]*Program of the Communist Party of the Soviet Union*, reprinted in *The Road to Communism*, Documents of the 22nd Congress of the Communist Party of the Soviet Union, October 17–31, 1961 (Moscow: Foreign Languages Publishing House, 1961), p. 454.

[55]*Ibid.*, pp. 470.

[56]*XX s'ezd Kommunisticheskoi Partii Sovetskogo Soiuza*, Stenagraficheskii otchet, Vol. I (Moscow: 1956), p. 10.

[57]Chossudovsky, *op. cit.*, p. 574.

[58]Brezhnev, "Report of the CPSU Central Committee to the 24th Congress. . . ." *op. cit.*, p. 11. The peaceful coexistence thesis, according to Moscow, originated as early as 1915. It is now held that Lenin argued at that time that if a revolution were successful in one country, "that socialist country will not fly away to the Moon, it will inevitably coexist side by side with capitalist countries. Thus life itself advances the thesis of one country existing side by side with countries where a capitalist or even a precapitalist mode of production prevails." M. Trush, *Soviet Foreign Policy: Early Years* (Moscow: Novosti Press Agency, Publishing House, 1971), p. 16. While "life itself" may have advanced this attitude in the early 1920s—after the attempts to encourage, promote or simply applaud revolutions in Central and Eastern Europe came to naught—this certainly was not part of Lenin's thinking in 1915 as now claimed. Reality (or "life") taught Lenin that his early hopes for "revolutionary war" were not practicable.

[59]A. Kaplin, "Lenin on the Principles of Socialist Diplomacy," *International Affairs*, No. 6, (June, 1969), p. 54.

[60]N. S. Khrushchev, *For Victory in Peaceful Competition with Capitalism*, (New York: E. P. Dutton & Co., Inc., 1960), p. 91.

[61]Leo Gruliow and Charlotte Saikowski, eds., *Current Soviet Policies IV* (New York: Columbia University Press, 1962), p. 184.

[62]Beloff, *op. cit.*, Vol. II, p. 401.

[63]A. Belyakov and F. Burlatskiy, "Leninskaya teoriya sotsialisticheskoi revolyutsii i sovremennkost'" (Lenin's Theory of the Socialist Revolution and the Present Time), *Kommunist*, No. 13 (1960), pp. 15'–16; quoted in Garthoff, *op. cit.*, p. 405.

[64]See Thomas W. Wolfe, "Communist Outlook on War," RAND Paper P-3460 (Santa Monica: The RAND Corporation, August, 1967), p. 30.

[65]*Pravda*, July 20, 1963; quoted in William Hyland and Richard Shryock, *The Fall of Khrushchev* (New York: Funk and Wagnalls, 1968), p. 128.

[66]N.S. Khrushchev, "Some Fundamental Questions of Present-Day International Development—Report of the Central Committee of the CPSU to the Twentieth Party Congress," quoted in Alvin Z. Rubinstein, *The Foreign Policy of the Soviet Union* (New York: Random House, 1960), p. 299.

[67]Herbert S. Dinerstein, *Fifty Years of Soviet Foreign Policy* (Baltimore: The John Hopkins Press, 1968), p. 38.

[68]Chossudovsky, *op. cit.*, p. 574.

[69]Robert C. Tucker, *The Soviet Political Mind* (New York: Frederick A. Praeger, Publishers, 1963), p. 207.

[70]*World Marxist Review*, December, 1962, editorial; cited in William Zimmerman, "The Soviet Union," Steven L. Spiegel and Kenneth N. Waltz, eds., *Conflict in World Politics* (Cambridge, Mass.: Winthrop Publishers, 1971), p. 46.

[71]N. S. Khrushchev, Interview with Gardner Cowles, broadcast TASS account, *Radio Moscow* (April 25, 1962); quoted in Garthoff, *op. cit.*, pp. 409–410.

[72]*Ibid.*, p. 410.

[73]*Pravda*, July 4, 1968.

[74]Moore, *op. cit.*, p. 392.

[75]Quoted in *The Economist*, March 8, 1969, p. 16.

[76]Richard Lowenthal, "Continuity and Change in Soviet Foreign Policy," *Survival*, XIV, No. 1 (January-February, 1972), p. 3.

[77]*The New York Times*, May 30, 1972.

[78]*The New York Times*, May 22, 1973.

[79]G. Arbatov, "The Strength of a Policy of Realism," *Izvestia*, June 22, 1972; translated in *CDSP*, Vol. XXIV, No. 25 (July 17, 1972), p. 6.

[80]Herbert S. Dinerstein, "Soviet Union and the Communist World," *Survey*, Vol. XIX, No. 2 (87) (Spring, 1973,), p. 147.

[81]*The Department of State Bulletin*, Vol. LXIX, No. 1778 (July 23, 1973), p. 160.

[82]Abraham Becker "The Superpowers and The Arab–Israeli Conflict, 1970–1973" (Santa Monica: The RAND Corporation), RAND Paper P-5167 (December, 1973), p. 67.

[83]*Ibid.*, p. 64.

[84]Adam B. Ulam, "Communist Doctrine and Soviet Diplomacy," *Survey*, No. 76 (Summer, 1970), p. 6.

[85]See Morton Schwartz, "The USSR and Leftist Regimes in Less-Developed Countries, *Survey*, Vol. XIX, No. 2 (87) (Spring 1973), pp. 209–244.

[86]A. Bovin, "In the Struggle for Unity," *Izvestia*, June 17, 1972; translated in *CDSP*, Vol. XXIV, No. 24 (July 12, 1972), pp. 8–9.

[87]I. Shatalov, "Leninist Foreign Policy and the National Liberation Movement," *International Affairs*, No. 1 (January, 1969), p. 72. (Italics added.)

[88]Schwartz, "The USSR and Leftist Regimes. . .," *op. cit.*, pp. 238–240.

[89]*The New York Times*, April 17, 18, 24, 27 and 29, 1972.

[90]*Ibid.*, June 20, 1972.

[91]Vadim Zagladin, "Principled and Consistent," *New Times*, No. 22 (May 1972), p. 5.

[92]"The Supreme Internationalist Duty of a Socialist Country," *op. cit.*

[93]Vernon V. Aspaturian, "Moscow's Foreign Policy," *Survey* (October, 1967), No. 65, p. 37.

[94]J. D. B. Miller, "Unlimited Competition of Spheres of Responsibility," *Soviet–American Relations and World Order: The Two and the Many,* Adelphi Papers, No. 66 (London: The Institute for Strategic Studies, March, 1970), p. 36.

[95]Francis B. Randall, *Stalin's Russia* (Glencoe, Illinois: The Free Press, 1965), p. 86.

[96]Cyril E. Black, "Soviet Society: A Comparative View," in *Prospects for Soviet Society, op. cit.,* p. 21.

[97]This point is well made in A. L. Rowse, *Appeasement: A Study in Political Decline,* 1933–1939. (New York: W. W. Norton & Co., Inc., 1961). The proximity of a revolutionary Russia may well have been a major factor in the success of Hitler himself. The sense of dread provoked by the constant attacks from the German Communist Party within the Weimar Republic and the fear of Bolshevism which Moscow's belligerent anti-capitalist propaganda engendered served to weaken the moderate political elements in Germany and, at the same time, became a pretext for building up of the Nazi forces.

[98]Marshall D. Shulman, "Relations with the Soviet Union," in Kermit Gordon, ed., *Agenda for the Nation* (Garden City: Doubleday and Co., 1968), p. 376.

[99]Ulam, *Expansion and Coexistence, op. cit.,* p. 131.

[100]*ABM, MIRV, SALT and the Nuclear Arms Race.* Hearings Before the Subcommittee on Arms Control, International Law and Organization of the Committee on Foreign Relations, U.S. Senate, 91st Congress, 2nd Session, March–June, 1970 (Washington: Government Printing Office, 1970), p. 22.

[101]A. Kovalev, *Azbuka diplomatii* (The ABCs of Diplomacy), 2nd ed. (Moscow: Institute of International Relations, 1968), p. 40. Moscow does admit of the theoretical possibility that, in clearly unusual circumstances, "some group of interests of the ruling class may temporarily be identical with the interests of the nation and states as a whole. This occurred, for instance, during the Second World War . . . but even then the identity of interest was partial, temporary and contradictory." Kapchenko, *op. cit.,* p. 44.

[102]Sh. Sanakoyev, "U. N. General Assembly: Fact and Fiction," *International Affairs,* No. 12 (December, 1968), p. 19.

[103]Platonov saw the Soviet Communist Party as "giving meaning to life for all the world." *The Fierce and Beautiful World,* Stories by Andrei Platonov. Joseph Barnes, Translator. (New York: E. P. Dutton and Co., 1970), p. 235.

[104]Quoted in Max Jacobson, *Diplomacy of the Winter War,* pp. 142—143; cited by Fischer, *Russia's Road from Peace to War, op. cit.,* p. 383.

[105]Quoted by Castro Delgado, *J'ai perdu la foi a Moscou* (Paris: Gallimard, 1950), p. 62; cited in Leon Goure, *The Siege of Leningrad* (Stanford: Stanford University Press, 1962), p. 8.

[106]One pre-1941 Soviet Book, *The First Blow,* suggested a revolt against Hitler's regime would occur by the second day of any war between Germany and the Soviet Union. Cited by Soviet historian A. N. Nekrich, *June 22, 1941,* Vladimir Petrov, translator (Columbia, S.C.: University of South Carolina Press, 1968), p. 126.

[107]Quaestor, "Leading the World Against Hitler," *Labour Monthly,* No. 13 (August, 1941), pp. 361–362; quoted in Gene D. Overstreet and Marshall Windmuller, *Communism in India* (Berkeley: University of California Press, 1959), p. 192. The author further declared that, given the Nazi attack on the Soviet Union a few months earlier, "the interests of the British imperialists [now] temporarily coincide with those of the Soviet Union and *therefore* with those of the British people." (Italics added.) That the interests of the British people were at one with those of the USSR is obviously taken for granted.

[108]T. B. Bottomore and Maximillian Rubel, eds., *Karl Marx, Selected Writings in Sociology and Social Philosophy*, (New York: McGraw-Hill Book Co., 1956.), p. 80.

[109]Quoted in "For the Cause of Peace and Socialism," *Pravda*, June 8, 1972; translated in *CDSP*, Vol. XXIV, No. 23 (July 5, 1972), p. 14.

[110]V. Kortunov, "New Tactics and Old Goals," *International Affairs*, No. 8 (August, 1972), p. 34.

[111]Alfred G. Meyer, "Communist Revolutions and Cultural Change," *Studies in Comparative Communism*, Vol. V, No. 4 (Winter, 1972), p. 351.

[112]Morris, *op. cit.*, p. 77. "The idea of the perfectability of men through an international society of justice" was the origin of the Communist movement, notes Morris. "Take away the internationalism," he asks, "and what remains?" (p. 76).

[113]*U.S. Foreign Policy for the 1970s: The Emerging Structure of Peace*. A Report to the Congress by Richard Nixon, President of the United States, February 9, 1972 (Washington, D. C.: Government Printing Office, 1972), pp. 17–18.

[114]This point is well developed in Zbigniew K. Brzezinski and Samuel P. Huntington, *Political Power: USA/USSR* (New York: The Viking Press, 1963), pp. 56–70.

5

The dynamics of Soviet
domestic politics: system needs

The influence of domestic politics on Soviet foreign policy is often a source of confusion. Unlike Western political systems, where domestic and foreign policy are generally seen to be highly interactive, a sharp division is often seen to exist between the two in the USSR. Those at the apex of power in all authoritarian regimes are said to be far freer of domestic political constraints than responsible foreign policymakers in democratic societies. Given their complete monopoly of political power and a highly centralized and disciplined system of political controls, the leading officials of the Communist Party of the Soviet Union (CPSU) have no need to concern themselves with public opinion. Furthermore, their monopoly of the means of communication makes it possible for them to give their own and only their own version of national and international developments to the Soviet people. Unconstrained by pressures from competing political groups (rival parties), the pulls and shoves of inter-est group politics, and mass opinion, Soviet policies are said to have great advantages—in terms of their cohesiveness, consistency, and flexibility—over those of their democratic adversaries.

This view, once rather popular, can no longer be considered valid. Recent scholarship demonstrates that there is a highly important inter-connection between Soviet domestic and foreign policy. In fact, some have argued, that the most distinctive features of the USSR's foreign policy are the product of the particular character and needs of the Soviet political system.

The insecurities of dictatorial power

The Soviet Union, as we saw in Chapter Four, is what Philip E. Mosely has called an "ideocracy."[1] That is to say, the power of the Soviet Communist party over the 240 million citizens of the USSR is justified in terms of ideological doctrines, those of Marxism–Leninism. The doctrinal tenets which perform this legitimizing function, which serve in effect as the psychological foundation for the Soviet political system can be crudely summarized in terms of two basic principles: "the leading role of the party" and "democratic centralism" in inner-party politics. The first insists that the Communist Party controls all state agencies and social institutions—that it dominates all spheres of Soviet public life. The Party determines all policy and oversees all performance. The principle of "democratic centralism," though designed ostensibly to ensure democratic processes within the Communist Party, in fact means not free debate but oligarchic rule. The emphasis in practice is on "centralism," not "democratic," the complete domination by the Party high command.

Set forth originally by Lenin,[2] these precepts are still the core of the Soviet political system. Despite recent efforts to modify political practices and to eliminate the more brutal and terroristic measures introduced by Stalin, these two principles persist. And their continued primacy is justified exclusively in terms of the Leninist doctrines which originally gave them life.

The importance of ideology as a source of Party legitimacy cannot be overemphasized. Doctrine, and doctrine alone, explains why the CPSU is the only Party, why it controls the state administration and all spheres of society, why the media is subject to censorship, and why the Party Politburo dominates political life. To the extent that a significant number of Soviet citizens come to doubt the validity of socialist (especially Leninist) ideas, the whole Soviet political structure may be jeopardized. Even more profound difficulties would arise if the leadership itself came to lose confidence in the verities of Leninist doctrines. Self-doubt at the top is a malaise which no regime can long endure.

Concern over legitimacy should, on its face, no longer be a problem for the Soviet regime. Having survived intact for over half a century, the authority of Leninist-type Party rule is by now a well-established tradition. Its presence, once threatened and uncertain, has become "normal," a fact of life, a historical given, for most Soviet citizens. Furthermore, the economic achievements of the past two decades led to a considerable improvement in the regime's popularity, especially during the late 1950s and early 1960s.

Despite their auspicious record, the Party leaders remain preoccupied with the problem of the regime's authority; they continue to worry about what Peter Reddaway has called the "health of party/people relations."[3] This was true even of Khrushchev, the most popular and self-assured Soviet leader since Lenin. In March 1963, for example, the usually genial First Secretary warned that a relaxation of the existing system of strict Party control over literature and art would result in political disaster. "As a first step," he predicted, "a blow would be dealt at our revolutionary gains in the sphere of socialist art. By the logic of the struggle," he continued, "things would hardly end there. It is not impossible that these people [those critical of "socialist art"] on gathering strength would make an attempt to come out in opposition to the revolutionary gains."[4] In Khrushchev's view, the danger of people "coming out in opposition" and of things getting out of hand was just below the surface. Though the Kremlin boasts incessantly about "the unshakeable and ever-growing unity between the Party and the people," this seems very much a case where the "lady doth protest too much."

The underlying explanation of the regime's uncertainty is complex. It reflects in part a deeply rooted fear of anarchy. For centuries, Russia has been shaken by violent peasant unrest. Rebelling against the barbarous conditions under which they were compelled to live, Russia's vast peasantry has periodically sought to wreak primitive vengeance against their enslavers. Naturally such outbursts commanded respect— and fear. "The elite, with good reason," notes Richard Pipes, "always had a tremendous dread of the barbarous masses of Russia, which they so exploited." Thus, while some enlightened members of Russia's ruling elite may have felt, and some do even today, that the introduction of democratic institutions in Russia might be a good thing, the fear persisted that once authority was relaxed, Russia's "dark masses" (*temnyi narod*) would rise up in an orgy of violent destruction.[5]

The country's long exposure to turmoil and disorder—in the 1770s, for example, and during the revolutions of 1905 and 1917—has helped instill an abiding respect for order and stability in Russian political thought. Basically distrustful of the Russian peasant masses and their potential for destructive violence, Lenin and his successors developed a system of centralized authority precisely to maintain control over them. Recent regimes have shared Lenin's concern with discipline and organization. As Khrushchev warned in 1958, "spontaneity, comrades, spontaneity is the deadliest enemy of all." To ensure that "anarchic self-will" not be allowed to "sow dissension and disorganize the life of society," he declared in 1963 that even in the ideal society of "full communism" the will of the individual "must be subordinated to the will of the collective." The traditional fear of anarchy apparently lives on.[6]

Another factor which may contribute to the regime's anxiety over internal political cohesion is the absence of any regularized succession mechanism. The procedure for transferring power in the USSR from one ruler or set of rulers to another is not fixed. This lack of any institutionalized succession procedures has serious consequences. First, it tends to make for intensive political infighting. Each incumbent in the Party leadership knows that his tenure in office depends solely on his ability to establish and maintain an effective political coalition against ambitious rivals ever on the lookout for an opportunity to replace him. Furthermore, if the major political figure in the Party leadership dies or is removed, the absence of established succession arrangements can create great uncertainty. Thus when Stalin was felled by a stroke in 1953, his successors were openly apprehensive and warned the Soviet populace against "disorder and panic." There is, in recent years, some evidence that a pattern of peaceful succession may be emerging in the Communist countries of Eastern Europe.[7] However, only one of the three major transfers of power in Soviet history occurred without bloodshed. The removal of Khrushchev in 1964 took place peacefully, but this single example does not yet demonstrate the existence of an institutionalized succession procedure. The potential for "disorder and panic" still exists.

Additionally, and somewhat related, the system of "collective leadership" which apparently still prevails in the Kremlin also creates uncertainty. Though we know rather little about the precise manner in which this system of group control actually works, no fixed mechanism seems to exist which establishes authority and responsibility for making decisions. Is the General Secretary of the Party always the top leader? With whom does he (must he) consult? What is the role of the Party's leading bodies (the Politburo, the Central Committee, and the Secretariat)? There seems to be no established answer to these questions; the particular importance of each of these factors varies with personalities and situations. The uncertainty that seems to exist on these critical political issues further intensifies the tensions and anxieties which prevail at the apex of the Soviet political system.[8]

Alexander Gerschenkron suggests a more general explanation. All modern dictatorships, he writes, including the USSR, face a permanent problem of maintaining authority over their citizens. Unlike a hereditary monarchy, which bases its legitimacy on its claim to divine sanctions and ancient traditions, or a democracy, which justifies its claim to rule on the consent of the governed as expressed in periodic elections, the power of a modern dictatorship is "at all times . . . jeopardized by doubt."

> The subjects—or, rather, the objects—of dictatorial rule are perennially moved to ask the simple but deeply probing and profoundly disturbing questions: Why should there be a dictatorship? Why should it continue in power? However aggressive the actions of the dictatorship, in a very real sense it always finds itself on the defensive.[9]

Unable to vindicate its claim to rule by historically traditional methods (which were rejected in 1917 when the Tsar was overthrown), the Soviet regime from the outset of its existence, has been hard at work to justify its power.

The main instrument of this justification is Marxism–Leninism, the official state ideology of the USSR. Though its doctrinal precepts, especially when interpreted and applied by Moscow's ideological experts, can supply answers to Gerschenkron's "disturbing questions," this important task is not always performed well. The high priests of Marxism–Leninism have found it difficult to explain abrupt reversals and contradictions in policy within the framework of the ideology. (For example, the attempt to explain Stalinist terrorism in Marxist–Leninist terms, using the pseudo-concept of "the cult of the personality," has never been convincing.) Still more important is the fact that a considerable discrepancy exists, as the Soviet leaders are very much aware, between the ideological goals of Marx and Lenin and the still tawdry reality of Soviet life. The leadership's inability to make good their much publicized intentions—to establish a classless and conflict-free society, to create economic abundance and "true" political freedom, and to promote a world-wide socialist revolution—must inevitably create doubts and uncertainties.

The Kremlin's anxiety on this score is not without some basis in fact. Given the utopian character of Soviet ideology, there is a virtually inevitable gap between promise and performance. This gap was widest during the years of the Stalin regime when the brutality of Soviet public life contradicted the goals of Marxist–Leninist doctrine in countless ways. The sense of cynicism regarding the regime's ideological claims which this experience produced was acidly expressed by the Soviet author, Andrei Sinyavsky, who wrote:

> So that prisons should vanish forever, we built new prisons. So that all frontiers should fall, we surround ourselves with a Chinese wall [or Iron Curtain]. So that work should become a rest and a pleasure, we introduced forced labor. . . . In the name of the Purpose [the achievement of Communism] we turned to the means our enemies used: we glorified Imperial Russia, we wrote lies in *Pravda* [Truth], we set a new Tsar on the now empty throne. . . . Sometimes we felt that only one final sacrifice was needed for the triumph of Communism—the renunciation of Communism.[10]

Though Sinyavsky was speaking of an earlier, far grimmer period, the disparity between the regime's rhetoric and the socio-political reality in which the average citizen lives is still very much apparent. Despite the country's vast economic achievements, the Soviet citizen feels that the Kremlin has not carried out its promise of a decent standard of living. The average Russian, according to Richard Pipes, is poor not only in comparison with his counterpart in other European countries (including those in Eastern Europe) but "also in comparison with his own grandfather. In terms of essentials—food, clothing and housing—the Soviet population as a whole is worse off than it was before the Revolution and in the 1920s."[11] In addition, the Soviet citizen is continually frustrated by the rigidities of the Soviet economic system. Looking at agriculture, for example, he knows the private plot is a vastly more efficient food producer than is the collective farm. Given this situation, one well known to all Soviet consumers, the question inevitably rises: Who needs so much planning and direction from above? The atmosphere of disappointment in the material accomplishments of the regime and the hollowness of its promises is reflected in the following anecdote, popular during the 1960s: "What's the difference between capitalism and socialism?" "That's easy," replies a young student. "Under capitalism you have the exploitation of man by man; under socialism, you have the reverse."

Official pronouncements and explanations of public policy have long been lacking in credibility. Despite this situation (or, more likely because of it) the Kremlin leaders place great emphasis on Marxism–Leninism: they pay considerable attention to Party dogma and continually undertake massive ideological indoctrination campaigns. This somewhat paradoxical fact makes sense, given the character of Party rule. Ideology, as we have seen, has been the sole justification of the power of the Soviet leadership. Furthermore, with the abandonment of reliance on overt terrorism, ideological indoctrination has become, in the eyes of the Party authorities, the prime method to ensure political conformity. Thus, continued stress on such hallowed Leninist principles as "the leading role of the Party" helps ensure that, even (or especially) in uncertain times, the established system of Party rule will remain the only conceivable method of organizing a socialist political system. The claim is constantly reiterated, in the words of Politburo member Nikolai Podgorny, that

> ... the Communist party guides the development of democracy ... it is precisely the Party that constitutes the nucleus of authority under socialism and acts as the principle element in the socialist state system. For the Soviet people the question of the role of our Party is clear: genuine democracy is impossible and inconceivable without the direction of the Communist Party. ... [12]

Such shibboleths are incessantly repeated. So, too, are the other major tenets of Marxism–Leninism on whose continued acceptance the authority of the Party ultimately depends. Thus, despite the fact that relations with "capitalist" countries are considerably better than those with some of their "socialist" partners, most notably China, the Soviet leaders continue to emphasize the traditional doctrines of the "international class struggle" and "proletarian nationalism." The achievements and purposes of the "world socialist system" are endlessly glorified while the "capitalist" states are denounced for their self-serving and immoral policies at home and abroad. When a Western government does act in a "positive" manner (for example, adopts a policy position favored by the Soviet government), it is invariably explained as a response to pressure—either from public opinion within the country or from the socialist states.

To the degree such a world view is accepted—and the average citizen has little opportunity to acquire any other—commitment to the Soviet regime is thereby reinforced. Under capitalism, after all, most of the people are poor and will become poorer while the wealthy grow ever richer. The moral is clear: "How lucky we are to live in a just socialist society which knows no inequity." Such myths also help remove all doubts regarding the wisdom of Marxist–Leninist doctrine. By insisting on a dichotomous image of the world, observes Jeremy Azrael, a world of "socialist heroes" and "capitalist villains," the Soviet leadership seeks "to inculcate a radical intolerance of ambiguity."[13] The certainties of doctrine, therefore, help overcome the uncertainties of authority.

The tenacity with which the Soviet leaders adhere to the canons of Marxism–Leninism should, therefore, be understood in terms of their domestic political needs. The Soviet authorities think and speak in terms of the international class struggle and the ultimate triumph of socialism; they believe, along with Politburo member Suslov, that the Communist Party enjoys the "unlimited support of the Soviet people who see in the party's activity and policy the expression of their fundamental interests and therefore actively support all of its measures"[14]—because they must! To abandon these doctrinal beliefs (or to revise them substantially) would endanger the psychological and philosophical underpinnings of Soviet political power. In a sense, the Soviet leaders are the victims of their own ideology. They are compelled to adhere to Marxism–Leninism by their need for reassurance and legitimation.[15]

Dependence on ideology affects Soviet behavior in various ways. It helps explain the abrasive style and messianic pretensions of Soviet diplomacy. Reflecting the Kremlin's distinctive approach to foreign policy, Khrushchev declared in 1958:

> The future is with our socialist system. Capitalism is at its ebb, heading for collapse. This does not mean that it is already lying down with its legs stretched out; much work has yet to be done to bring it to such a state. But this is inevitable, just as death inevitably comes to the living organism or plant after a specific stage of development.[16]

In uttering such bellicose remarks, as he did so often, the Soviet leader was not simply trying to propagandize his countrymen regarding the eventual triumph of socialism over capitalism; he was also expressing his conviction that such, indeed, was the future of the world. Khrushchev, then, as well as his successors, accept the Marxist–Leninist view of the world, for their whole political universe rests on their continued faith in such doctrines.

Continued adherence to Party orthodoxy also helps explain the relative technological backwardness of the Soviet economy and its slowness to change. Wedded to a set of beliefs purported to explain all of human history, the Kremlin rulers tend to regard all of their economic institutions and procedures—such as central planning, collective agriculture, direct political management—as necessarily sanctified by the "scientific laws" of Marxism–Leninism. These practices, many of which were actually adopted for reasons of expediency, thus tend to become hallowed principles of a socialist economy. They are also sustained by vested bureaucratic interests. Little wonder that they are so resistant to change.

The tendency to ideologize places severe limitations on innovations in all spheres of public life. The Soviet leaders have been extremely slow to implement fundamental economic reforms, especially any that seem tinged with "capitalism," such as the use of "profit" rather than plan fulfillment as an economic indicator, or modification of the command economic system in the direction of a decentralized, market economy.

The following remark, attributed to an East European planning official, gives some hint of the frustration this attitude fosters:

> . . . Marx was the world's greatest philosopher and Lenin the world's greatest man, but the issues we face, such as those requiring increasing numbers of computors and automatic machinery, were not foreseen by these men, one of whom died almost 90 years ago, and the other almost 50 years ago. In short . . . we turn not to Marx and Lenin to resolve our economic problems, but to the Harvard Business School and to Western technology, which do provide some answers.[17]

Though basic changes in the Soviet-type economic system are regarded by most economists (even in the USSR and especially in Eastern Europe) as long overdue, the elite's dependence on Marxist–Leninist orthodoxies makes reform difficult. And so, the problems confronting the Soviet economy referred to in Chapter One—especially its lack of technological innovation—are not easily overcome.

The USSR is a land of paradox. The ideology of revolution has become a major source of conservatism. Rather than spurring rapid social change, Marxism–Leninism serves to reinforce the Soviet *status quo*. Underlying this paradox is another even more profound. Though the Soviet regime is rigidly centralized, highly disciplined, and control-oriented, the Party dictatorship which dominates this autocratic political structure is psychologically insecure.

Whatever the actual state of "party/people relations," the evidence suggests that the party elite remains strikingly uncertain about its basic authority position. Though its mood shifts, depending somewhat on changing circumstances and personnel, the Politburo continues to worry about political instability—about preserving the ideological and social cohesion of the Soviet people.

This simmering authority crisis imposes important constraints on Soviet behavior. It leads to ideological rigidification and conservatism. It also tends to create a built-in bias in favor of an atmosphere of tension, internally and internationally. To bolster their fragile psychological foundations, suggests Alexander Gerschenkron, modern dictatorships often seek to maintain "a permanent condition of stress and strain." Only "by creating enemies at home or abroad and/or by imposing upon the population gigantic tasks that would be unlikely to be carried out in the absence of dictatorship," he writes, will the "stability conditions" of dictatorial power be ensured.[18]

While the dynamics of dictatorial power described here are hardly unique to the USSR (or to "modern dictatorships"), they do help to explain many aspects of Soviet behavior. In fact, Kremlin policy, domestic and foreign, often cannot be intelligently understood unless it is recalled that the Soviet political system virtually requires a crisis atmosphere to survive. Only in a climate of permanent emergency can the Kremlin rulers justify their continued monopoly of power and the Party–police control apparatus which sustains their rule.

To help create the psychological environment on which their system rests, the Soviet leaders continually refer to the mortal dangers created by their "enemies." In a sense, the regime is heavily dependent on its enemies. Every dictatorship, notes Louis Fischer, "must have enemies. When it cannot find them it creates them." By focusing attention on adversaries, real or fancied, he goes on, the dictator can rally his people

> . . . around the government, their shield against those who threaten. By striking down the internal dissident and denouncing the hostile outsider the ruling oligarchs proclaim themselves the vigilant guardians of the people's interests and hope thereby to establish an identity between the dictatorship and the nation.[19]

In its ceaseless quest "to establish an identity" between government and people, the Kremlin seeks to implement Aristotle's twenty-three-century-old injunction to "foster alarms" and "bring distant dangers near." For this purpose, enemies are indispensable.

The "need for enemies" has long been a basic feature of the Soviet political system. Since the death of Lenin (in 1924), whose personal authority was widely respected, all Kremlin leaders have warned of the mortal danger from "hostile forces." This was a favorite stratagem of Stalin. In 1927, for example, he deliberately encouraged rumors about an impending war with England. "Everybody in Moscow was talking war," declared Soviet Foreign Commissar Chicherin. "I tried to dissuade them. 'Nobody is planning to attack us,' I insisted. Then a colleague enlightened me. He said, 'Shh. We know that. But we need this against Trotsky.' "[20] Stalin, apparently, invented a "war scare" to strike at his major domestic political rival.

The most elaborate attempt to apply the indispensable enemy stratagem came in Stalin's famous thesis on "capitalist encirclement." The Soviet Union, he repeatedly pointed out, was politically isolated in a world of predatory imperialist powers. If it was to survive, it had to take severe measures to increase its military strength and tighten internal political security. This was Stalin's rationale for the massive Five-Year Plans, the harsh methods involved in the collectivization of agriculture, and the brutal political purges of the 1930s. As Demaitre has observed, "in picturing the Soviet Union as a beleaguered fortress surrounded by implacable enemies, the Soviet leadership sought to divert attention from domestic problems and at the same time to strengthen the individual citizen's identification with the Soviet state."[21] The purported dangers from "capitalist encirclement" served to stimulate the enormous expansion of Soviet industrial and military power and simultaneously helped justify the Stalinist dictatorship.

Obviously, the Stalinist system thrived in a psychological atmosphere of crisis and fear. The regime's unceasing concern with "capitalist encirclement" was not a species of paranoidal madness, but part of a rational strategy to bolster and consolidate an internally insecure political system. Stalin, like other dictators, sought personal security through perennial public insecurity.

Maintenance of a cold war climate also enabled Stalin to avoid too close contact between Soviet citizens and those of other countries.[21] As we saw in earlier chapters, xenophobia has deep roots in Russian political culture. While derived in part from religious and cultural traditions, this scorn of things foreign also reflects the profound authority crisis that has long troubled the political leadership. "Russia's rulers," writes George Kennan,

> have invariably sensed that their rule was relatively archaic in form, fragile and artificial in its psychological foundations, unable to stand comparison . . . with political systems of Western countries. For this reason they have always feared foreign penetration, feared direct contact between [the] Western world and their own, feared what would happen if Russians learned [the] truth about [the] world without or if foreigners learned [the] truth about [the] world within.[22]

Thus, despite their internationalist ideology, the Soviet leadership has generally felt a sense of uneasiness about too intimate contact with foreigners. Uncertain of their own authority, the Kremlin rulers, as Kennan suggests, have continually scorned close relations with alien populations. Soviet citizens have continually been urged to be vigilant and loyal, to avoid becoming contaminated by alien influences. When they do become "excessively interested" in things foreign, political repression invariably follows.

Stalin's policy in the 1940s toward the "returners"—the many thousands of Soviet citizens who found themselves tossed by the winds of war outside the borders of the USSR (either as war prisoners or as forced labor)—dramatically illustrates the regime's deep insecurity and fear of foreign penetration. Prior to their being allowed to return home, these exhausted and sickly survivors of Hitler's camps were subjected to intensive interrogation by the Soviet secret police. As a result of the NKVD "investigations," large numbers were sent to forced labor camps in the USSR—on suspicion of disloyalty or traitorous conduct.

How can this bizarre behavior be explained? Soviet writer Alexander Solzhenitsyn, himself a political prisoner for eleven years, suggests that the regime feared the "returners" had been "recruited by the enemy."[23] In light of Soviet policies during the aftermath of World War I, this possibility could not be ignored. After all, had not the Bolsheviks won recruits to the Communist cause by agitating among Russia's war prisoners in 1918? According to one report, about 90,000 people, mainly Hungarians, became active in the Communist movement as a result of such recruitment efforts.[24] These newly won converts became, according to Lenin, "the bacilli of Bolshevism," carrying the cause of proletarian revolution to Central Europe. Given this limited though nonetheless real success (a short-lived Soviet republic was set up in Hungary by Bela Kun, himself a former POW) and Stalin's own acute political anxieties, the Soviet dictator may well have feared that the defeated Germans would try to wreak their revenge on recruiting among Soviet forced laborers and POWs. To protect the exhausted and weakened regime against such a possibility, these "potentially dangerous" elements either had to be eliminated, as many were, or isolated from the "healthy elements" of Soviet society.

Thus, to the extent that the Soviet regime feels insecure politically, that it seems uncertain of the sense of cohesion between various parts of Soviet society on the one hand, and the governing authorities on the other, it retains a vested interest in preserving a psychological climate of perpetual national emergency. External enemies and isolation from foreign influences are veritable necessities for the survival of such a regime. This was precisely the sort of political environment that Stalin sought to create. Thus, Soviet policy in the immediate post-war period—the abrupt and complete termination of all contacts with the West and the vitriolic anti-Western propaganda campaigns—was, in considerable measure, the product of domestic imperatives. The Iron Curtain was designed mainly to help Stalin consolidate his power—both domestically and in Eastern Europe.

With the death of Stalin in 1953, the situation changed dramatically. Traditional patterns and perspectives were drastically altered. The notion of "capitalist encirclement"—which in view of the Communist regimes established in Eastern Europe and China, was no longer tenable[25]—was finally abandoned in the mid-1950s. As Khrushchev remarked, with characteristic exaggeration, "At present it is not known who encircles whom."[26] Further, acceptance of the "peaceful coexistence" thesis indicated that the hated and feared capitalist enemies could at least be dealt with (even though they were still not to be trusted). And, as part of the post-Stalin détente, international contacts were greatly enlarged, especially with the West; tourist travel in the USSR was greatly expanded; scientific and technological exchange programs were developed; Soviet citizens began to travel abroad more frequently; and the volume of foreign trade was increased.

If our previous discussion is at all near the mark, the modification—in some instances the outright discarding—of traditional Bolshevik perspectives on international relations indicates a concomitant improvement in the regime's sense of internal security. Changes in domestic policy point in much the same direction. The marked reduction in the power of the secret police, the toleration of more open political discussion and within strict limits, some criticism of policy (a practice greatly stimulated by Khrushchev's attack on Stalin's "cult of the personality" in 1956), and the growing attention to the production of consumer goods—all indicate that recent leaders no longer felt themselves as dependent as Stalin had on permanent crisis and external enemies to secure their power base.

The post-Stalin regime had good reason to feel more self-confident. As a result of the enormous changes produced by Stalin's forced modernization programs, the internal political environment had been dramatically altered. Soviet industry and the vast ministerial bureaucracies were now being run by a group of well-trained and reasonably well-informed specialists—engineers, government officials, and technicians—who were overwhelmingly loyal and grateful to the Party for granting them the opportunity for social advancement. The political basis of Party rule clearly had improved. As a result of such developments, the USSR has achieved, as Frederick Barghoorn has written, "a substantial degree of external and domestic acceptance, legitimacy, prestige and prosperity."[27]

Khrushchev's rule seemed remarkably free of the internal insecurity which marked the Stalin era, especially in the late 1950s and early 1960s after Stalin's system of police terror was relaxed, the forced labor camps closed, and consumer goods became relatively more plentiful. Nevertheless, even under Khrushchev, considerable evidence of leadership anxiety could be found. This was especially true in the aftermath of Khrushchev's domestic de-Stalinization campaign, when increasing signs of restiveness began to appear, in both the USSR and in Eastern Europe. In 1956, this led to open rebellion in Hungary. The scourge of anarchy seemed to threaten Soviet rule.

The Kremlin faced a dilemma. While he was very much interested in improving Soviet living standards and emancipating his countrymen from the brutalities of Stalinism, Khrushchev very much feared, as Ulam suggests, that "excessive concessions and unkindled freedom would bring the whole system crashing down."[28] To preserve Marxist–Leninist "law and order," Red Army tanks forcibly repressed the Hungarian revolution in the fall of 1956. Furthermore, though Party–police constraints were never allowed to resume their Stalinist dimensions, political controls in the USSR were tightened. Soviet writers, artists, scientists and students were put on notice that while they would not be subject to wholesale imprisonment, as under Stalin, there were nonetheless sharp limits to the "thaw" which had taken place in post-Stalin Russia.

The persistence of what we have called leadership anxiety, a feature apparently endemic to the Soviet system, became strongly apparent once again after the ouster of Khrushchev. Less optimistic and less self-confident than their exuberant predecessor, the "collective leadership" led by Brezhnev and Kosygin has reverted back to a more traditional Kremlin posture of apprehension and defensiveness. They have been confronted with considerable pressures from below—from writers and scientists, from economists and national minorities—to modify specific aspects of government policy. While the Party's apparent willingness to suffer such expressions of dissidence may indicate some growth in self-confidence and tolerance,[29] many leading dissidents were arrested or imprisoned in psychiatric hospitals in 1971 and 1972, and their main journal, the remarkable underground publication entitled "The Chronicle of Current Events," was suppressed. In 1973 and 1974, a number of prominent dissident leaders, including Alexander Solzhenitsyn, were sent (sometimes forcibly) into exile abroad.

To legitimize its continued monopoly of power and ward off these pressures from below, the regime falls back on the need for unity in a hostile world. The USSR is thus still depicted as a nation under siege. "The entire enormous apparatus of imperialist propaganda," notes Politburo member Grishin, "is aimed at . . . undermining socialism from within and at instilling bourgeois ideology and morality in the consciousness of Soviet people, especially young people."[30] The new strategy, warns the Party leadership, is "to undermine socialism *from within.*" To carry out its pernicious plans, imperialism is said to be dissecting every sphere of Soviet life, making "microscopic studies of each cell of the Soviet organism, probing for spots where infection could be introduced."

> They are seeking out *the scum among us, the chronic failures and paranoiacs* [!] *The dregs of society*—this is the foundation on which they construct their "scientific" conclusions about the "crisis" of Soviet power.[31] (Italics added.)

In March 1968, Brezhnev warned that bourgeois ideologists were attempting to "ferret out morally unstable, weak and politically immature people . . . susceptible to self-advertisement . . . deceitful people." To combat such influences, to create a healthy socialist society, "iron discipline" in Party ranks was essential.[32]

The regime evidently remains nervous and continues to distrust its own citizenry. To overcome its fears and ensure its power, the bogey of external danger is invoked. Those deviating from official Soviet policy —the "scum, renegades, parasites . . . paranoids, crooks, rascals," and "morally unstable, weak and politically immature people"—are said to be either unwitting dupes or, in some instances, conscious supporters of Western propaganda. Such people cannot be ignored. As Brezhnev warned, "there can be no political indifference, passivity or neutrality with respect to the aims pursued by the enemy."[33]

To combat the risk of "infection from within," the Party periodically renews its demands for internal unity and vigilance. "Closely rallied around the Leninist party and under its tested leadership," declares *Pravda*, "the Soviet people, steeled in work and in battles against the enemies of socialism, are confidently marching into their communist future. They will let no one encroach upon their historic gains."[34] The essence of the regime's stratagem was revealed by Soviet novelist Alexander Solzhenitsyn. In a letter to the Russian Writer's Union (which had just summarily expelled him) he explains how the Party's literary bureaucrats could justify their arbitrary behavior—expulsions without warning, secret meetings, secret appointments and personnel changes:

> "The enemy is listening." That's your answer. These external enemies are the basis of your existence. What would you do without your enemies? You would not be able to live without your enemies. Hate, hate no less evil than racism, has become your sterile atmosphere.[35]

Soviet nuclear physicist Andrei Sakharov testifies in a similar vein.

> Truthful information about our shortcomings and negative phenomena is kept secret lest it be "used by hostile propaganda." Exchange of information with foreigners is restricted out of fear of "penetration of hostile ideol-

ogy." Theoretical conceptions and practical proposals which may seem
bold to some are suppressed immediately without any discussion because
of fear that they may "undermine the foundations."[36]

The specter of eternal omnipresent enemies—now, as under Stalin—
remains essential to legitimize the Party's repressive system of rule.

Policy implications—the need for tension?

The implications of this endemic authority crisis for domestic policy are
obvious: in order to secure its "leading role" in Soviet society, the Communist Party must maintain a permanent system of administrative, ideological, and policy controls. Thus, though the harsher features of the
Stalin era have been largely abandoned, the insecurities of leadership
place limits on how far the main principles of dictatorial rule can be
modified. The Soviet authorities are still too concerned with their own
self-preservation to risk significant internal reforms which might endanger
their monopoly of power.[37]

Persistence of leadership insecurity would seem to have profound
implications for foreign policy as well. If the preceding argument is
sound and Soviet autocratic structures need a cold war atmosphere to
endure—a judgment somewhat more accurate than the old Marxist
axiom that capitalism requires war to prosper—does not "system need"
impel the Kremlin to favor a tension-producing foreign policy? The post-
World War II era of constant international crisis and danger was an ideal
environment for perpetuation of authoritarian rule. ("War," notes the
Polish philosopher Leszek Kolakowski, "is the ally of tyranny."[38] Exactly
the same may be said of cold war.)

Détente, on the other hand, would appear to undermine the
regime's internal position. With the General Secretary of the CPSU and
the titular head of the "world revolutionary movement" personally visiting such capitalist bastions as Washington and Bonn and hailing the President of the United States and the Chancellor of the Federal Republic of
Germany as "sober statesmen who have taken a realistic and constructive
approach" to their relations with the USSR, the postulate of an implacably
hostile external environment hardly seems creditable. The question logi-
cally arises: if Richard Nixon and Willy Brandt, then leaders of the most
powerful capitalist nations, were seen as the diplomatic and trading
partners of the USSR, who then is the "enemy" against whom "vigilance"
is so indispensable?

The Soviet leadership does seem more comfortable politically during periods of crisis and it may well be said to have a vested interest in
perpetuating a climate of international tension. Such, indeed, is believed
to have been the mainspring of traditional Russian imperialism. The
Tsarist drive "to aggrandize the national territory, its 'gathering of land,'
placed great premium on military strength." By means of this policy,
suggests Robert Tucker, the government was able to "bind all classes"
in compulsory service to the autocracy. The motive force underlying

Tsarism's policy of territorial expansion, in his view, was the drive to consolidate autocratic power.[39]

The extraordinary outward thrust of the Russian Empire did produce a highly centralized state with an autocratic ruler, the Tsar, whose very title still remains the code word for unlimited power. Concentration of authority was required by the Russian Empire's foreign policy successes. The very size of the empire, the problems of administration and taxation, and the maintenance of an army to secure it against predatory neighbors in all directions contributed to the creation of a political system in which the greatness of the state dominated society and where there were no interests outside the state. As the Russian historian Kliuchevsky described it, "the expansion of state territory, straining beyond measure and exhausting the resources of the people, only bolstered the power of the state without elevating the self-confidence of the people. . . . The state swelled up; the people grew lean."[40]

Richard Pipes offers a similar analysis of Soviet foreign policy behavior. The policies of the CPSU, he argues, like those of the Tsars, "are primarily internally generated." Here, too, the mainspring of policy is leadership anxiety. Soviet behavior, he suggests "is motivated by fear . . . only the fear is not of other peoples but of its own, and for that reason it is incapable of being allayed by concessions. Fear breeds insecurity which in turn expresses itself, in nations and individuals, in aggressive behavior." Thus, concludes Pipes, if the USSR seeks to pursue an aggressive policy (which he argues it does), if it continually strives to expand, "it is precisely because its expansion is in large measure determined by internal rather than external factors, above all, by the tragic relationship of the government to its people."[41]

The Soviet system, therefore, would seem to have a built-in tendency toward aggressive behavior. At the same time, however, history has taught Russia's rulers the bitter lesson that wars have political consequences far beyond those contemplated by their originators. While the Tsar's ministers often sought to promote internal cohesion through limited military engagements, these policies ultimately contributed to their undoing. "All the important concessions which the Imperial government had made before the revolution," Pipes reminds us, "were the consequences of long wars: the Crimean War, which compelled it to free the serfs and institute local self-government; the Russo-Japanese War, which forced it to grant a constitution, and World War I which caused it to abdicate."[42]

Thus, whatever the internal political pressures, the Soviet leadership is not likely to seek a way out of its domestic problems through an aggressive foreign policy. The Kremlin rulers know, from the legacy of their predecessors and from their own experience with internal defection during the early stages of World War II,[43] that wars—especially protracted wars—place enormous strains on relations between a government and its people. Thus, the same factor which produced its need for an aggressive posture—the regime's lack of self-confidence—also forces it to act cautiously. Fear of its own population has thus compelled the Soviet government to pursue a generally prudent policy in which the avoidance of general war has always been of the highest priority.

"System need," therefore, is seen to impose a curious and rather neurotic pattern of demands on Soviet diplomacy. The internal Soviet political system tends to require an atmosphere of continued international tension and, at the same time, a policy of low risk and crisis avoidance. Precisely these domestic necessities, according to advocates of the "system need" school, explain the persistent tendency toward apparently purposeless expansion so often noted by observers of the Russian scene. The outward thrust of Soviet policy, they argue, is to be understood not in terms of any real or tangible objectives but as an attempt to satisfy the Soviet leaders' need for an environment of political tension. Their expansion, as a result, is bereft of any discernible pattern. Soviet policy, notes Pipes, focuses on "targets of opportunity"; it is "motivated less by needs than by opportunities, less by what its elite wants than what it can get."[44]

The recent pattern of Soviet foreign policy is a case in point. Despite the fact that the Kremlin leaders have had no discernible purpose in mind—the USSR clearly has more than enough territory, sufficient access to raw materials and markets, and military power adequate to protect its security—they have maintained an aggressive, forward stance since the mid-1940s. Focusing first on Eastern Europe, then on Iran, Turkey, Germany, Korea, the Middle East, with occasional forays into more distant regions (Africa, the Caribbean, India), they have continually pushed outward, testing and probing for weak spots and advantages—but exercising extreme prudence at times of international crisis.

Moscow's expansion is said to be without specific objective; it is expansion for expansion's sake. Having no particular purpose. or end in view—save the prospect of success—the Soviet leaders sought to exploit any situation or opportunity where serious resistance seemed unlikely. Where firm resistance was encountered (as in Western Europe, Korea, Cuba), they simply moved on. Held in one area, they sought opportunities in another.[45]

This analysis, though in some ways compelling, is not entirely persuasive. It has several weaknesses. First, it assumes that the basic character of Soviet foreign policy is shaped by internal factors. It is true that Soviet conduct does spring in some measure from internal sources. Such, indeed, is the main argument of this book. However, while recognizing the influence of economic, political, historical, and ideological factors, it would be a mistake to exaggerate their importance. It has also been argued that the foreign policy of the USSR is essentially reactive—that it is determined more by the challenges and opportunities presented by the international environment than by domestic imperatives. It would not be unreasonable to suggest, for example, that the expansion of Soviet influence in Eastern Europe in the 1944–1948 period was related more to anxieties regarding the dangers that the West, particularly a revived Germany, might again pose for Soviet security than to internal political requirements.

It may be that the anxieties of a particular leadership will encourage efforts to foster a climate of international tension. This was clearly true of the post-1945 period. However, the USSR's behavior at this time seems to have been more a function of the troubled personality of Stalin (to whose pathological insecurities even his daughter, Svetlana, has testified)[46] than a necessary product of the Soviet political system *per se*. Subsequent Kremlin rulers—from Malenkov through Brezhnev—have apparently felt more secure. They clearly have been less dependent on a "besieged fortress" environment and have generally sought to reduce (or at least control) world tensions. This has been the thrust of the Soviet policy of peaceful coexistence—now almost two decades old—despite possible damage to "system needs."

Furthermore, the "purposeless expansion" which some analysts see in Soviet behavior may be understood in various ways. The Kremlin's current foreign policy posture and its deepening international involvements and commitments in the Middle East, South Asia, and the Caribbean (Cuba), may be an expression of the "restless ambition" of an insecure authoritarian regime. However, Moscow's assertive policies may also be interpreted in terms of the traditional drive of a very large and very strong nation for world power and prestige. Thus, while the USSR's desire for primacy and eminence may reflect deeply buried psychological and political anxieties, history teaches that nonanxious and even nonauthoritarian leaders are themselves not completely free from such ambitions.

Finally, even if we are to grant that Soviet policy is best explained primarily in terms of internal needs, the implications for Soviet policy are not quite as clear as has been suggested. While internal political needs may require a tense international atmosphere, internal *economic* needs seem to demand precisely the opposite. A leading Soviet Party official presented this argument in 1966 when he wrote:

> The resolution of many economic problems now facing our country requires a further increase in the well-being and culture of the working people, an increase in the material and cultural benefits offered them by society. Naturally it is possible, based on the revolutionary enthusiasm and high consciousness of the people and on their internationalism to conduct matters in the course of a relatively brief historical period so as not to raise the living standard but at the same time to engage in successful economic construction. But no kind of high-consciousness permits the transformation of such a situation into a permanent state. The economic laws will inevitably prove to be stronger; they will begin to take revenge, they will revenge themselves in a thousand ways, and in the end there will be a drop in labor productivity and a slowing down of economic development.[47]

Top Kremlin leaders since Khrushchev have assumed that the successful performance of the Soviet economy depends on improving per capita consumption. They are aware that these same "economic laws" may "take their revenge" on the political system as well. To the extent it was still necessary, the economic riots in Poland in December, 1970—which resulted in the burning of Communist Party headquarters in two cities

(Gdansk and Szczecin), the death of 45 persons, and the injury of over 1,000 others (according to official figures); and which led to the resignation of Wladyslaw Gomulka, long-time leader of the Polish Communist Party—convinced the Kremlin that the viability of the Soviet system depends ultimately upon a steady increase in the living standards of the Soviet population. Thus, though détente may be counter-productive in one sense—in that it undermines the Cold War atmosphere on which insecure Party officials depend—an improvement in relations with the West which results in massive financial and technological assistance and gives a significant boost to the troubled Soviet economy may help strengthen "party/people relations." Détente, in this sense, helps reinforce the "stability conditions" of the Party regime.

Thus, to the extent that "internal needs" are the mainsprings of policy, they would seem to have contradictory implications for Soviet external behavior. It is clear, however, that abandonment of the Cold War posture and adoption of the relatively benign doctrine of peaceful coexistence has complicated the regime's internal political situation. The established system of Party rule clearly functions best during periods of tension, crises, and threats. Détente, on the other hand, is more conducive to internal relaxation. In an era of international cooperation and accommodation, the need for eternal vigilance seems less compelling.

In order to shore up its domestic position, the Kremlin's strategy has been to insist that there is no "peaceful coexistence" in the sphere of ideology. In fact, an increasingly intense struggle between the two systems is now said to be taking place on the ideological plane. As Politburo chief Brezhnev declared shortly after the first Nixon visit to the USSR, the policy of détente does not "signify the possibility of relaxing the ideological struggle. On the contrary, we must be prepared for this struggle to be intensified, for it is to become an increasingly crucial form of the confrontation of the two social systems."[48] Vigilance, is ever more necessary. Chief Party ideologist Mikhail Suslov put the matter bluntly when he declared:

> ... we must permit no weakening of any sort in the struggle against reactionary bourgeois ideology. With the changes in the world situation that favor socialism, the hopelessness of any attempts to bring military, economic or political pressure to bear on the Soviet Union or the socialist commonwealth as a whole becomes more and more obvious. This being the case, the struggle becomes particularly acute in the area of ideology, an area in which there is not and cannot be peaceful coexistence between socialism and capitalism.[49]

Détente, apparently, tends to heighten the domestic ideological struggle. If the capitalist states are no longer the hated bogey men, there is nothing—save doctrine—to justify the Party's system of rule. Once again, in time of uncertainty, ideology is called upon to reinforce the Soviet regime.

The psychological difficulties which could result from détente were alluded to Army General A. Yepishev, chief of the Main Political

Directorate of the Red Army when he warned that "détente must not give rise to elements of pacifism and complacency and the advocacy of non-violence in class relations."[50] An ideological functionary writing in a Polish Army journal spelled out the apprehensions underlying the leadership's worries.

> The climate of international relations necessary for our offensive in favor of a détente may generate trends toward demobilization inside the country, (particularly in the ideological sphere); it may contribute to the emergence of illusions about the possibility of permanent and all-embracing agreements between the two systems, about the disappearance of "political and social differences" between them. It may make for a "softening" of attitudes, a weakening of social vigilance vis-à-vis imperialism.[51]

Détente, it is feared, will encourage trends toward ideological and eventually political "demobilization."

Thus, to preserve the venerable methods of Party rule—censorship, police controls, arbitrary arrests, persecution of dissidents, restriction on travel and on foreign contacts—the Kremlin authorities have refurbished the slogan of "ideological struggle." This is precisely the leadership's justification for its recent tightening of ideological and political controls. It remains a matter of urgency, declares a Pravda editorial, to struggle against "certain immature people" who "still fall under the influence of bourgeois propaganda and are provoked into antisocial actions."[52] To discourage Jews, Ukrainians, other ethnic minorities, writers, and scientists who have been openly advocating changes in Party policies, the Committee on State Security (the KGB), the Soviet secret police have harassed and in several instances have arrested such nonconformist elements.[53] The danger of "subversive" threats from the West is thus used to justify vigilance against unorthodox ideas from within.

The Kremlin is seeking to contain the effects of détente at the Soviet border. Whether they will be able to insulate Soviet society permanently from the warm winds of peaceful coexistence is, however, open to question. In a more relaxed international atmosphere, the justification for continued repressive policies is increasingly strained. Furthermore, recent waves of nonofficial political activity—from the publication of underground (samizdat) literature to the demands of Soviet Jews to be allowed to emigrate to Israel—indicate that the traditional techniques of dictatorial control are not working with their usual efficiency. In such times of "disorder" (or, even "anarchy"?), nervous Party officials see what Gerschenckron called the "stability conditions" of Soviet rule to be in jeopardy. The campaign for vigilance against "contamination by bourgeois ideology" will undoubtedly continue as détente develops.

While internal political dynamics may not have prevented a rapprochement with the West, it would be an error to exclude them from consideration completely. Soviet–American relations, it should be remembered, have long been the prisoner of the Party oligarchs' political needs. The Kremlin's dependence on Marxist–Leninist doctrines and on the appearance (if not the reality) of continued international tension makes the United States, as the world's leading capitalist power, Moscow's "indispensable enemy." Such shibboleths have undoubtedly been an obstacle to the recent improvement in relations between the Kremlin and the White House. (It has taken two critical problems—severe economic difficulties and a fundamental and apparently worsening dispute with China—to stir Moscow from its traditional posture. And, as we shall see, some Party leaders have opposed any such changes.)

Whatever the initial inspiration, the thaw in Soviet–American relations will probably be of a limited character. A regime grounded on the myth of a "war-mongering imperialism" bent on annihilating "the gains of socialism" in the USSR cannot embrace the leader of the imperialist world too closely. Furthermore, residues of old attitudes and suspicions remain. While the principle of international trade and cooperation is being celebrated in the official press, the Kremlin has been reluctant to tell the Soviet people that enormous supplies of grain were purchased from the United States in 1972. (Mention of wheat imports from this country has been made by some public lecturers but not by the Soviet press.) Furthermore, although the regime has encouraged speculation about vast, long-term (twenty to thirty year) agreements to promote development of Siberian resources, especially natural gas, Western specialists were only reluctantly permitted to examine the Soviet fields. Fear of foreign espionage persists.

A basic policy decision has been made to turn westward, especially to the United States, for the new technology and capital needed to modernize the Soviet economy. However, traditional secretiveness and apprehension of the "capitalist" world continues. Moreover, dependence on Western assistance raises important questions about the domestic claims of the regime. For example, a Soviet television viewer has asked, "Why must we suddenly be dependent on the Americans after all these years?" Having traditionally boasted that everything was invented in Russia and that there was nothing to be learned from the decadent West, Soviet officials are hard-pressed for an answer. (The usual reply is, "We have some things the capitalists can use and they have some things that we can use."[54]) Given the persistence of such attitudes and the Kremlin's dependence on the ideological cant of continuing "struggle" between "socialism" and "capitalism," a broad scale Soviet–American accommodation seems unlikely—unless or until the Soviet leaders substantially overcome the psychological uncertainties of their system of rule. Only then will a full relaxation of ideological controls be conceivable.

A "special relationship"

What we have termed "system need" has had a much more profound influence on relations between the states of the Communist world. These relationships are affected by the specific character of the Communist Party regimes. The authority of all Party leaders, as we saw earlier, is based on their claims to be the executors of a universally valid "scientific" creed. Their confidence in their own legitimacy and their survival as rulers depend upon the widespread acceptance of the leadership's claim that the principles of Marxism–Leninism are indeed "correct" and that they are being properly interpreted and applied.

When the USSR was the only Communist state and, in the early post-World War II period, when it was the dominant nation in the "socialist" camp, Moscow was the recognized authority and sole source of interpretation of Marxist–Leninist doctrine. However, in the late 1940s and especially in the mid-late 1950s, after Peking's relations with the Kremlin worsened, Soviet primacy and doctrinal authority came under increasing attack. Since they were all equally "ideocracies," each regime—the Yugoslav, the Chinese, as well as the Soviet—sought to demonstrate that their policies and institutions were "legitimate"—that they were based on a "correct" interpretation of Marxism–Leninism. Convinced that Marxism–Leninism is the one "true" faith, each believed that there could be only one "true" doctrine—their own.

Each national Party sought to legitimize its policies by appealing to Party dogma. Such differences as occurred between them, therefore, became not simply disagreements on policy or differences in national interests but conflicts of Party principles. Thus, political disagreements were elevated into intense ideological conflict. Mutual accommodation became much more difficult. "In doctrinal conflict, . . . all claims tend to be absolute and cumulative—disagreement breeds hostility, hostility breeds suspicion of deviation, deviation breeds charges of heresy."[55]

This pattern has been especially characteristic of the Sino-Soviet dispute. As the conflict between the two largest powers in the Communist world became serious in the mid-1950s, each side began to insist that its policies were more Marxist–Leninist than the others'. And, as Heldman has observed, the attack of each upon "the truth or reality" of the other system's ideology "constitutes or is at least perceived . . . as constituting an attack upon his legitimacy. . . ."[56] Thus, when economic difficulties prevented the USSR from providing China with the funds needed for its industrialization drive, the Chinese leader Mao Tse-tung launched his famous Great Leap Forward of 1958. In announcing this policy, however, Mao declared not only that China would industrialize using its own resources, but that the methods it would adopt, especially the introduction of the People's Communes, were a shortcut to a "higher stage" of socialism.

This announcement was construed in Moscow not only as an attack on the USSR's traditional claim to ideological leadership in the Communist world but, equally important, as an oblique criticism of existing Kremlin policy. There was only one right way, in the Soviet view, one Marxist–Leninist way to industrialize, and that was the Soviet way. Any deviation, any attempt to introduce major innovation, implied that the Kremlin rulers were ideologically wrong.

Thus, internal developments within other Communist countries feed back into the Soviet Union, especially when they deviate from Soviet practice. Each ideological assertion in support of innovative programs becomes a threat. ". . . Though initially designed to engender domestic compliance and support for the commune program," Mao's justifications "challenged the Soviet Union's validity and legitimacy both internally and internationally in such a way as to cast doubt on Soviet experience as correct or relevant, efficient or effective."[57]

Common adherence to Marxist–Leninist doctrines elevates political differences into ideological conflicts which, as a result, become much more difficult to resolve. Each regime claims that "truth" is on its side and that the position of the other is doctrinally in error and, therefore, unworthy of support. There is considerable truth in *Pravda*'s claim that, according to Peking, "Everyone who does not agree with Mao Tse-tung is imperiously excommunicated from Marxism–Leninism, the revolution and socialism and is declared an enemy."[58] The Kremlin takes much the same position regarding critics of its policies, domestic and foreign.

There are other problems which irritate Sino-Soviet relations. Interests and policies clash on a variety of both domestic and foreign policy issues. Moscow and Peking are rivals for influence in the international Communist movement. They have had important differences on various political problems—de-Stalinization in the USSR, Middle Eastern diplomacy, Soviet economic assistance, the Taiwan Straits crisis, Soviet–American relations, Bangladesh, and many others. In addition to policy differences, two other factors influence and aggravate Sino-Soviet relations—geography and history. China and Russia share the longest common frontier in the world—over 4000 miles in length. Furthermore, according to Chinese claims, the USSR occupies vast territories forcibly annexed by "unequal treaties" that Tsarist Russia imposed on China in the nineteenth century. The land involved has been estimated to include about 1.5 million square kilometers of territory in Soviet Central Asian and Far Eastern provinces. According to a 1964 statement by Chairman Mao, China has "not yet presented its account" for these lands. Peking thus remains a potential threat to Soviet territorial security.

The Kremlin's fear of China is also racial. Russia's experience 700 years ago at the hands of Genghis Khan and his successors—which led to 250 years under what Soviet history books refer to as the "Mongol–Tatar Yoke"—has bred in the Russian psyche a deep fear and suspicion of the "danger from the East." The startling thing about the cries of "Yellow Peril" emanating from Moscow a few years ago is that this "scare" campaign apparently sparked a genuine response among the Russian people. The vandalism and the uncontrolled behavior of the Red Guard during the Cultural Revolution and the shedding of Russian blood on the Ussuri by the Chinese in 1969 convinced many Russians that Mao was a latter-day Genghis Khan. The Red Guard, according to an *Izvestia* correspondent, "In an impotent rage . . . threatened to pull out the entrails of the Soviet people, burn them and scatter the ashes, and to wipe the Soviet Union from the face of the earth."[59] The Soviet poet Andrei Voznesensky captured this fear in his 1967 "Prologue to a Poem" where he warned that the Cultural Revolution threatened to destroy all of civilization.

Will the astronauts who fly to Mars tomorrow
Return the next day to the era of cattle-breeding feudalism?

Will Shakespeare be forced to make public confessions of ignorance of
"isms"?

Will Stravinsky be dragged through warring streets
With a garbage pail on his grey head?

"Why all the centuries of history," he asks, "if it's to be back on all fours?" Leaving no room for doubt as to the source of this degeneration, he blames all on Chairman Mao.

The barn rats chew at Marx,
Pull down the Comparty [Communist Party], thirst for a hogparty.
Genghishogism swells like dough rising. . . .[60]

The fear of oriental barbarism returning is never very far beneath the surface.

Though the origins and sources of the Sino-Soviet conflict are to be found in the conflicting interests and values of their national leaderships, a common ideological heritage has magnified the divergences between the two Communist powers. The stakes are extremely high at this level because they involve questions of political power and, perhaps, domestic political stability. To the extent that Peking can effectively argue (as they have tried) that the Soviet state has been captured by the "bourgeoisie," the revolutionary respectability and prestige of the Kremlin will decline and its political strength will be diminished in Communist and "progressive" circles around the globe.

More important (though considerably less likely) is the fact that Mao's criticisms of Soviet policies might find support within the ranks of the Soviet Communist Party, even among the top Soviet leadership. (Such was briefly the case until Molotov was removed in mid-1957.) Here, again, the Chinese could undercut the political authority of the Kremlin leadership, this time within the Soviet Communist Party itself. Ideologically based criticisms, therefore, may be (and, in fact, have been) a stimulus to factionalism within the Soviet Communist Party. To our knowledge, no Western sources have such potential for influence within the Kremlin.

Thus in a sense, Communist China represents a threat to the USSR largely because she is Communist—and is challenging the revolutionary authority of the Soviet leaders abroad and at home—in other Communist states, among the leftist-oriented regimes and movements in the Third World, in the world Communist movement and possibly in the CPSU itself.

Ideological disagreements among socialist states are of the greatest importance. What look like religious disputations over esoteric doctrines are actually powerful political struggles between Communist nations. The very survival of these regimes may be at stake. It is little wonder that the Soviet leadership is constantly on the lookout for "ideological subversion" from within the Communist system. They are "preoccupied with heresy," as Herbert Dinerstein notes, "since it challenges their justification for being."[61] Doctrinal deviation not only threatens the legitimacy of the regime but challenges the specific features of Soviet Party rule. Such innovations are also—and properly—seen as threats. Thus, when Alexander Dubcek attempted to create a "socialism with a human face" in Czechoslovakia in 1968 by introducing dramatic political reforms, Moscow reacted sharply. Dubcek's reforms were considered heretical. While still proclaiming loyalty to Communist doctrinal principles, the reformers in Prague attempted to reduce Communist Party controls in various spheres, especially in the economy. They were seeking to democratize the Communist Party internally by allowing open criticism of Party policy and choices among candidates for election to leading Party posts. To make matters worse, from the Kremlin's point of view, censorship was ended and political activity by non-Party groups was permitted.

For the orthodox leaders in Moscow, Prague was the scene of a tumult and disorder hitherto unknown under Communist rule. Not only was Dubcek suggesting that the Soviet political system was seriously deficient—if he sought to create "socialism with a human face" in Czechoslovakia, the face of socialism in the USSR was obviously something less than human[62]—but political life in Prague seemed to be veering out of control. Debate was open and intense, political demonstrations were spontaneous and undisciplined, and there was considerable disunity within the ranks of the Czechoslovak Communist Party. The black flag of anarchy seemed to have replaced Communism's red banner. To stem the onrushing tide of chaos and disorder, and to protect the "achievements of socialism" in Czechoslovakia from "counterrevolutionary forces" and "hostile foreign influences," a Soviet-led army of 500,000 Warsaw Pact troops invaded. The Soviet Politburo ordered the invasion to restore Marxist–Leninist law and order. In order to preserve "socialism" in Czechoslovakia, it was essential to reestablish Party controls. Under the watchful eye and guidance of Soviet occupation authorities, "democratic centralism" was restored to the Czechoslovak Communist Party. "Discipline" and "unity" replaced the untidiness of open discussion and dissenting opinion. "Erroneous" views were denied a forum. Above all, "the leading role of the Party" was again secured, as political control of the press, television, the universities, and political and social organizations was reasserted.

Moscow acted with such alacrity (and disrupted important negotiations with the United States) because, in the view of the Soviet leadership, the issues involved were of the gravest seriousness. The Kremlin deemed it urgent to act, and to act decisively, not only to protect Czechoslovakia from the danger of anarchy and "counterrevolution" (which, in the eyes of some, would lead to a restoration of "bourgeois" political rule), but, more importantly, to prevent the spread to the Dubcek heresy to other countries of Eastern Europe and especially to the

USSR itself. The Kremlin authorities knew that, despite Dubcek's disclaimers (he insisted throughout 1968 that his policies were relevant (only to Czechoslovakia), the political reforms being attempted in Prague would evoke sympathetic reverberations within the Soviet Union. They obviously feared that if the Czechoslovak Communist Party could end censorship, allow free speech, permit real choices during elections, and allow non-Party political groups to engage in political activity, Soviet citizens and possibly even Party members would ask why the Kremlin Party leaders could not consider adopting similar policies.[63] To "stop the rot" before it spread, the Politburo approved armed intervention. The Dubcek heresy was exorcised, the practices of "anarcho-liberalism" condemned, and Marxist–Leninist methods of rule restored.

The "ideocratic" character of authority in these states, therefore, greatly affects relations among Communist Party regimes. Because each side continually needs to justify its domestic rule ideologically, doctrine remains a powerful influence on their relations. However, as Herbert Dinerstein has suggested, "A case exists for the proposition that ideology is the solvent of alliances, not the cement."[64] This generalization clearly applies to the once vaunted (and much feared) "Moscow–Peking axis" and to relations between the Czechoslovak and Soviet members of the Warsaw Pact Treaty Organization. Furthermore, as a result of their common doctrinal basis, relations among Communist states belong somewhere "in the twilight zone," in Marshall Shulman's phrase, between domestic and foreign policy. The Soviet leaders tend to regard political life in other Communist countries as more or less part of the Soviet political system —which, in a sense, they are. As we have seen, major reforms anywhere in the Communist world threaten to feed back into the USSR itself. As a result, relations with other Party regimes tend to become part of—or at least greatly influence—Soviet domestic policy as much as they do foreign policy. In this sense, intra-Communist relations reflect a "special relationship."[65]

Here, too, the trend toward détente has taken its toll. In the past, to keep the Communist states (the so-called socialist commonwealth) together ideologically and politically, the Kremlin continually emphasized the danger of international conflict and exaggerated the menace of imperialist aggression. Now that major agreements have been signed both with the West German "revanchist" forces and with the American organizers of the "aggressive NATO bloc," the threat hardly appears creditable. The traditional rationale for tightly knit socialist unity is no longer very persuasive.

Concerned that their alliance system might disintegrate in the new international environment, the Soviet leaders continually warn their European comrades about the dangers of subversion "from within." Having been deterred by the defensive might of the USSR from attacking the socialist camp, as Suslov noted earlier, imperialism seeks to employ new, more subtle methods to achieve its purposes. It now places greater stress on the ideological struggle and seeks to introduce bourgeois, nationalist, non-Marxist notions into Eastern Europe. It hopes, thereby, to undermine the foundations of Marxist–Leninist rule within these countries and to incite artificial conflicts between them and the Soviet Union. Such subversive influences, it is said, played a significant role in Czechoslovakia in 1968. In order to protect the socialist commonwealth from internal erosion and splintering, Party rule and close ties with Moscow must be preserved.

While eager to maintain controls over the basic trend of developments, the Kremlin may be modifying its traditional posture. The Soviet authorities seem to be increasingly tolerant of programmatic experimentation and policy variances in Eastern Europe. Hungary, for example, has introduced a series of reforms which, by Soviet standards, has created a decentralized and profit-oriented economic system. Furthermore, Western media and cultural influences are increasingly present in Eastern Europe as are Western consumer goods and investment funds. There is also greater tolerance of religion, political cabarets, and critical sociological inquiry probing beneath the clichés of Party rule. While the pattern varies—with Hungary and Poland the most open and experimental, Bulgaria the least, and with East Germany, Rumania and Czechoslovakia somewhere in between—the differences in the system of Party rule between Eastern Europe and the USSR are quite marked.[66]

Moscow confronts a number of dilemmas in its policy toward Eastern Europe: fearing that insistence on strict imitation of Soviet practices will tend to aggravate conditions in these countries and possibly result in internal explosions—as in Poland (1970)—the Kremlin has allowed the East European Communist regimes greater internal flexibility to deal with their own problems. At the same time, however, the Soviet leaders are apprehensive that permitting increased domestic autonomy will increase the risk of disrupting Communist political controls—as in Czechoslovakia (1968). The Kremlin today is trying to walk a tightrope between "Poland" and "Czechoslovakia," that is to say, it is allowing each Communist government to make more decisions for itself without, however, permitting political or ideological ties to become too loose. Should this policy be successful, the Soviet authorities will still face the difficult problem of isolating their own population from developments in Eastern Europe. Given much greater contact with the peoples of this region and the special ideological kinship referred to earlier, Moscow will undoubtedly face considerable difficulty in stopping word of the East European variations on the Marxist–Leninist theme from reaching the USSR. The Soviet leaders clearly expect to be able to control and largely neutralize the effects of such "feedback." Whether they will be successful is far from clear.

Notes

[1] See his *The Soviet Union, 1922–1962, op. cit.*, p. 441.
[2] See Leonard Schapiro, *The Origin of the Communist Autocracy.* (Cambridge, Mass: Harvard University Press, 1956).
[3] Peter B. Reddaway, "Aspects of Ideological Belief in the Soviet Union," *Soviet Studies*, Vol. XVII, No. 4 (April, 1966), p. 381.

[4]*Pravda*, March 10, 1963; quoted in *ibid.*, p. 476.

[5]Testimony of Richard Pipes, "The Limitation of Strategic Arms. . . ." *op. cit.*, p. 26. This dread of chaos helps explain why many intelligent people in the USSR remain politically apathetic. Thus, in justifying his general indifference to the goings on in the Kremlin, a writer-friend commented to Arthur Miller, the American playwright: "We don't bother with what happens there. They know what they are doing." The willingness to tolerate arbitarary power which this statement expresses, writes Miller, reflects Russia's classical fear of disorder and need for strong leadership. "It was as though there were an anarchy at the center of their being which, if left to itself, would expand into a demoralization of all order." Inge Morath and Arthur Miller, *In Russia* (New York: The Viking Press, 1969), p. 11.

[6]Khrushchev's 1958 statement can be found in Erich Goldhagen, "The Glorious Future: Realities and Chimeras," in Abraham Brumberg, ed., *Russia Under Khrushchev* (New York: Frederick A. Praeger, 1962), p. 626. His latter remarks are cited in Allen Kassof, "The Administered Society: Totalitarianism Without Terror," *World Politics*, Vol. XVI, No. 4 (July, 1964), p. 570). The regime's recent stress on consumer goods production may reflect its agreement with the prediction of a dissident Russian historian who foresees that a slowdown in the improvement of living standards will "arouse such explosions of anger, mixed with violence, as were never thought possible." Andrei Amalrik, *Will the Soviet Union Survive Until 1984?* (New York: Harper and Row, 1970), p. 33. As supporting evidence, Amalrik reminds us that several hundred people were shot in a "hunger riot" in the southern Soviet city of Novocherkassk in 1962.

[7]Zygmunt Bauman, "Twenty Years After: The Crisis of Soviet-Type Systems," *Problems of Communism*, Vol,. XX, No. 6 (November-December, 1971), pp. 45–53.

[8]As Herbert Dinerstein has noted, "the political base of the most powerful leader or leaders is in constant motion. . . ." *Fifty Years of Soviet Foreign Policy, op. cit.*, p. 34.

[9]"The Stability of Dictatorships," in *Continuity in History and Other Essays* (Cambridge: The Belknap Press, 1968), p. 314.

[10](A. Tertz) A. Sinyavsky, "On Socialist Realism," *Dissent* (Winter, 1960), p. 45.

[11]Testimony of Richard Pipes, "The Limitations of Strategic Arms. . . ." *op. cit.*, p. 21.

[12]*Pravda*, June 11, 1971; quoted in *CDSP*, Vol. XXIII, No. 24 (July 13, 1971), p. 5.

[13]"Soviet Union," in James S. Coleman, ed., *Education and Political Development* (Princeton: Princeton University Press, 1965), p. 241.

[14]M. Suslov, "Leninism and the Revolutionary Transformation of the World," *op. cit.*, p. 21.

[15]On the general problem of authority and ideology, see Alfred G. Meyer's perceptive discussions in his "Authority in Communist Political Systems," in Lewis J. Edinger, ed., *Political Leadership in Industrialized Societies* (New York: John Wiley and Sons, 1967), pp. 84–107 and "The Function of Ideology in the Soviet Political System," *Soviet Studies*, Vol. XVII, No. 3 (January, 1966), 273–285.

[16]*Moscow Radio*, April 10, 1958; quoted in *Soviet World Outlook*, Department of State Publication 6836 (Washington, D.C.: Government Printing Office, 1959), p. 5.

[17]Quoted in Robert F. Byrnes, *Eastern Europe: The Unstable Element in the Soviet Empire*. Memorandum Prepared at the Request of the Subcommittee on National Security and International Operations of the Committee on Government Operations, United States Senate (Washington, D.C.: Government Printing Office, 1970), p. 6.

[18]"On Dictatorship," *The New York Review of Books* (June 19, 1969), p. 4.

[19]Fischer, *Russia's Road From Peace to War, op. cit.*, p. 183.

[20]Quoted in *ibid.*, p. 172. Though Anglo–Soviet relations at that time were strained, there was, as Chicherin and others then knew, little real substance to the "war scare."

[21]Demaitre, *op. cit.*, p. 13.

[22]Kennan, *Memoirs, op. cit.*, p. 550.

[23]*The First Circle* (New York: Harper and Row, 1968), p. 305.

[24]Elsa Brandstrom, *Among Prisoners of War in Russia and Siberia* (London: Hutchinson and Co., Ltd., 1929), pp. 234–240.

[25]This position was apparently held by some ranking Party leaders. The argument, Stalin replied, was confused. Encirclement was a political not a geographical notion; the danger to Soviet security would thus remain as long as capitalism existed in the major capitalist countries. See Tucker, *The Soviet Political Mind, op. cit.*, pp. 27–28.

[26]*Moscow Radio*, March 27, 1958; quoted in *Soviet World Outlook, op. cit.*, p. 8.

[27]Frederick C. Barghoorn, "The Security Police," H. Gordon Skilling and Franklyn Griffiths, eds., *Interest Groups in Soviet Politics* (Princeton, N.J.: Princeton University Press, 1971), p. 93.

[28]Ulam, *Expansion and Coexistence, op. cit.*, p. 607.

[29]Not since the 1920s has the USSR been witness to public sit-ins and mass protest visits to Party and government offices by Soviet citizens as it did in the early 1970s when Jews from various parts of the country began to demand the right to emigrate freely. Neither has it seen the birth of opposition groups known collectively as "The Democratic Movement," nor the flowering of an underground [*samizdat*] press. Though some interpret this startling development as part of "liberalization" process, a gradual widening of the area of freedom, others, such as the dissident Soviet historian Andrei Amalrik, view it as reflecting "the growing decrepitude of the regime." "The regime is simply growing old and can no longer suppress everyone and everything with the same strength and vigor as before. . . ." Amalrik, *op. cit.*, p. 30.

[30]"Speech by Comrade V. V. Grishin, First Secretary of the Moscow City Party Committee," *Pravda*, April 1, 1971; reprinted in *CDSP*, Vol. XXIII, No. 14 (May 4, 1971), p. 17.

[31]This quotation appeared in an article in *Komsomolskaya Pravda*, July 22, 1967, with the curiously revealing title "They Are Afraid," reprinted in *ibid.*, Vol. XIX, No. 29 (August 9, 1967), p. 4. (Italics added.)

[32]"Speech by Comrade L. I. Brezhnev at 19th Conference of Moscow City Party Organization, March 29, 1968," *Pravda*, March 30, 1968; reprinted in *ibid.*, Vol. XX, No. 13 (April 17, 1968), pp. 6, 3.

[33]*Ibid.*, p. 6. As part of its appeal for "eternal and constant vigilance," the Soviet press has warned against "chatterboxes" who are said to reveal valuable secrets to foreign espionage. "The wartime aphorism 'Loose talk helps the enemy,' " *Nedelya* reminds its readers, "retains its importance in our divided world." Cited in *ibid.*, Vol. XXII, No. 48 (December 29, 1970), p. 20.

[34]December 17, 1970; reprinted in *ibid.*, Vol. XXII, No. 49 (January 5, 1971) p. 18.

[35]"Letter of a Soviet Writer," *The New York Times*, November 15, 1969. Solzhenitsyn had been denounced because his novels *The First Circle* and *Cancer Ward* (though banned in the Soviet Union) had been printed abroad and used to criticize the Soviet system. The conservative writer Mikhail Sholokhov clearly had Solzhenitsyn in mind when he denounced "those who eat Soviet bread but who want to serve Western bourgeois masters and send their works there through secret channels. Soviet men of letters want to get rid of them." Quoted in *ibid.*, November 28, 1969.

[36]"Letter of A. D. Sakharov. . . ." *op. cit.*, pp. 112–113. The Soviet writer Anatoly Kuznetsov recounts that in the reissue of a book written earlier, Boris

Polevoi cut out some material which had quoted Göring on the Nazi policy in Czechoslovakia in 1939 as follows: "Arrest the Government, compromise the others. Form another government. Then have them issue a program and make some declaration. And keep tanks at the crossroads." Explaining his decision, Polevoi tacitly recognized that Göring's description also applied to the recent Soviet policy in Czechoslovakia. "Today," he observed, "that [quote] would be a trump card in the hands of our enemies. We mustn't put cards in the enemy's hands, so we have to cut things out of history. And it's right to do it. We must make use of such factors as suit our purposes and not the enemy's." Quoted in *The New York Times*, August 21, 1969.

[37]The same concern for internal cohesion helps explain the Kremlin's resistance to economic reforms. Fearful that the political sphere could not be insulated from fundamental changes in the economy, the regime opposes any significant decentralization of economic decisionmaking. The adoption of a meaningful market mechanism to replace the present system of central planning—the key demand of the reformers—can only lead, it is charged, to "*anarcho*[!]-syndicalism." The fear of internal disintegration is still alive. See Gregory Grossman, "The Solidary Society: A Philosophical Issue in Communist Economic Reforms," in Gregory Grossman, ed., *Essays in Socialism and Planning in Honor of Carl Landauer* (Englewood Cliffs, New Jersey: Prentice-Hall, Inc., 1970), pp. 184–211.

[38]"Hope and Hopelessness," *Survey*, Vol. XVII, No. 3 (80), (Summer, 1971), p. 40. Even democratic governments tend toward authoritarian practices (restraint on freedom of the press, on freedom of movement and speech, on economic and political activities) in time of perceived national emergency. It is in this sense, as Kolakowski notes, that wars are "a grave for democracy."

[39]Tucker, *op. cit.*, p. 71.

[40]Quoted in *ibid.*, pp. 71–72. The reverse argument—that it was the hostility of Russia's external environment rather than "internal political needs" which fostered a concern with centralization of power and militarization of Russian society—is the more traditional one. (See Chapter Three above.)

[41]"Testimony of Richard Pipes," *op. cit.*, pp. 39–40, 20, 24.

[42]*Ibid.*, pp. 23–24.

[43]See page 44, this text.

[44]"Testimony of Richard Pipes," *op. cit.*, p. 24. Some critical observers have likened the Soviet Union in its foreign relations to a burglar who will "try every door in the house, enter all the rooms which are not locked, and when they come to one that is barred, if they are unsuccessful in breaking through it, they will withdraw and invite you to dine genially that same evening." Winston Churchill, quoted in Ulam, *Expansion and Coexistence, op. cit.*, p. 424.

[45]As Pipes, Bolsover, Lewis and numerous others have noted, nineteenth century Tsarist expansion revealed a similar "pendulum" effect. Concentrating on four major areas—Europe, the Near East, Central Asia and the Far East—the Tsars would tend to focus on one particular region at a time until, like the current regime, formidable obstacles forced them to change the focus of their attention.

[46]Alliluyeva, *op. cit.*, pp. 181–182, 394. Stalin, according to Svetlana, was obsessed by a need to protect his authority. "With cold calculation he had cemented his own power, afraid of losing it more than anything else in the world." *Ibid.*, pp. 181–182.

[47]Georgi Arbatov, "The Building of Socialism in the USSR and the World Revolutionary Process," *Pravda*, September 7, 1966; quoted in D. Bruce Jackson, *Castro, The Kremlin and Communism in Latin America* (Baltimore: The Johns Hopkins Press, 1969), p. 140.

[48]"In a Fraternal Cordial Atmosphere," *Pravda*, June 28, 1972; translated in *CDSP*, Vol. XXIV, No. 27 (August 2, 1972), p. 12.

[49]"Serve the Cause of the Party and the People," *Pravda*, June 21, 1972; translated in *CDSP*, Vol. XXIV, No. 25 (July 17, 1972), p. 19. Translation

copyright 1974 by the Current Digest of the Soviet Press; published weekly at The Ohio State University by the American Association for the Advancement of Slavic Studies; reprint by permission.

[50]*Krasnaya Zvezda*, February 1, 1974, p. 2.

[51]*Wojsko Ludowe* (May 5, 1972); quoted in Leopold Labedz, "Shadows Over Helsinki," *Encounter*, Vol. XL, No. 6 (June, 1973), p. 84.

[52](Editorial) "Urgent Tasks in Ideological Work," *Pravda*, July 8, 1972; translated in *CDSP*, Vol. XXIV, No. 27 (August 2, 1972), p. 31.

[53]*The New York Times*, January 19, 1972; June 3, 11, 13, 1973.

[54]Theodore Shabad, "Russians Seeking Investment and Trade as Spur for Lagging Economy," *The New York Times*, June 17, 1972, Sec. 3, p. 5.

[55]Huntington and Brzezinski, *op. cit.*, p. 404.

[56]Dan C. Heldman, "The Sino-Soviet Split and Party Legitimacy," *Survey*, No. 77 (Autumn 1970), p. 52.

[57]*Ibid.*, p. 54.

[58]P. Fedoseyev, "On the Ideological and Political Essence of Maoism," *Pravda*, December 5, 1971; translated in *CDSP*, Vol. XXIII, No. 49 (January 4, 1972), p. 8.

[59]S. Yurkov, "Unwise Course," *Izvestia*, August 26, 1971; translated in *CDSP*, Vol. XXIII, No. 34 (September 1, 1971), p. 5.

[60]*Literaturnaya gazeta*, March 24, 1967; translated in *CDSP*, Vol. XIX, No. 13 (April 19, 1967), p. 17. Translation copyright 1974 by the Current Digest of the Soviet Press; published weekly at The Ohio State University by the American Association for the Advancement of Slavic Studies; reprint by permission. In a state of nationalist fervor, Voznesensky depicted Russia as the savior of the world from barbarism.

> Are we to carry the world on our backs once more?
> Time!
> Pray to Russia for her incredible destiny!
> For our selflessness, eternal, as the skies,
> All the bullets for Rome, for Vienna, sinking into us!
> Russia the savior! Whatever Batus* may come—
> Always Russia,
>   Russia again.
>   Always Russia.
>
> *Batu, grandson of Genghis Khan

[61]Herbert S. Dinerstein, "The Future of Ideology in Alliance Systems," *Journal of International Affairs*, Vol. XXV, No. 2 (1971), p. 256.

[62]This formulation, set forth originally by Zvi Y. Gitelman, is cited in *ibid.*, p. 247.

[63]Some Soviet intellectuals did see Dubcek's liberal reforms as a model that they hoped the CPSU would emulate. See, for example, Sakharov, *Progress, Coexistence and Intellectual Freedom*, *op. cit.*, p. 67.

[64]Herbert S. Dinerstein, "The Soviet Union and China," in Steven L. Spiegel and Kenneth N. Waltz, eds., *Conflict in World Politics* (Cambridge, Mass.: Winthrop Publishers, 1971), p. 78.

[65]Writing about Sino-Soviet relations, Heldman observes that "domestic needs and foreign policies constitute a 'seamless web' in which actions generated by one power demand responses by the other." Heldman, *op. cit.*, p. 53.

[66]See the excellent series of articles on Eastern Europe by Hedrick Smith, Moscow correspondent of *The New York Times*, June 10-13, 1973.

6

Soviet foreign policy formulation

The single party, by its nature, must present an apparent front of unity; and the discussions within its ranks, when they touch the raw nerve of real difference, will be conducted in secret and fought out in the dark. This constitutes a deep and genuine difference between the State of a single Party and the State of a plurality of parties. The one may seem divided, and even distracted. But the division of the one is the public and open division which leaves a central core of unity: the unity of the other is a screen which hides both the secret differences of the single party and the suppressed opinions of the dissidents.

Reflections on Government
—Ernest Barker

That we leave consideration of Soviet internal political institutions and processes for last does not imply that they are lacking in importance. Clearly, the distinctive character of domestic decisionmaking arrangements within the USSR is among the most significant determinants of policy, internal as well as external. However, given the secretive nature of Kremlin rule, our information in this area is imperfect, both regarding the precise details of Soviet political structures and their influence on the character and direction of Soviet foreign policy.

Analysis of foreign policy decisionmaking is an elusive undertaking under the best of circumstances. Much information vital to understanding the issues thoroughly is usually classified. However, the nature of the problem varies considerably from country to country. For example, analysts of American foreign policy have access to valuable materials unearthed by skeptical Congressmen and inquisitive journalists. Students of the Soviet Union are not so fortunate. Soviet newspapermen display little of the curiosity which characterize many of their American counterparts and usually limit themselves to explaining and embellishing government policy statements. Probing for weaknesses, inconsistencies, and failures of official policy is simply not part of their mission. Furthermore, Soviet policymakers are under no obligation to the Supreme Soviet (the USSR's parliament) to submit to the detailed and often dogged scrutiny of their policy decisions to which American officials are often subjected by Congressional committees.

What this suggests is that while we may know a great deal about what the Soviet government actually does in specific instances, we know rather little about the particular motivations of its leaders, about who participated in reaching the decisions, about disagreements which may have occurred among the top leaders, and about possible alternatives that may have been considered and the reasons for their rejection. With these caveats, we turn to the task of describing the basic mechanisms and processes of internal Soviet politics.

Soviet political institutions

There is a strong temptation when discussing international politics to view other nations as though they are monolithic entities. All actors on the world stage are seen as single, unified "states." This tendency is especially marked in the analysis of Soviet international behavior since the Soviet political system is dominated by the highly centralized and disciplined political apparatus of the Communist Party of the Soviet Union (CPSU). There does seem to be a far greater degree of unity of leadership opinion and greater internal domestic solidarity in support of official policy in the USSR than elsewhere. The Kremlin appears to speak with one voice, especially on questions of foreign policy; indications of internal disagreement are rare. Thus, when referring to the policies of "Moscow," of "the Soviet authorities," or of "the Kremlin," there is a strong presumption that one is speaking of a policy generally agreed upon by the leadership and accepted (however passively) by the Soviet population.

This description grossly distorts Soviet reality. While the Soviet policymaking process is indeed more centralized than most, there is considerable evidence of policy differences and conflicts within and among the groups participating in formulating decisions. However, before we seek to evaluate the politics of Soviet foreign policy decisionmaking, a word about its institutional structures.

According to the Soviet Constitution (Article 14), the *Supreme Soviet* decides governmental policy on questions of war and peace. In principle, the legislature is the supreme policymaking body in external affairs. However, as is well known, the Supreme Soviet serves less as a parliamentary organization than as a sounding board for the political leadership. Meeting for only a few days a year, its functions are necessarily very limited. The *Presidium of the Supreme Soviet,* which carries out the legislature's functions when it is not in session, also acts as the collective head of the Soviet state. As such, it performs many ceremonial functions—ratification of international treaties, appointment and recall of ambassadors, reception of foreign diplomatic representatives, and so on. In fact, these are its only foreign policy functions. The Presidium, like the Supreme Soviet itself, remains a rubber-stamp body.

Power emanates from the Communist Party. Reflecting the general pattern of policymaking in the USSR, the formulation of Soviet foreign policy is the responsibility of the Party *Politburo.* While the Supreme Soviet formally ratifies policy—usually by making and applauding speeches heralding the most recent triumphs of the USSR and by passing whatever legislation and budgets are deemed necessary—it is the Politburo that makes policy. The *Council of Ministers* (the head of the executive branch of the Soviet government) and the two main governmental agencies devoted to foreign policy—the Ministry of Foreign Affairs and the Ministry of Defense—also implement policies set by the Party leadership in the Politburo. While any governmental ministry or specialized state committee (such as the KGB) can initiate a specific policy proposal and submit it through the Council of Ministers for consideration, Party approval is needed before it can be implemented.

Soviet Foreign Minister Andrei Gromyko attested to Politburo predominance in foreign policy decisionmaking in his speech to the 24th CPSU Congress (1971). In contrast to the Politburo, which he described as being constantly concerned with matters of foreign policy, Gromyko noted that the main activity of the Supreme Soviet has been the issuance of appeals and statements on major foreign policy questions to the peoples of the world. It also supervises the work of the Foreign Affairs Committees of both houses of the parliament (which hear reports by the Foreign Minister but, according to the evidence available, have no discernible policy influence), and the activity of the Parliamentary Group, which arranges visits, talks, and exchanges with parliamentary delegations from other countries. Even the role of the Party's *Central Committee (CC),* the second highest organ of the CPSU, is a minimal one. The Foreign Minister notes, for example, that while the "plenary sessions of the Central Committee . . . have considered questions of foreign policy several times . . . ," they have, on these apparently infrequent occasions, "invariably approved the Politburo's foreign policy activity."[1] While in theory they both can modify or even reverse Politburo decisions, neither the Central Committee nor the Supreme Soviet actually play much of a role in foreign policy formulation. The Politburo sets the course of Soviet foreign policy.

The pattern of authority at the apex of the Soviet political system has changed considerably over the years. During the Stalin era, the dictator himself determined all internal and external policy. One of the distinctive features of the Stalinist system was the famous "Special Sector" of the Party's Central Committee by means of which the General Secretary directed the enormous machinery of Party and government. This "Special Sector" had a foreign section with special representatives through whom Stalin conducted Soviet foreign policy. According to a Russian emigré, "Through the Special Sector, Stalin directed the foreign Communist parties, received reports on the work of military and political services abroad, gave directions to ambassadors, guided the fifth columns . . . and so on. . . . Foreign policy was made in the Kremlin by Stalin and transmitted downward through the Special Sector."[2] By creating a mechanism to serve much like a personal secretariat, Stalin obviously sought to bypass the normal Party and governmental apparatus. He could thereby avoid the possibility of resistance to his commands, should any top bureaucratic official feel sufficiently secure to contemplate offering any.

In the last two decades, the situation at the top of the Soviet political pyramid has changed dramatically. Policy decisions are no longer unilateral. Under both Khrushchev and Brezhnev, the views of other top leaders in the Party Politburo and the Council of Ministers have been listened to. Khrushchev, it is true, often made light of the role of others. In characteristically crude fashion, he once derided the influence of his foreign minister by observing that if he were to ask Mr. Gromyko to take off his trousers and sit on a block of ice, the Foreign Minister would have to comply.[3] Nevertheless, both during Khrushchev's reign and since, the top Party leaders solicit the views of the Council of Ministers, especially the Foreign and Defense Ministers and their staffs, and also consult with professional academic specialists.

The Party's domination of the whole foreign policy scene is safeguarded by a number of mechanisms. The Central Committee *Secretariat*, the Party body which verifies fulfillment of leadership policy, maintains a special apparatus to oversee foreign policy. Its International Department, currently headed by Politburo candidate–member and Party Secretary B. N. Ponomarev, a veteran Party ideologist, is in charge of relations with Communist Parties in non-Communist countries and with supervising relations with the West and countries of the Third World. K. F. Katushev, also a member of the Central Committee, now heads up the Department for Liaison with Communist and Workers' Parties of the Socialist Countries. The primary function of Katushev's department is the development and maintenance of close ties with fraternal brethren parties in the other Communist states. Since the Communist Parties are the ruling Parties in these countries, Party-to-Party relations supervised by this Department are more important than official state-to-state relations. In this area especially the CC apparatus overshadows the respective country desks for Eastern Europe, China, and others in the Foreign Ministry. Here as elsewhere in the Soviet system, the Party commands the cooperation of the state bureaucracy. In addition, the Party Organs

Department of the Central Committee controls all personnel appointments to diplomatic posts abroad and to important positions in the foreign policy apparatus in Moscow.

The importance attached to control over foreign policy by the top leadership is also evidenced by the Kremlin's appointment priorities. The Politburo assigns its most trusted representatives to carry out its purposes in this area. For example, of the 101 heads of Soviet diplomatic missions abroad in 1972, the key positions were held by members of the Party's Central Committee; all of the ambassadors to the "socialist commonwealth" (Eastern Europe including Yugoslavia, China, Outer Mongolia, and Cuba) and to the United States, India, France, and Chile were full members of the Central Committee. Indicating a slightly lesser ranking, the Soviet ambassadors to Bulgaria, Finland, and the UAR were candidate members of the CC while those to North Korea, North Vietnam, the United Kingdom, and Italy were members of the Party's symbolically important Central Auditing Commission.[4] Similarly, the leading academic institutions in the foreign policy area are controlled by the Party. N. N. Inozemtsev, director of the Institute of World Economy and International Relations of the Soviet Academy of Sciences (of which he is a full member), is a candidate member of the CC while G. A. Arbatov, director of the recently established Institute for the Study of the USA, also of the Academy of Sciences, is a member of the Central Auditing Commission. While all of these officials are sophisticated professionals, the very high Party ranking of leading foreign policy personnel clearly indicates that primary responsibility rests with the Party rather than the Foreign Ministry or any other governmental agency.

Communist Party dominance in foreign affairs is perhaps best symbolized by the recent diplomatic activities of Leonid I. Brezhnev, its General Secretary. Brezhnev clearly has been the moving force behind the Party's "Peace Program," the adoption of which he secured at the 24th Party Congress in March, 1971. Not only did he personally receive, in 1971 and 1972, Georges Pompidou, President of France, Willy Brandt, Chancellor of West Germany, and Richard Nixon, President of the United States, but, in 1973, he led Soviet delegations on much publicized return visits to all of these countries. On each occasion, Brezhnev was received with the honors due a head of state, and signed major international agreements in the name of the USSR—despite the fact that he does not hold an official governmental position![5] Soviet Prime Minister (formally, Chairman of the Council of Ministers) Alexei Kosygin and Soviet President (formally, Chairman of the Presidium of the Supreme Soviet) Nikolai Podgorny have undertaken important diplomatic missions on frequent occasions. However, in the most recent period, they have been overshadowed by General Secretary Brezhnev. Symbolically as well as in reality, the Party dominates foreign policy.

Party control of this area may suggest that Party political and ideological considerations have a greater influence in matters of foreign policy than would be the case were the foreign affairs apparatus staffed by professional diplomats. Such, indeed, has been the case regarding the Communist countries. As relations with Yugoslavia, Hungary, China, Rumania, and Czechoslovakia reveal, the Soviet embassies in these countries are often involved with matters of a political and ideological character as well as with more traditional diplomatic concerns. Leaders in each of these countries—Tito, Nagy, Mao, Ceausescu, and Dubcek— have all been charged with some form of ideological deviation. It is not surprising, therefore, that the Kremlin should appoint experienced and ideologically trustworthy Party officials to deal with such problems. This appointment pattern reinforces our earlier observation that relations with other socialist nations are very closely intertwined with internal Soviet political life. As leading officials of the Soviet Party elite, these CC members bring to their embassies the Party-political and doctrinal values and objectives of the Kremlin rulers. It is precisely for such purposes that they are chosen for these diplomatic posts.

While many Soviet ambassadors, especially those to Eastern Europe, were selected because of their political skills and experience, a number of ranking Foreign Ministry officials have been appointed to important posts in the Communist Party in recognition of highly successful diplomatic careers. For example, Anatoli F. Dobrynin, USSR Ambassador to the United States since 1961, and Vasili V. Kuznetsov, First Deputy Minister of Foreign Affairs, have been named full members of the Party's Central Committee. Similarly, Soviet Foreign Minister Andrei A. Gromyko, who has been in diplomatic work since 1939—he was USSR Ambassador to Washington from 1943–1945 and permanent USSR representative on the UN Security Council from 1946–1948—was recently appointed to the Party's Politburo. Unlike the case of V. S. Tolstikov, who presumably was named Ambassador to China in 1970 because of demonstrated political competence (he was formerly head of the important Communist Party organization in Leningrad), Gromyko, Dobrynin, and Kuznetsov were elevated to very high Party positions as a result of important contributions to governmental service.[6]

This pattern is characteristic of a more general development in Soviet political life. In their efforts to govern effectively, the Party leaders have been according greater weight and authority to those groups in society which possess the knowledge and skills necessary to make the increasingly complex Soviet system work. To maintain control of this process, they have sought to assimilate the most highly trained and technically proficient representatives of all groups in Soviet life into the ranks of the Party. Leading scientists, engineers, plant managers, and government officials are, wherever possible, inducted into the CPSU. This policy, while in many ways enlightened, is not without its problems. To the extent that it is successful and that such elements are brought in and are advanced in high positions, the Party risks becoming increasingly dominated by these new groups. Thus, rather than the Party controlling society by co-opting leading elite groups, "society" may be taking over the Party which now becomes a motley array of diverse, specialized, highly trained administrators and representatives of functional and sectional interests rather than an ideologically inspired political vanguard.

This point of view has some merit. It is generally not relevant, however, when talking about the Politburo. Although many top Party leaders have a considerable degree of technical training (Brezhnev was a metallurgical engineer, Podgorny a graduate of the Kiev Technological Institute of the Food Industry), they virtually all made their real careers as Party functionaries. Nevertheless, this technical competence and experience at the very highest echelons of the Party, along with growing numbers of state administrators and specialized officials in its leadership ranks, cannot help but strengthen the more pragmatic tendencies in the formulation of policy.

The recent inclusion of the three major "national security" ministries in the ranks of the Politburo seems to have reinforced this trend. (Marshal A. A. Grechko, the Minister of Defense, and Y. A. Andropov, head of the Committee on State Security (the KGB), the Soviet secret police and intelligence agency, were elected to full membership along with Foreign Minister Gromyko in April 1973.) Their promotions suggest that traditional patterns of relations between Party and State agencies in the USSR may be undergoing change. The role of the governmental ministries has, in the past, been largely technical and advisory. Their job has been to describe a given problem, offer suggestions and advice, and discuss various alternative approaches to its solution. Their primary function has been not to recommend policy decisions but to consider how best to implement policies once they have been decided in the Politburo. Now, however, with the "national security" agencies themselves represented in the Politburo, they will actually participate in the making of policy. The role of the governmental ministries, therefore, seems to have been given somewhat greater weight.

The political significance of this development is hard to gauge. On the one hand, it seems to be a victory for the forces of moderation. Though the principle of party primacy clearly remains intact, the new Politburo will probably reflect pragmatic departmental interests more than it has in the recent past.[7] In principle, the presence of additional ministerial heads should tend to temper the influence of the Party ideologues at the very apex of the Soviet system. On the other hand, given the political orientation of the KGB and the Ministry of Defense, this change clearly does not imply a strengthening of the moderate influences in the top Party leadership. In fact, it has been speculated that the more conservative elements in the Party leadership agreed to accept Brezhnev's policy of détente only at the price of strengthening their forces in the Politburo by bringing in Grechko and Andropov. Though the trend toward pragmatism and professional competence in Party decisionmaking seems to be growing, the influence of the traditional system of conservative political control still seems well entrenched.

Though little is known about the workings of the top Party organs, we do have some information. The Ministry of Foreign Affairs, according to available evidence, reports directly to the Politburo on a regular basis. Thus, questions of foreign policy seem to be on the agenda as a matter of routine. Foreign Minister Gromyko admitted as much at the 24th Party Congress when he observed that

> ... the international situation never freezes over, and it never goes on vacation as people do, for a month or even a day, even if it has a fever. .... Every day, the Politburo deals in depth with questions of foreign policy, ensuring timeliness and foresight in the decisions it adopts.[8]

Some specialization exists in the Politburo's handling of matters of policy. Under Khrushchev, there were several "teams" within the top organ which were primarily responsible for policy in specific areas. Khrushchev tended to rely on leaders with the greatest experience to deal with specific problems.[9] Presumably, a similar pattern exists today. It would seem likely that the current foreign policy "team" consists of Brezhnev (who, as General Secretary, heads all policy "teams"), Gromyko, Marshal Grechko, Andropov, Suslov (both Andropov and Suslov have had foreign policy experience), Prime Minister Kosygin, and President Podgorny.

However, unlike Khrushchev, who tended to dominate the Politburo and often acted on his own, Brezhnev probably brings the policies evolved by his foreign policy task force before the whole Politburo for approval. The "collective" character of the current Soviet leadership was dramatically symbolized during the 1968 Czechoslovak crisis when, in the final futile efforts at negotiation, virtually the whole Politburo took part in the last minute talks with the Dubcek leadership in the Czechoslovak village, Cierna nad Tisou. More recently, however, Brezhnev seems to have become *primus inter pares*, first among equals, especially in foreign policy. Nevertheless, the tradition of broader consultation with the Politburo seems established. In an interview with a group of American journalists, Brezhnev noted that 99.99 percent of the time, the Politburo reach its decisions by unanimous agreement, after lengthy discussions. If there is not consensus, he said, the disputed issue is resolved by a small group within the Politburo.[10] The public emphasis today is on broad discussion, not one-man rule.

The ministry of foreign affairs

In the conduct of relations between the USSR and the one hundred-odd nations with which it has diplomatic ties, the major day-to-day responsibilities belong to the Ministry of Foreign Affairs. In terms of structure and organization, the Soviet Foreign Ministry is very similar to its counterparts among the other Great Powers. The headquarters staff in Moscow consists of about sixteen geographic divisions or desks that deal with specific groups of countries: the desks are the Near East, Southeast Asia,

Far East, U.S., Latin America, six separate European divisions, three African, plus two separate departments for international organizations (mainly the United Nations and its affiliated bodies) and international economic organizations. It also includes several functional divisions with responsibility for such matters as protocol, legal questions, and press relations. Relations with Communist countries are handled largely by the CC Department for Liaison with Communist and Workers' Parties of the Socialist Countries, rather than by the Foreign Ministry. Thus, this formal organizational structure is less significant for the "socialist commonwealth" than for the rest of the world.

A unique feature of the Foreign Ministry is its *collegium,* or directing staff. The collegium, chaired by the Minister, includes all Deputy Ministers and some of the more important division chiefs. It advises the Minister on policy and at the same time serves as a coordinating agency, pulling together the activities of the various divisions, planning future policy, as well as translating general policy directives into specific assignments and overseeing their implementation.[11] The collegium is unusual in that it is, in theory, entitled to disagree with the Foreign Minister and appeal his decisions to the Council of Ministers.

While this prerogative seems largely an imaginary one—since the ultimate arbiter of policy is neither the Foreign Minister nor the collegium nor even the Council of Ministers but the Politburo—the collegium mechanism does broaden and "collectivize" the base of foreign policy decisionmaking. The existence of these arrangements, according to one author, "tends to demonstrate that the Kremlin leaders are not given to hasty decisions but increasingly are relying on carefully planned policies."[12] The growing influence of academic institutions such as the Institute for the Study of the USA (ISShA) and the Institute of World Economy and International Relations (IMEMO) bears further witness to this trend. Given the extraordinary complexity of Soviet foreign relations, the Kremlin leaders seem increasingly willing to place heavy reliance on expert advice. Both the burdens of office and the fact that they are more familiar with internal political and administrative problems than with matters of foreign policy seem to have compelled the members of the Politburo to turn to specialists in the Foreign Ministry and the Academy of Sciences. The influence of foreign policy specialists clearly has been increasing. For example, G. A. Arbatov, the knowledgeable head of ISShA, was included in the official party which accompanied Brezhnev on his 1973 visit to the United States.[13]

Here, too, there are countervailing tendencies. The increasing stress on more traditional aspects of diplomacy and on professional expertise must be seen against the background of conservative Party attitudes still to be found in Party and government foreign policy institutions. This is especially true of Soviet missions abroad where political controls on diplomatic officials tend to be tight. All individuals proposed for overseas assignment must be cleared by a special Party body which probes both their suitability for foreign assignment (their ability to withstand exposure to the alien influences of foreign societies), and their political reliability. To ensure that diplomatic personnel do not waver in their commitments, each overseas mission includes a number of Party officials who guard the political orthodoxy of the embassy staff.

Besides maintaining internal security within the foreign missions —even tourist delegations abroad are under close scrutiny by Party guardians—Soviet diplomatic staffs often engage in espionage activities. According to reports by former Soviet officials, about 60 percent of the diplomatic staffs in Soviet embassies are full-time intelligence officers working for either the KGB or GRU (military intelligence). As a result of these activities, Soviet diplomats have been expelled from thirty-six countries for espionage and related activities in the past dozen years. The Soviet secret police have also been involved and exposed in political plots, as with the expulsion of five Soviet diplomats (including the Chargé d'Affaires) from Mexico in March, 1971, for recruiting Mexican students to be trained in North Korea for guerrilla warfare, and as in similar cases in the Third World (Ethiopia, Bolivia, Kenya and elsewhere). The most embarrassing of such instances came in 1961 when Soviet Ambassador Daniel Solod was expelled by the Marxist regime of Sekou Touré for interfering in the internal politics of Guinea.[14]

The need of the Party apparatus for control over "exposed" Soviet diplomatic officials abroad is not conducive to the development of normal relations with other countries. To encourage the proper atmosphere for détente, Foreign Ministry and other Soviet representatives abroad must be allowed relatively free contacts with their Western counterparts. Though this undoubtedly makes for nervousness among the Party orthodox, the leadership in recent years has openly encouraged easier relations with foreigners. At the same time, political controls remain to ensure that contamination by foreign ideas or goods does not become too serious.

The regime's continued reliance on espionage is more significant. The virtues of "peaceful coexistence," with its stress on "noninterference in the internal affairs of other states," seemed rather hollow in 1971 when the normally cautious British government felt compelled to expel 105 members of the Soviet Embassy in London for espionage activities. (A letter from Lord Douglas-Home, the British Foreign Secretary, to Soviet Foreign Minister, Andrei Gromyko, complained that "The Soviet Union conducts espionage against Great Britain on a large scale."[15]) Despite increasing reliance on competence and professionalism, the institutions of Soviet foreign policy are still influenced by traditional Bolshevik attitudes toward diplomatic relations with the capitalist world. To the extent such attitudes persist, they will inevitably act as a brake both on détente and on the more moderate trends emerging in the apparatus of Soviet foreign policy.

Power, bureaucratic politics and foreign policy

While Soviet policymakers operate in an environment very different from that prevailing in democratic societies, one quite free of the constraints and pressures built into their institutions and political culture, they are not totally free of tensions and conflicts. The tugging and pulling between what has been referred to as "moderate" and "conservative" tendencies and "ideological" and "pragmatic" orientations indicate that the Soviet political elite is far from unitary. Though policymaking in the USSR is determined by a single unit, the Politburo, decisions are made by men of varied outlooks and interests. Furthermore, the makers of policy are subject to pressures from specialized advisory groups in both Party and government offices. Thus, though it does not have to confront the diversity of views and pressures characteristic of democratic systems, the Kremlin does not always speak with a single, clear voice. In fact, there exists within the Soviet political elite a considerable range of attitudes, interests, and objectives which frequently lead to differing and sometimes conflicting positions on foreign policy.

Issues of foreign policy often become entangled in the bitter controversies and intrigues of factional politics in the USSR. As has often been noted, the Soviet political system is seized by an endemic struggle for power. There are periods of relative political stability, such as between the early 1930s and 1953 when Stalin had firm control over the machinery of power; and since 1964, when the Kremlin rulers seem to have regularized relations among themselves and created a workable "collective leadership." Still, political authority in the Soviet system is never secure. In the absence of any institutionalized mechanism for leadership selection, it is fully conceivable that Brezhnev will suddenly find himself removed from office by a political conspiracy of his former Politburo associates. Such was the fate of Khrushchev in 1964.

To protect against such a possibility, the incumbent leader must strive constantly to secure his position against possible opponents. This concern for power invariably requires a concern for policy because the successes and failures of Brezhnev's decisions and the political implications of his policy choices—the supporters he attracts and the enemies he makes—may well determine his tenure in office. Khrushchev was ousted both because of policy setbacks (the missile crisis, China, agriculture) and because he had managed to offend nearly everyone in the Kremlin leadership by his decidedly brusque and, according to some, high-handed political style. Soviet politicians must seek winning issues and strive to maintain effective political coalitions in support of their leadership. The battle over policy becomes part of the struggle for power.[16]

Stalin's foreign policy posture was often bound up with his internal political situation. This was especially true during the early years of the post-Lenin succession struggle when Stalin shaped his foreign policy views with an eye of bolstering his position against his arch rival, Leon Trotsky. Soviet support of Chiang Kai-shek's Kuomintang in the mid-1920s, for example, was at least partly the product of Stalin's wish to embarrass Trotsky who had argued (correctly) that such aid would have disastrous implications for the revolutionary cause in China. Thus, largely for *internal* Soviet reasons, the Chinese Communist Party was compelled by the Kremlin to remain allied with Chiang and, in 1927, became the victim of his cruel anti-Communist pogrom.[17]

Foreign policy issues became involved in the struggle for power between Georgi Malenkov and Nikita Khrushchev which followed Stalin's death in March, 1953. Although Malenkov had initially been outmaneuvered—Khrushchev was elected Party Secretary while Malenkov became Prime Minister—it was not clear for a while where ultimate political power actually resided. Hoping to promote their own political interests, each assumed different positions on policy questions. Malenkov sought support for his leadership by emphasizing a marked shift in policy from Stalin's harsh approach to both domestic and foreign policy. He argued that nuclear weaponry endangered the survival of human civilization and urged a policy designed to relax international tension and to expand production of consumer goods and services. Khrushchev, on the other hand, argued along more conservative lines. He insisted that the predatory character of Western imperialism did not allow the Soviet Union the luxury of reducing its defense budget or cutting allocations to heavy industry. On the question of nuclear weapons, he argued that the enormous power of the new weapons technology in no way jeopardized what he declared to be the superiority of the USSR's military might. Furthermore, he declared, should the imperialists provoke a war, only they—and not all of civilization—would be destroyed.

That these positions were taken partly for partisan political reasons—by Malenkov to distinguish himself from Stalin; by Khrushchev to undercut Malenkov—is obvious, particularly in Khrushchev's case. Although Khrushchev secured predominant support for his position, especially from traditionalist Party leaders and the armed forces, and succeeded in having Malenkov removed from office, upon gaining power he adopted (much as Stalin did after Trotsky had been defeated) a number of policies which had been advocated by his ousted rival. After Malenkov's forced resignation as Premier in February, 1955, Khrushchev endorsed his former competitor's appeal for reducing international tensions. Not only did he participate in a summit meeting with the heads of the major Western governments in Geneva in 1955 but, at the 20th Congress of the CPSU (February, 1956), he introduced important modifications of traditional doctrine (peaceful coexistence abroad and welfare at home) in support of his new policy posture.

This new twist in policy was also partly politically inspired. Stalin's old henchman, Vyacheslav Molotov, was still on the scene. He not only defended Stalin's hard line on foreign policy in principle, but opposed and tried to obstruct Khrushchev's peaceful coexistence policies. For example, Molotov was against any rapprochement with Yugoslavia or with the United States, he regarded economic assistance to the countries of the Third World as wasteful, and he considered Khrushchev's performance at the 20th Congress—peaceful coexistence, the attack on Stalin, and revision of established Leninist doctrine on imperialism—as verging on heresy. In June, 1957, Khrushchev succeeded in having Molotov removed from the Party leadership for his "reactionary" and "obstructionist" views.

From this description, Khrushchev appears to be nothing more than a political opportunist, supporting only those policies which helped promote his political career. Such was not the case. Though political necessity at times moved him to adopt an orthodox traditionalist stance, once he had achieved victory over Malenkov, Khrushchev moved steadily along a relatively moderate course; and he often did so at considerable political risk. Nor, as might be inferred, is foreign policy merely in Linden's phrase "the pawn of power."[18] While policy decisions are often influenced by political considerations, it is not a one-way relationship. Power and policy interact. The way in which issues are defined and the actual results of policy decisions affect the outcome of power struggles as much as factional conflict shapes policy.

Another source of policy conflict arises from basic differences in attitudes and priorities among the Soviet leaders. Just as there are "hawks" and "doves" in American politics, so there are "moderates" and "conservatives," "softs" and "hards," in Soviet politics. Perhaps the traditional Marxist dichotomy, "Right" and "Left," might be more appropriate. As Alexander Dallin has suggested, the attitudinal differences that shape "Right"/"Left" cleavages on foreign policy are often congruent with similar differences on other issues. Thus, a "Left" (or "hard" or "conservative") orientation on world politics, which would stress a tough anti-imperialist posture, avoidance of contact with the West, and high levels of military spending, would also support concentrating resources on heavy industry, tight internal political controls, and a centralized command economy. A "Right" (or "moderate" or "soft") foreign policy posture, which would emphasize relaxation of international tension, expansion of foreign economic and cultural contacts, and moderate defense budgets, would also support increased production of consumer goods, greater internal tolerance of divergent views, and a "market socialist" economy.[19]

Such differences in policy orientation, both domestic and foreign, often reflect conflicting philosophical and even psychological values and orientations. Some Soviet leaders are predisposed toward a conservative posture on all issues. This was notably true of Stalin. Sullen, morose, and secretive, Stalin was the example *par excellence* of the warrior personality. His sole concern, at home and abroad, was *kto-kogo?* ("who [will defeat] whom?"). To protect and enhance his power and that of his country, his policies were "hard." Khrushchev, on the other hand, had a distinctively different temperament from that of this predecessor; he was outgoing, ebullient, and expansive. Not surprisingly, their styles of rule were quite different. Under Stalin, the Kremlin was closed to the public. The *vozhd'* (supreme leader) was only to be seen at a great distance, usually on the tribune of the Lenin mausoleum in Red Square, waving benignly to the hundreds of thousands of Soviet citizens who paraded by on May Day or November 7th (the anniversary of the Bolshevik Revolution) eagerly struggling for a glimpse of the tyrant who held them in thrall.

During the Khrushchev era, the open, free-wheeling, gregarious Party Secretary continually and openly traveled about the country, talking (and lecturing) to as many people as possible. His policies were also different. The more self-confident Khrushchev launched a de-Stalinization program that resulted in a relaxation of domestic political and ideological tension; he reduced the power of the secret police, greatly increased production of consumer goods, abandoned Stalin's overt hostility toward the outside world, and traveled abroad frequently.[20]

While international and domestic political considerations also were involved, Khrushchev's adoption of the "peaceful coexistence" line reflects the significance of the personality factor in shaping policy. It is difficult to imagine that, had he lived beyond 1953, Stalin would have opted for détente, improved living standards, and internal political relaxation. The old warrior's options would have been selected from a rather narrower, less generous, set of alternatives. Stalin's political personality tended him toward a "Left, hard, conservative, and militant" posture; Khrushchev, on the other hand, was more inclined toward a "Right, soft, moderate, and pragmatic" outlook.

Though rather scanty, there is some evidence of "Left"/"Right" political cleavages on policy issues in the more recent period. For example, the Soviet leaders apparently differed among themselves in connection with the Middle East crisis of 1967. The demotion shortly after the crisis of Nikolai G. Yegorychev from his position as First Secretary of the important Moscow Party organization has been interpreted as punishment for his outspoken militancy at the June 22–23, 1967, plenary session of the Central Committee. Identified with a tough line domestically, having previously castigated permissiveness in the arts and literature, Yegorychev is said to have urged more forceful Soviet intervention in the Arab–Israeli war. A more moderate faction, headed by Brezhnev, Kosygin, and Podgorny, is reported to have ousted Yegorychev as an object lesson to supporters, real and potential, of his "hawkish" position.[21]

Still more recently, the ouster of Pyotr Shelest as leader of the prestigious Ukrainian Party organization on May 21, 1972, the day preceding President Nixon's arrival in Moscow, also indicates sharp disagreements within the leadership. Coming at a time when the Kremlin would normally want to present a solid front, the removal of Shelest indicates that he had opposed the summit talks. As much was confirmed by *Pravda* a few weeks later when it reported that the Moscow summit had taken place "in the face of the sometimes direct opposition of those who like to warm their hands by fanning the fires of hostility and tension." Shelest, who had reportedly been an ardent advocate of the Soviet invasion of Czechoslovakia and who was generally critical of the Kremlin's policy of improving relations with West Germany, may have favored canceling Nixon's visit to protest the U.S. mining of Haiphong harbor a few weeks earlier. In April, 1973, presumably (at least in part) because of his continued opposition to accommodation with the United States, Shelest was removed from the CPSU Politburo.[22]

Such Kremlinological analysis is, needles to say, a hazardous undertaking; it is based on the most uncertain of evidence. Since neither

Yegorychev nor Shelest nor any other ousted or demoted Soviet official has given interviews to the media, and since no credible public explanation has ever been given for their removal (more often than not, ousted leaders simply "go into retirement" or, if they are lucky, are "transferred to other duties"), one can only infer that political conflict among the top Party leaders reflects such differing "Right"/"Left" political perspectives. Such judgments are made even more difficult by the fact that the record is plagued by internal inconsistencies. In American politics, as Dallin notes, "not all 'doves' are liberals; not all politicians assume ideologically coherent or consistent postures on all issues that arise."[23] Such is also the case in the USSR. For example, although Suslov and Ponomarev (head of the CC's International Department) have been identified as leaders of the hard-line faction, they are reported to have been "doves" on the invasion of Czechoslovakia. (They are said to have taken a conciliatory position in the hope of salvaging the planned international conference of Communist Parties, scheduled for that November, for which they were responsible.[24])

The most pronounced incongruencies are associated with the policies of Khrushchev. While a relative moderate on domestic politics and the eager advocate of peaceful coexistence, the jovial Party Secretary was a tough and militant combatant and something of a gambler. He actively sought to promote Soviet interests and took numerous and sometimes bold initiatives to achieve his purposes. Furthermore, his openness and exuberance should not blind us to a high degree of ruthlessness. In 1956, for example, he crushed the Hungarian uprising with a Stalin-like brutality. He was not averse to attempting nuclear blackmail, as during the 1956 Suez conflict and at the time of the ill-fated U-2 flight when he issued stern warnings of possible Soviet military action; nor was he afraid of taking risks, as he did in placing Soviet strategic missiles in Cuba in 1962. Obviously, a reformist orientation does not necessarily imply a benign foreign policy. In fact, the more conservative Stalin was much less prone to engage in risky ventures than his more moderate successor. Thus, "hard liners" are not always "hawks," nor are "moderates" invariably "doves."

Though there are inconsistencies, themselves often the result of transitory power political considerations, the same leaders *tend* to line up the same way over time on a variety of issues. Stalin, Molotov, Andrei Zhdanov (militant Politburo member from Leningrad associated with the harsh post-war domestic political crackdown in the USSR, known as the *Zhdanovshchina*), Suslov, and Shelest have tended to be militant conservatives on foreign, domestic, and ideological issues; Khrushchev, Malenkov, Kosygin, Podgorny, and Arbatov tend to be "dovish" and moderate in their views. Such "Right"/"Left" political cleavages may be partially explained in terms of variations in political temperament. More frequently, however, the regularities and consistencies of political alignment in the USSR reflect differing bureaucratic interests, especially below the very highest levels of the Party.

The crucial importance of bureaucratic influences on policy formation in all political systems is an incontrovertible but often neglected fact. The basic argument was eloquently expressed by James Schlesinger (currently U.S. Defense Secretary). Policy decisions in the United States, he astutely observed, "are nominally made by senior political figures who are harried, have insufficient time to study problems in detail, who are gripped by emotions of their youth or by prior experience, and who are susceptible to claims made by subordinate groups which are couched in a way to appeal to their prejudices. Below them," he notes,

> are a set of mutually jealous and warring bureaucratic groups, clamoring for resources and anxious to protect established preserves. To the extent they are not closely watched, the subordinate bureaucratic groups will attempt to achieve their objectives quietly or even surreptitiously. Moreover, their capacity for resistance to high-level objectives enunciated from above, but to which they have taken exception, is breathtaking. Actual programs and allocative decisions will consequently diverge quite sharply from those that would be predicted on the assumption of a rational intelligence. Instead they will be strongly influenced by prejudice, incompetency, and by infighting, deviousness and bootlegging within the bureaucracies. Changes which appear rational and desirable will be compromised half to death, and the compromises themselves will be slow in coming.[25]

Thus, policies are not made by an abstraction called "the government," but result from the constant sharp interplay and competition of conflicting interests and bureaucratic agencies. Schlesinger's analysis applies to the USSR as well. The Ministries, departments, committees, and commissions of the Soviet government and the Communist Party exert, or seek to exert, a powerful influence on national decisionmaking. And they seem to do so in a relatively predictable and regular fashion—certain bureaucratic groups tend to have definite foreign policy preferences.

The particular policy orientation favored by an individual Party or state is best understood if we keep in mind the close relationship between foreign and domestic policy. In all societies, but perhaps especially in the Soviet Union (where resources have been in short supply and where all economic investment decisions are centrally planned), foreign and defense policy decisions have vitally important implications for domestic policy. For example, a Kremlin decision that the international situation is improving and, therefore, that military spending can be reduced and appropriations for new weapons systems cut back may well permit greatly expanded investments in the agricultural sector of the economy. On the other hand, should the Soviet leaders feel that the world situation requires enlarged military outlays and increased allocations for defense-related industries, a cut in appropriations for consumer goods and services is highly likely.

Thus, the requirements of the international situation, in the words of Vernon Aspaturian, exercise a "tyranny" on Soviet budgetary allocations which in turn "have a fortuitous and objective impact on the fortunes, status, regards and deprivations of various groups in Soviet society." He elaborates:

The foreign policy and defense posture of the Soviet state established a certain configuration of priorities in the allocation of budgetary expenses and scarce resources. Various individuals and groups develop a vested interest in a particular foreign policy or defence posture because of the role or status it confers upon them. Correspondingly, other individuals and groups in Soviet society perceive themselves as deprived in status and rewards because of the existing allocation of expenditures and resources. . . .[26]

Further, Aspaturian suggests, not only do bureaucratic groups that benefit from international tension (or détente) develop "a vested interest" in such an environment, but they may even "initiate proposals that could alter existing foreign and defense postures. . . ." For example, beneficiaries of tension would tend to manipulate their assessments of the world scene, emphasizing the darker, more pessimistic trends at home and abroad; they may even use their resources to encourage the belief that tension is increasing.

The important point is that different foreign policies create different budgetary priorities that affect various bureaucratic interests differently. Some groups tend to benefit from, and not unnaturally, to prefer policies and allocation decisions normally associated with a tense world situation; others gain more from a relaxed international environment. As a result of their specialized roles and interest, Aspaturian divides bureaucratic agencies, departments, and individual Soviet politicians into "two competing constellations": "a security–productionist–ideological grouping" and a "consumptionist–agricultural–public services grouping."[27]

These two "demand sector coalitions" tend to take opposite stands on their assessment of the international situation and on their priorities regarding the distribution of investments and resources. The former, led by the military and heavy industry groups, and the intelligence services, continually emphasizes conflict, struggle, and international tension. Military leaders, the most visible members of this coalition (in part because they have their own newspaper, *Krasnaya zvezda* or *Red Star*) are continually stressing the unchanging character and aggressiveness of American imperialism. Typical of this is Defense Minister Grechko's warning in March, 1973: "Acute crisis situations that are at any moment capable of rocking the entire system of world relations are arising in the world through imperialism's fault, as before. . . . Imperialism," he declared, "is not reconciled to the existence of the socialist states and is not about to lay down its arms."[28] While such gloomy and worrisome utterances stood in sharp contrast to the Kremlin's generally rosy evaluations of the world scene at that time, they reflected the natural skepticism of the Soviet military regarding the intentions of their American counterparts in the Pentagon. Grechko's prime objective, however, was to ensure that Soviet armed forces continued to receive sizable budgetary appropriations. Thus, he noted that "imperialism reckons with force above all else in international relations." The moral is clear: Only by maintaining powerful defense forces could the security interests of the USSR be protected.

The military is obviously fearful that the Politburo's détente policy will cause their role to be reduced. To protect their interests, they have attempted to slow down the rapprochement with the West. For example, there are indications that some elements in the Soviet military opposed the SALT talks. In a speech on July 27th, 1968, when he informed the Supreme Soviet that the Kremlin was prepared to enter negotiations on "the mutual limitation and later reduction" of offensive and defensive missiles, Foreign Minister Gromyko caustically observed:

> To the good-for-nothing theoreticians who try to tell us . . . that disarmament is an illusion, we reply, "By taking such a stand you fall into step with the most dyed-in-the-wool imperialist reaction, and weaken the front of struggle against it."[29]

Gromyko's "good-for-nothing theoreticians" were undoubtedly military officers and civilian "defense intellectuals" close to the Ministry of Defense.

The secret police, the intelligence service, and the Party ideologists also have a vested interest in a climate of tension. Only in such an atmosphere can their demands for vigilance and tight political controls (as well as their claims for budgetary support) be justified. Paraphrasing Solzhenitsyn, Where would the KGB and the Party militants be without their enemies? According to some evidence, Soviet secret police officials have attempted to block rapprochement with the West by provoking embarrassing incidents. For example, in order to impede a then incipient accommodation between the USSR and West Germany and a projected visit by Khrushchev to Bonn, the police are said to have been responsible for the physical attack on a member of the German embassy staff in Moscow in September, 1964.[30]

Finally, the "metal eaters," the managers of heavy industry who urge continued priority to investment in capital goods production, especially steel, rather than in light industry or agriculture, also are beneficiaries of a cold war atmosphere. Only in such a climate can enlarged allocations for defense-related industrial production be legitimized. This position is often supported by the professional military as well as by conservative Party leaders. The argument usually made by these groups runs as follows: heavy industry, "as everyone knows," is a "basic" indicator of a "country's economic strength" and "vital" to maintaining its defense posture. These groups are not enthusiastic about allocating scarce resources in the consumer sectors; they warn against allowing the desire for improved living standards to detract from the country's defense needs.

What this analysis suggests is that there is something akin to a "military–industrial complex" in the USSR. Groups do exist which, in Aspaturian's phrase, have "a vested interest" in a tense international environment. While not united on all issues, the Soviet military establishment, heavy industries (especially defense-related), the secret police, and the conservative wing of the Party are bound together by their knowledge that the interests of all can best be advanced in a state of international tension. They often make common cause, either as a result of collusion or simply by expressing their own departmental view of the world, in attempting to demonstrate the need to remain "strong" and "vigilant" in the face of external danger. It is difficult to determine whether they actually perceive high levels of tension and danger, or, given their stake in doing so, unconsciously distort the objective situation and see enemies and threats where none exist. Whatever their motivations, the various components of the Soviet "military–industrial–political complex" continually press their policy preferences on the Party leadership by describing the outside world in negative terms, in the hope of legitimizing their claims for funds and supports.[31]

Not only does a "military–industrial–political" complex exist in the USSR, but it has become a thriving concern, especially in recent years. The industrial establishment supporting the Soviet armed forces, as we have seen, enjoys considerable privileges denied other sectors of the economy. Furthermore, the steady build-up of Soviet offensive and defensive weaponry in recent years suggests that the Ministry of Defense and its coalition partners have been very successful in their efforts—that they have convinced the Party leadership that national security expenditures must be maintained at a high level.

Who, if anyone, speaks for détente? Who represents the interests of the "consumptionist–agricultural–public services sector?" In the Soviet Union, as perhaps elsewhere, this latter group is relatively weak politically. The Soviet military, police, and heavy industrial managers not only receive high priority treatment in terms of resources but have acquired extraordinary political power. This is especially true of the professional military, which is very well represented in the Party's top organs. For example, in 1971, 31 military representatives were elected to the Central Committee (7.8 percent of the total membership) and 287 delegates from the military were at the 24th Party Congress (5.8 percent of the total).[32] In April, 1973, the Defense Minister, himself a professional military man (in contrast to some earlier defense ministers like Marshals Bulganin and Voroshilov who were senior Party officials appointed to bird-dog the Red Army) was elected to the Politburo. No combination of representatives from the textile industry, the Ministries of Housing or Agriculture, the Soviet trade unions, the Union of Writers or the kolkhoz peasantry can compete with such an array of power. An there is little likelihood of a Ralph Nader or a consumer protectionist group organizing a sustained challenge to governmental policies and economic priorities on behalf of the unorganized and long-neglected citizens of the USSR.

Though relatively powerless institutionally, those who favor "détente" policies and "détente" budgets are not without their supporters. Party and state officials responsible for consumer-related industries develop a vested interest in the welfare of their constituencies. A well-known incident illustrating this phenomenon occurred shortly after Khrushchev was ousted. In early 1965, the Party Central Committee approved a massive investment program for agriculture. The Central Committee agreed to allocate forty-one billion rubles ($45.5 billion) to agriculture for the period 1966–1970, double the amount invested in the preceding five years. However, by 1967, the budgeted farm investment funds were sharply slashed. In an article in *Kommunist*, the Party's leading ideological journal, First Deputy Prime Minister and Politburo member Dmitri S. Polyanski strongly protested the cutback. He argued that a flourishing agriculture was vital to the welfare of the entire economy. "Unfortunately," he asserted, "the urgency of a correct decision of this issue has not always been recognized."[33]

This rare glimpse of a Party conflict on economic priorities is significant on several counts. First, it indicates that the "consumptionist" sector does have its advocates. Polyanski, as the Politburo member responsible for agriculture, vigorously and publicly sought to protect this sector of the economy. In an unusual display of temper, Polyanski openly denounced those who had endorsed the slashing of funds: "The only explanation for such behavior," he declared, "is political myopia." Second, it appears that what we have called the "consumptionist" sector is a not very cohesive grouping. While agricultural funding was cut back in 1967 (after a good harvest the preceding year), funds for the consumer goods sector were increased. And the target of Polyanski's article was not the supporters of heavy industry or the military, but the advantaged light industry grouping promoted by Premier Kosygin.

The "military–industrial complex," it should be noted, is itself a diffuse coalition of groups and interests which, at times, is also internally divided. For example, the Soviet armed forces face intra-service rivalries. In addition, there are reports of occasional conflicts between the professional officer corps and those Party officials who serve in all branches and at all levels of the armed services to ensure the political orthodoxy and loyalty of both offices and troops. Each service is also plagued with internal divisions between "radicals" and "traditionalists,"—between young, technically sophisticated, missile-oriented officers, who emphasize reliance on modern weaponry and new strategic orientations, and older, conventionally trained officers who favor tried and true weapons and strategies. However, internal divisions here are not as serious as in the "consumptionist" sector, if only because greater political influence and budgetary supports make the scramble for scarce resources less intense.

Finally, it seems quite evident that, in the long run, the interests of the "consumptionist" sector are advanced best by the top Party leadership itself. It was Party Secretary Brezhnev who in 1965 pushed the original program to enlarge agricultural investments. He did so to prevent recurrence of the disastrous harvest of 1963. Thus, when confronted with what appear to be serious problems, the Politburo itself may take the lead. This was especially true during Khrushchev's tenure in office. After the ouster of Malenkov, Khrushchev became the champion of programs that had the creation of a more abundant society as their primary objective. He was politically committed to the goal that, in the words of the slogan of the 22d Party Congress (1961), "The present generation of Soviet people shall live under Communism." To create the conditions of material abundance which, according to Marx and Engels, are necessary to arrive at this happy state, Khrushchev strongly urged policies designed to expand agriculture, consumer goods production, housing, and to improve the lot of the average Soviet citizen.

What Khrushchev had in mind was to reorient domestic priorities and to move the Soviet economy away from its traditional focus on heavy industry in favor of a more broadly based economic growth. Expansion of the consumer sector would at last begin to reward the long-deprived Soviet workers for their labors—and thereby would act as an incentive to greater productivity. Khrushchev hoped both to improve the lot of the Soviet consumer and to stimulate economic growth.

To improve living conditions and enlarge investments in agriculture, Khrushchev had to reduce the size of Soviet military outlays. The political problem for Khrushchev was to persuade the other Kremlin leaders that the defense budget could be reduced without risking Soviet security interests. To achieve these purposes, Khrushchev's strategy was to dovetail his pro-consumer approach at home with a policy of détente abroad. It is in this context that, beginning in 1956, he urged his policy of peaceful coexistence with stress on an ameliorating international environment. Khrushchev, as no one in Soviet history before him, spoke for détente and the consumer.[34]

With considerably less fanfare, Khrushchev's successors have taken a similar stance. Though he has been generally sympathetic to high levels of defense spending, Brezhnev did initiate the program for expanded investment in agriculture. Kosygin has consistently favored expanding the consumer sector, with special emphasis on light industry and consumer durables. Both leaders seem persuaded of the need to shift greater attention to satisfying consumer needs. When the Ninth Five-Year Plan was announced in 1971, it was publicized as the first in Soviet history to project a faster growth for the consumer sector than for heavy industry. Apprehensive, perhaps, that the Polish riots of the preceding December might spill over onto Soviet territory, Party Secretary Brezhnev boasted of "saturating the market with consumer goods."[35] To achieve thier economic goals, the current Soviet leaders have pursued a policy of international détente. Their basic strategy was explained by a Soviet analyst who wrote in late 1969: "Experience has shown that only under conditions of a relaxation of international tensions is it possible to concentrate a maximum of resources on accomplishing the plans for the building of communism."[36]

When they believe that internal socio-economic circumstances require it, the Party leaders may speak for the consumptionist sector. Thus, to achieve his domestic economic program, Khrushchev sought to divert funds from the military budget and from heavy industry. In doing so, he knowingly incurred the enmity of Party conservatives, especially Suslov and Kozlov—"those comrades who displayed an overly developed appetite for metals"—and most of the military leadership. The military, led by Soviet Defense Minister Marshal Malinovski, were skeptical of Khrushchev's assessment of the international situation and generally regarded his foreign and defense posture with grave suspicion. Partly as a result of the enemies these policies created, Khrushchev's political position disintegrated and he was ousted in 1964.

Perhaps to avoid a similar fate, Brezhnev and Kosygin have tried to steer a middle course between "guns" and "butter." They have attempted simultaneously to expand appropriations for the consumer sector and agriculture and to maintain high levels of expenditure on defense. They are in a much better economic position than was Khrushchev. Because of the considerably larger Soviet economy, they *can* invest in both guns and butter. However, their flexibility is limited. As its poor performance in 1972 indicates, the Soviet economy still faces considerable problems, not the least of which is agriculture. The regime's recent efforts at modernization and expanded productivity is an attempt to maintain maximum economic, hence political, flexibility. The larger the economic pie, the more resources available for distribution, and the less likelihood of alienating (at least on these grounds) any of the major factional bureaucratic interests.

* * *

Behind the facade of "monolithic unity" exists a strikingly heterogeneous Soviet political leadership. While the leaders share much in common, the top echelon of the Party power structure is characterized by a considerable diversity of values, attitudes, and outlooks. Struggles for power, variations in ideological orientation and temperament, and clashing bureaucratic interests combine with personal rivalries and petty jealousies to create a degree of internal political conflict far greater than usually imagined. Political disagreements on foreign policy may become so sharp at times that there appear to be two separate Soviet governments, "a 'government A' and a 'government B' tugging away in different directions."[37]

Policy conflicts, it must be stressed, should not be perceived along simplistic institutional lines—as for example between Party officials and the military. While such bureaucratic conflicts of interest do occur, disagreements on policy more typically occur between inter-institutional coalitions whose compositions vary from issue to issue. As one informed source has noted, the various sections of the Party apparatus may be divided among themselves.

> In general, the International Department [of the Party's Central Committee] would be more interested in détente than the Department for Liaison with Workers and Communist Parties, which would be preoccupied with preservation of the *status quo* in Eastern Europe. Both, however, would be more inclined to favor a relaxation of tensions within prescribed limits than would the Department for Agitation and Propaganda. Similar differences of opinion might be expected to exist within components of the Foreign Ministry and the military. The defense industry usually exhibits great skepticism toward détente and disarmament but might, in fact, welcome some measures in this direction if . . . [they] provided the Soviet Union with greater access to American advanced technology and know-how.[38]

Soviet policymaking is shaped more by relations among issue-oriented coalitions with shifting memberships than by clashes among fixed institutional interest groups.

Such a situation can create problems. Government by shifting factional coalitions tends to move rather slowly. This is especially true as the political process has become more "open." As more people and diverse interests have become involved in the formulation of policy, it becomes increasingly difficult to reach decisions: policies tend to be watered down in order to take the interests of all into account. The regime's ability to act effectively is made especially difficult in the absence of a single authoritative source of power. Group rule, or "collective leadership," compounds the problem of decisionmaking in a government composed of many internally divided factions.

It is not surprising, therefore, that the strong thrust which can be detected in Soviet foreign policy since the early 1970s coincides with the rise of Brezhnev to preeminent position in the Politburo. His vigorous leadership seems to have been necessary to push through the Party's new "Peace Program." But Brezhnev's position is not one of complete political supremacy. He seems to have been compelled to include political opponents, Grechko and Andropov (whose institutional affiliations with the military and the secret police hardly make them supporters of international détente), in his government. As a result, policymaking in the USSR today is likely to continue to be a process of slow and often difficult compromise.

Notes

[1]"Speech by Comrade A. A. Gromyko, U.S.S.R. Minister of Foreign Affairs," *Pravda*, April 4, 1971; translated in *CDSP*, Vol. XXIII, No. 17 (May 25, 1971), p. 33.

[2]Quoted in F. S. Northedge, ed., *The Foreign Policies of the Powers* (New York: Frederick A. Praeger, Publishers, 1968), p. 85.

[3]Ulam, *Coexistence and Expansion, op. cit.*, p. 622.

[4]"List of Soviet Ambassadors Abroad," *Radio Liberty Dispatch*, May 30, 1972.

[5]While Brezhnev is a member of the Presidium of the USSR's Supreme Soviet, this is a ceremonial post lacking executive authority. Thus, every time he signed an agreement during his June 1973 trip to the United States—he signed four, including the joint final communique summarizing the results of his week-long summit meeting with President Nixon—the Soviet Foreign Ministry handed over an official statement which asserted that Brezhnev was authorized to do so on behalf of the Soviet Government. *The New York Times*, June 26, 1973.

[6]On the career patterns of Soviet Foreign Ministry officials, see *The Soviet Diplomatic Corps 1917–1967* (Metuchen, N.J.: The Scarecrow Press, Inc., 1970).

[7]The Politburo has not been graced by the presence of these three key branches of the bureaucracy in many years. The last internal security head to serve was Lavrenti P. Beria, Marshal Georgi K. Zhukhov was the last Defense Minister and Vyacheslav M. Molotov the last Foreign Minister. It is instructive to recall that Beria was executed for treason in 1953 and Molotov was purged as foreign policy chief in 1956. Zhukhov attained Politburo status in 1957, after the

other two had been removed, but a few months later fell into disgrace and was ousted.

[8]"Speech by Comrade A. A. Gromyko. . . ." *op. cit.*, p. 33.

[9]*Staffing Procedures and Problems in the Soviet Union.* A study submitted by the Subcommittee on National Security Staffing and Operations to the Committee on Government Operations, United States Senate (Washington: Government Printing Office, 1963), p. 25. "Khrushchev made the decision to withdraw Soviet offensive weapons from Cuba in consultation apparently with Mikoyan, Kosygin, Suslov, Brezhnev and . . . Kozlov. These men appear to form a kind of . . . inner cabinet which at least in this case functioned as a Soviet 'national security council.' "

[10]*The New York Times*, June 15, 1973. The tradition of consultation was again confirmed when diplomatic negotiations with Secretary of State Kissinger in Moscow in March, 1974, were temporarily suspended so that Brezhnev could meet in an unusual Wednesday session with his Politburo colleagues. *Washington Post*, March 28, 1974. With such weighty matters as strategic arms limitation agreements under consideration, the General Secretary presumably wanted to (or was obliged to) get the views of other top Party leaders.

[11]*National Policy Machinery in the Soviet Union.* Report by the Subcommittee on National Policy Machinery, Committee on Government Operations, United States Senate (Washington: Government Printing Office, 1960), pp. 41–42.

[12]Kurt London, *The Making of Foreign Policy East and West* (Philadelphia: J. B. Lippincott Co., 1965), p. 189.

[13]On this general point, see Vladimir Petrov, "Formation of Soviet Foreign Policy," *Orbis*, Vol. XVII, No. 3 (Fall, 1973) pp. 819–850.

[14]"Espionage, Politics and Trade," *Soviet Analyst* (London), I, No. 19 (November 16, 1972), pp. 5–6 and *The New York Times*, December 21 and 27, 1961.

[15]*Keesing's Contemporary Archives* (October 23–30, 1971), p. 24885.

[16]See Carl A. Linden, *Khrushchev and the Soviet Leadership, 1957–1964* (Baltimore: The John Hopkins Press, 1966), pp. 7, 15.

[17]Given their experience at his hands, Chinese Communist expressions of devotion to Stalin are obviously feigned. Fealty to Stalin was Mao's stick with which to attack the anti-Stalinist policies of Khrushchev.

[18]Linden, *op. cit.*, p. 7.

[19]This discussion is based on Alexander Dallin, "Soviet Foreign Policy and Domestic Politics: A Framework for Analysis," *Journal of International Affairs*, Vol. XXIII, No. 2 (1969) pp. 259–263.

[20]For a fuller discussion of the differences in personality and political style between Stalin and Khrushchev, see Morton Schwartz, *The "Motive Forces" of Soviet Foreign Policy: A Reappraisal*, Monograph Series in World Affairs, Vol. VIII, No. 2 (1970–1971), The Social Science Foundation and Graduate School of International Studies, University of Denver, pp. 15–24.

[21]*The New York Times*, July 12, 1967. A somewhat different interpretation argues that Yegorychev was not ousted for supporting a "hawkish" position but, rather, for criticizing the Party leadership for "squandering Soviet arms and prestige in support of the Arab states." Wolfe, *Soviet Power in Europe, op. cit.*, p. 339, fn. 117. Whichever view ultimately proves to have been correct, the existence of a serious internal split on the issue of Soviet policy in the June War is established.

[22]*The New York Times*, May 22 and June 16, 1972 and April 28, 1973. That Shelest's opposition was linked to U.S. Vietnam policy is hinted at when, in its attack on "obstructionist actions by rightist and leftist foes of relaxation," *Pravda* noted defensively that "negotiations conducted from principled positions and with reasonable tactical compromises . . . are not a sign of weakness or softness. . . ."

See Yu. Chernov, "Real Force of International Development, *Pravda,* June 15, 1972; translated in *CDSP,* Vol. XXIV, No. 24 (July 12, 1972), p. 2.

[23]Dallin, *op. cit.,* p. 260.

[24]*The New York Times* March 4, 1969.

[25]James R. Schlesinger, "The 'Soft' Factors in System Studies," *Bulletin of the Atomic Scientists,* Vol. XXIV, No. 9 (November, 1968), pp. 14–15.

[26]Vernon V. Aspaturian, "Internal Politics and Foreign Policy in the Soviet System," in R. Barry Farrell, ed., *Approaches to Comparative and International Politics* (Evanston: Northwestern University Press, 1966), p. 252.

[27]Vernon V. Aspaturian, "Moscow's Options in a Changing World," *Problems of Communism,* Vol. XXI, No. 4 (July–August, 1972), p. 6.

[28]"Fifth All-Army Conference of Party Organizations Secretaries: Report by Marshal of the Soviet Union, A. A. Grechko, USSR Minister of Defense," *Krasnaya zvezda,* March 28, 1973; translated in *CDSP,* Vol. XXV, No. 13 (April 25, 1973), p. 29.

[29]*Pravda,* June 28, 1968; quoted in Newhouse, *op. cit.,* p. 104.

[30]See Michel Tatu, *Power in the Kremlin* (New York: The Viking Press, 1969), pp. 388–390.

[31]For a perceptive discussion of this intriguing issue, see Vernon V. Aspaturian, "The Soviet Military–Industrial Complex—Does it Exist?" *Journal of International Affairs,* Vol. XXVI, No. 1 (1972), especially pp. 23 and 25. See also, William T. Lee, "The 'Politico–Military–Industrial Complex' of the USSR," *ibid.* pp. 73–86.

[32]Aspaturian, "The Soviet Military–Industrial Complex. . . ," *op. cit.,* p. 9.

[33]*The New York Times,* October 29, 1967.

[34]See Linden, *op. cit., passim.*

[35]*The New York Times,* February 4, 1973. As a result of serious failures in 1972, however, the consumer sector (light industry, the food industry and, especially, agriculture) fell far short of planned goals. Overall, basic heavy industries met the projected growth rate of 6.8 percent but the 7.1 percent goal for consumer industries (excluding agriculture) was not met; they went up only 6 percent. The revised 1973 plan called for 6.8 percent growth in heavy industry and only 4.5 percent in the consumer sector. *(Ibid.)*

Actually, the Second Five-Year Plan (adopted in 1934) also called for more rapid growth in the consumer goods sector. It, too, failed to fulfill this promise to the consumers as priority in fact went to heavy industry. Nove., *op. cit.,* pp. 224–228.

[36]Ivanov, *Leninskiye osnovy vneshnei politiki SSSR, op. cit.,* p. 50.

[37]This view has been attributed to Henry Kissinger. See Ross Terrill, "The 8,000,000 China and the World," *The Atlantic* (January, 1972), p. 43.

[38]Dmitri Simes and Gordon Rocca, "Soviet Decision Making and National Security Affairs," Georgetown University Center for Strategic and International Studies, Memorandum 20–KM–11–1, November, 1973, pp. 25–26.

7

Domestic policy determinants: their weight and direction

In the preceding chapters, we have attempted to introduce some of the main factors which must be taken into account in the analysis of Soviet foreign policy behavior. It has been our contention that domestic circumstances exert a powerful influence on Soviet policy in various ways, directly and indirectly. The material context in which the Soviets function—the geographical position of the USSR, the country's economic resources, its population mix—has implications which no Soviet leader can escape; further, Russia's historical and ideological heritage and cultural traditions help mold the Kremlin authorities' world view. In addition, internal economic and military capabilities provide—or fail to provide—the physical wherewithal to support Soviet diplomacy and, thereby, shape policy choices by helping to determine which policies are feasible and can be afforded and which not. Thus, the USSR's relations with the outside world—with the major areas of concern (Eastern Europe, China, the United States, Germany, the Middle East), its view of the character of each (whether it is seen as a threat or as an opportunity), and its evaluation of the specific resources available to deal with them, are in very considerable measure a function of what we have called domestic determinants of Soviet foreign policy. Clearly, though somewhat obviously,

Soviet policy has taken on its particular direction and features precisely because it is the policy of the government of the USSR. Were Brezhnev and his fellow Politburo members in charge of the government of New Zealand or Tunisia, with their very different geographic, economic and military circumstances, historical experiences, cultural traditions, political beliefs, and internal political structures, the course of their foreign policy would undoubtedly be vastly different.

Domestic factors, therefore, exert a profound influence on Soviet international behavior. While reinforced by other factors, Russia's historical traditions and experiences, the philosophical commitment of the Soviet government to Marxist–Leninist doctrines, and the anxieties of the Soviet political leadership all contributed to the Kremlin's largely hostile foreign policy orientation toward the West between the Bolshevik Revolution of 1917 and the mid-1950s, a policy marked by suspicion, xenophobia, and isolation. In addition, the personality of the political leadership has been a crucial influence on Soviet policy. Throughout much of its history, Stalin completely dominated the Soviet scene. Not only was he primarily responsible for the revolutionary policies of the 1930s—the Five-Year Plans, the collectivization of agriculture, and the cruel and highly disruptive political purges—but Stalin led the Soviet Union to victory in World War II and expanded its hegemony into Central and Eastern Europe. He was the prime author of Soviet policies which led to the nonaggression pact with Hitler, the "grand alliance" against Hitler, and the cold war with the West. Without Stalin, the USSR's relations with the outside world would have taken a decidedly different course.

The decisive role of Stalin cannot be exaggerated. It is held by many that without Stalin there would not have been a cold war. Typical of this view is the argument of Adam Ulam. Writing of the immediate post-1945 period, he asserts that " . . . it was impossible for the Soviets to abandon their suspicions about the intentions of the Western Powers. Not the most intensive credits [economic assistance], not even the turning over to the Russians of sample atomic bombs could have appeased them or basically affected their policies. Suspicion was built into the Soviet system; it was inherent in the character of its ruler."[1] Stalin's suspiciousness and anxieties were indeed so profound that it is hard to see how Soviet foreign policy could have been very different, regardless of what the Western powers did or did not do. As Ulam writes, "Internal policy dictated isolation from and hostility toward the West," and "internal policy" was, of course, Stalin's policy.

However, Stalin's extraordinary influence on Russian and world history has been a source of confusion. The Soviet system was so much a product of Stalin that outside observers—and even those within the Soviet Union—tended to regard Stalinist institutions and practices as inherent features of the Soviet political system. While understandable, given the length and impact of Stalin's rule, this identification left many analysts unprepared for and resistant to the possibility of change in the USSR after Stalin's death.

And change there has been, in domestic as well as in foreign policy. The internal political atmosphere has improved considerably as the role of the secret police has been reduced, far more attention has been given to consumer necessities and demands, and a greater concern shown for economic efficiency and rationality. In foreign affairs, the hostile posture of Stalin's Russia toward the West has given way to the far more amicable stance expressed in the post-Stalin policy of peaceful coexistence. This has resulted in an increased willingness to resolve long-vexing political issues (Germany), increased cooperativeness in dealing with complex international problems (arms control), greater political contacts, and expanded trade, scientific, and cultural exchanges. Soviet relations with Eastern Europe are, furthermore, very much more relaxed than in Stalin's day. In both domestic and foreign policy, it is true, changes have not been uniform in pace or direction. The Secret Police, Lenin's "sword of the revolution," is occasionally brandished (as when dealing with political recalcitrants). Similarly, Kremlin behavior toward the outside world has not become completely benign, as evidenced by the Cuban missile crisis and the Soviet invasions of Hungary and Czechoslovakia. Generally, however, the changes since the Stalin era have been dramatic.

While the broad dimensions of change are apparent to most observers, its causality is less clear. To what extent has the direction of post-Stalin foreign policy been the product of changing internal conditions in the USSR? Has it been primarily a function of the new political leadership? Is it simply the result of the rise to power of men more confident and less anxious than Stalin and, hence, less needful of a cold war? Perhaps developments occurring in Soviet society, especially the rise of less doctrinaire, more pragmatic cadres to positions of authority in the political elite, produced more conciliatory tendencies with the Party leadership. Or it may be a product of the self-assurance and sense of security which the USSR's improved military position affords the Soviet policymakers. It is also conceivable that domestic economic problems required that increased attention and resources be devoted to internal developments. These and other domestic factors certainly pointed the Kremlin in a policy direction different from that previously taken by Stalin.

Such domestic developments, while of considerable importance, were not of themselves sufficient to alter the course of Soviet foreign policy. The new approach which the Kremlin began to take in the mid-1950s was also influenced by important international developments. The suggestion and adoption of the policy of peaceful coexistence was in very considerable measure a response to the dangers of the new weapons technology. Apprehensive that nuclear war would cause enormous damage to the USSR, the post-Stalin political leadership felt it urgent to reduce the level of international tension.

Not only did they believe that the nuclear weapons environment demanded some limited effort at East–West accommodation but, by the mid-1950s, the Soviet leadership had also come to the view that the

United States did not pose a threat to core Soviet security interests. The Kremlin leaders seemed persuaded that Washington was not interested in provoking a general war, despite its great preponderance in strategic power. The Soviet leaders had survived living with a United States that had a monopoly of nuclear weapons for several crucial years and which, by the end of the Korean War, had achieved an operational capability of destroying the USSR. Yet the U.S. had not used or threatened to use its vast strategic superiority. Thus, by the mid-1950s the Kremlin authorities "had time to observe that the mere existence of this massive force was no threat to Soviet security. They had learned to live with SAC [the Strategic Air Command]. Moreover, despite Soviet propaganda against 'the imperialist warmongers,' they had also come to realize that the American leadership was not bellicose" and that, despite the Eisenhower Administration's rhetoric of "massive retaliation," the United States was not about to attack the USSR.[2]

Perhaps most reassuring to the Kremlin, however, was Washington's refusal to intervene in the turbulent developments in Central and Eastern Europe in the years immediately after Stalin died. The unwillingness of the United States to intervene in the uprising in East Berlin in June, 1953, or at the time of the Poznan riots in western Poland in June, 1956, and, particularly, during the Hungarian Revolution in the fall of 1956 was most reassuring to the Soviet leadership—despite much official American talk (especially by John Foster Dulles, the Secretary of State) about "liberation" of the "captive nations" and the "rollback" of Communism in Eastern Europe. Washington's failure to act, as Herbert Dinerstein has written, "was correctly interpreted to mean communist power in Eastern Europe was not to be subject to direct American intervention. . . . This inaction on Eisenhower's part was perhaps his most significant contribution to the Soviet belief in the possibility of coexistence."[3]

The policy of détente initiated by the post-Stalin leadership, therefore, was a function of both internal and external factors. The new political leadership wanted to reallocate scarce resources in favor of consumer needs—agriculture, housing, and consumer goods. Some degree of international stabilization was necessary before any significant diversion of funds from heavy industry and armaments could be considered safe. The policy of peaceful coexistence made sense—indeed, was only conceivable —in an increasingly safer international climate, or at least one perceived as less dangerous. Had Khrushchev felt that Soviet security was in any jeopardy, détente and resource reallocation to the civilian economy would have been quickly jettisoned.

What this suggests is that though domestic factors seem, at times, to be of prime importance and, at other times, external factors seem to compel certain policies, these two environments are highly interactive. That is to say, Soviet foreign policy is shaped by both internal and external factors, and developments in each sphere tend to influence the other. Foreign policy was largely a function of internal policy during the Stalin years; yet, even then, the external environment was not totally ignored.

For example, many of Stalin's policies in the late 1930s and during the Second World War were a response to the threat from Nazi Germany. Soviet policy toward postwar Europe was, in some measure at least, designed to protect Russia's vulnerable Western frontier.

However, while he could not ignore the dangers to Soviet interests from abroad, Stalin's main concerns were internal. He began talking about "capitalist encirclement" during the 1930s to justify his demands for "iron discipline, unceasing vigilance and the strictest centralization of leadership."[4] He saw dangers to Soviet security well before the international environment became hostile. In the post-war years, he contrived a posture of bellicosity and suspiciousness against former allies and domestic adversaries to satisfy internal political objectives. (Even those closest to Stalin were victims of his purges; members of the Molotov and Mikoyan families were exiled and imprisoned.) Stalin's anxieties and suspiciousness—not Soviet security interests—were primarily responsible for the cold war.

It can also be argued that internal needs were also the predominant influence in Khrushchev's foreign policy. The post-Stalin leaders may have pursued a policy of international détente precisely to allow them to concentrate on internal developmental needs—they sought international stability as a setting for internal development. Therefore, peaceful coexistence can be interpreted as reflecting a commitment to domestic reform and development.[5] However, a policy of détente and the reallocation of internal resources were conceivable only in an environment of reduced danger and threat. Though Soviet declarations and pronouncements could be manipulated to create the illusion of détente, world realities would not allow Khrushchev simply to invent it. The post-Korea international environment gave the Soviet leader creditable grounds for arguing that some form of accommodation was both conceivable and necessary.

The dynamic interaction between the domestic and external environments can also be illustrated by examining the changing fortunes of militant and pragmatic elements in the Party hierarchy. For example, during the Second World War, the role of anti-Western elements in the Party apparatus was diminished somewhat by the need to cooperate with the Allies in the common struggle against Nazi Germany. However, as post-war tensions with the West became more severe, the influence of these conservative groups again increased and their advice was eagerly sought. Among the reasons for the post-war ideological campaign spearheaded by Andrei Zhdanov, an arch-type Party militant, was the need to eliminate those officials who had developed sympathy for and perhaps even personal contacts with "bourgeois" cultures during the war.[6]

A time of stress and crisis, therefore, tends to promote the interests and status of conservative elements—in the Party, in the military, in the police, and in the bureaucratic offices of the government—who in turn encourage conditions that promote their prosperity and prestige. Zhdanov and his sympathizers prospered during the *Zhdanovshchina*. However, a period of declining tension erodes the apparent need for the instruments and budgeting on which militant groups depend. By weakening the influence of such elements, détente tends to encourage a relaxation of internal controls.

Such has been the case recently. The striking achievements in the direction of international accommodation in Europe and, particularly, the successes of West Germany's *Ostpolitik*—Bonn's treaties with the Soviet Union, Poland, Czechoslovakia and East Germany which apparently resolved the outstanding territorial issues left over from the Second World War, including the status of Berlin—have produced a considerable loosening of political ties in Eastern Europe, both within each country and between Moscow and the individual Communist states. As a result of *Ostpolitik*, the Soviet-led Warsaw Pact has become "less and less soldierly and more and more of an Imperial Diet in which the members of the alliance haggled out their differences and settled their conflict. . . . This is not to say that the Russians did not get what they wanted. But they had to bargain for it."[7] Furthermore, the attempt to create a "socialism with a human face" in Czechoslovakia in 1968 was conceivable only in a climate of détente in Europe. The need for a tight system of Party–police controls and the conservative demands for Marxist–Leninist orthodoxy seemed less compelling among intellectuals and even Party officials in Prague as the threat of West German "revanchism" diminished.

While foreign policy and domestic policy are highly interactive, the Kremlin leaders have striven mightily to eliminate the untoward effects of détente. External relaxation of tension has led, as we have seen, to increased internal vigilance. And, in view of the "special relationship" between Moscow and Eastern Europe, it seems all too clear that basic changes in this part of the world ultimately depend upon prior reforms in the Soviet Union itself. Given the USSR's present commitment to the principle of "the leading role of the Communist Party" and its desire to preserve the "achievements of socialism" in Eastern Europe, the Kremlin leaders are not likely to tolerate manifestations of "anarcho-liberalism" or "bourgeois nationalism."

*   *   *

To what extent is Soviet foreign policy an extension of internal processes? Perhaps the best reply to this question was given by Maxim Litvinov, for many years Soviet Commissar (Minister) of Foreign Affairs. The formulation of foreign policy in the USSR, he noted, is a highly complex matter. Unlike the economy, which could rest upon five-year plans drafted on the basis of Soviet "aspirations and wishes" and "a calculation of our own potentialities," there could be no such "five-year plans" for foreign policy. As Litvinov wrote:

> . . . in examining the development of foreign policy we have to deal with a number of factors that are scarcely subject to calculation, with a number of elements outside our control and the scope of our action. International affairs are composed not only of our aspirations and actions, but of those of a large number of countries . . . pursuing other aims than ours and using other means to achieve those aims than we allow.[8]

Thus, while highly important, the domestic environment is only a part of the reality which gives shape to Soviet policy.

A second point, by way of conclusion, relates to the relative weight and fixedness of the variables influencing foreign policy. The particular significance of each domestic factor, as we have seen, has changed over time. The most dramatic changes have occurred in the area of economic and military capabilities, which, in a relatively brief period, have catapulted the USSR into its current role as a global power. Less dramatic, perhaps, but equally important, have been the shifts which have occurred in the views of the Soviet political leadership. The evidence strongly suggests that many of the traditional attitudes and concerns of the Kremlin rulers have been significantly modified.

Let me give some examples. It has long been a characteristic Bolshevik assumption that the "scientific truths" of Marxism–Leninism would guide the Communist Party leaders along a clear and unswerving path. Armed with knowledge of the "laws of historical development," the Kremlin authorities—at least in their public utterances—always seemed fully convinced of the wisdom and righteousness of their policies. The actions of the Soviet state were always identified as appropriate, steadfast, wise, and, above all, correct. While much official commentary still takes this form, there are occasional hints that the traditional Bolshevik sense of certainty and rectitude is being modified. Despite their continued adherence to "scientific Marxism," Soviet writers are increasingly willing to confess doubts, uncertainties, and even errors. Soviet officials have been expressing an unusual degree of skepticism in dealing with current developments, especially in the economy. Not only is the Party press more willing to admit shortcomings, mistakes, and inefficiencies (which are still blamed on the faulty leadership of lesser-ranking officials) but there are indications of leadership uncertainty as to how such problems can best be handled. Thus, Party Secretary Brezhnev notes that in the management of the economy "as in other fields of social life, let us add—there are in practice *no definitive solutions* that could rid us of all problems once and for all."[9] (Italics added.) A close associate expresses a similar view:

> "... the tasks confronting the social scientists have become more complicated. ... This is connected above all ... with *the profound contradictoriness* of the present epoch, with *the immense heterogeneity* of the class forces participating in the social, economic and political struggle in the world arena and with the rapid changes ... and the emergence of new problems. ..." [Italics added.]

Quoting Brezhnev, he concludes that "the repetition of old formulas . . . and an inability or reluctance to approach new problems in a new way—all this harms the cause. . . ."[10]

This pragmatic tone, this willingness to admit that "life itself" is often complex, that there are "no definite solutions" to problems, and that "creative new approaches" must be ventured, increasingly seems to characterize the utterances of high Soviet policymakers. The classic Bolshevik sense of infallibility seems to have given way to a willingness to concede errors and to admit doubt. In speaking of the future, Brezhnev notes that the creation of a truly Communist society in the USSR will be difficult and will "take us quite a long time, since human psychology is remade far slower than the material foundations of human life."[11] It is slowly being recognized that it is easier to build a new hydroelectric plant than to create a "new Soviet man."

A modification of traditional attitudes has revealed itself in the sphere of foreign policy as well. Moscow's emphasis on pragmatic concerns were especially noticeable during the Soviet–American summit conferences of 1972 and 1973. Throughout this period, Soviet officials stressed the need for mutual accommodation and cooperation. During a talk to a group of American businessmen in Washington, Brezhnev went so far as to imply that the Soviet leaders themselves bear some of the responsibility for the antagonisms and hostilities of the cold war. He confessed that "we have certainly been prisoners of those old tendencies, those old trends, and to this day have not been able fully to break those fetters and to come out into the open air not only in the political field but in trade and economic ties."[12] Brezhnev was seeking to persuade his audience of Soviet sincerity and fair-mindedness. In his eagerness to expand trade relations with the United States, he was even willing—in a rare departure from Soviet practice—to hint at possible Soviet wrongdoing.

Another indication of changing perspectives can be found in the more accurate Soviet assessments of world political developments, especially in regard to the United States. The popular press can be depended upon to reflect the political line of the day, from the vitriolic distemper displayed during the late 1960s to the virtual absence of coverage of the Watergate scandal of 1973 (to avoid disturbing the growing accommodation in Soviet–American relations[13]); but specialized Soviet journals have been increasingly sophisticated and realistic in their analysis of internal political and economic developments in the United States.

For example, in contrast to the crude Marxist stereotypes of earlier years, American socio-economic and political processes and institutions are described as internally complex and differentiated; and, to a surprising degree, American policy is considered uncertain. Although Soviet writers adhere to the classical view that the methods and objectives of White House policymakers are determined by their capitalist class interests, the implications of this Marxist principle seem much less clear than in the past. In recent years, some important American leaders have been identified as "realists"; Presidents Kennedy and Nixon and Secretary of State Henry Kissinger are leading practitioners of this school, according to Soviet sources. The existence of such "realistic, sober" elements among American ruling circles with whom the Soviet Government can reach agreements, Soviet sources stress, does not indicate that the class character of the American system has changed. It does suggest, however, that important American policymakers are "realistic" in their assessment of the world power alignment—they recognize the power and influence of the USSR. It is in this sense, in this willingness to adjust to the new "correlation of forces," that President Nixon's visit to Moscow and the agreements reached with the USSR are seen as reflecting "realism."

Thus, while the traditional Bolshevik view held that the "nature" of the capitalist system shaped its aggressive, imperialistic character, the particular course and direction of White House policy today is not considered immutable but is said to reflect the specific balance of political forces in Washington (the influence of the "realists" in policymaking) and of the policies of other states. According to G. Arbatov, American foreign policy "depends, in the last analysis, on the course of the intricate political struggles in the United States itself which is developing under the influence of internal as well as foreign policy factors."[14] Thus, current American policy is seen as both changeable and subject to external influence.

Particularly interesting, for our purposes, has been a remarkable shift in the policy implications drawn from the Soviet analysis of capitalist foreign policy formation. Traditionally, the profit-making mechanism of capitalist societies was believed to propel them along militaristic and aggressive paths. Furthermore, the menace of Communism was seen virtually to necessitate an anti-Communist and anti-Soviet thrust to Western foreign policy. In the most recent period, this analysis has been revised. It is currently being argued that, in light of the internal (particularly economic) strains it generates, maintenance of a militaristic anti-Communist posture is no longer in the interests of the ruling classes. Contrary to classical Bolshevik dogma, it is now held that large-scale military expenditures exert "not a stimulating but, on the contrary, a destructive influence on the American economy." The American leadership is now said to realize that basing its policies on "a platform of militant anti-communism . . . can do substantial damage to its own class interests." More specifically, the ruling American bourgeoisie know that "in squandering a huge part of its natural resources on the arms race and military adventures, the U.S.A. is only undermining its position in the competitive struggle with other capitalist powers, dooming itself to monetary–financial upheavals and loosening the foundations of its economic and political influence in the world."[15]

Of course, this analysis has been designed to legitimize current Soviet foreign policy toward the United States. Brezhnev could not sign arms limitation agreements nor seek long-term trade relations and other accommodations if America were still depicted as a "predatory imperialist power." For Soviet détente policy to be creditable, especially at home, the image of the United States had to be considerably modified and Washington somehow had to be described in Arbatov's phrase, as an "acceptable partner."[16] In so doing, the traditional Bolshevik analysis of American foreign policy formulation has been substantially altered. The dynamics of monopoly capitalism are no longer seen as fueling the arms race, but as compelling the capitalist powers to abandon their aggressive militaristic stance and to improve relations with the USSR.

Assuming these new perspectives actually reflect views held in the leadership, what is their basis? The trend away from Bolshevik orthodoxies and the de-emphasis of simple-minded ideological formulae as a basis for policy formation can tentatively be associated with two related developments: First, the Soviet leadership seems increasingly persuaded that "life itself" is more complex and recalcitrant than the doctrinal principles of Marxism–Leninism would have one believe. Second, given the "profound contradictoriness" of the problems they confront, appropriate policy choices seem less clear than they once did. As Alexander Dallin has written, there seems to be "greater confusion about the shape of things to come and uncertainty about the 'proper' priorities and policies to be pursued."[17] To what can this "confusion" and "uncertainty" be attributed? This does not reflect loss of purpose on the part of the leadership—anyone rising to the upper reaches of the Soviet political elite cannot be suspected of lack of energy, discipline, or will. It may partly be a function of the collective character of the current Kremlin leadership; group rule does tend to blur and slow executive decision-making, and even to allow outside groups and interests to influence Politburo deliberations. But the evidence implies that something even more profound is at work. Leadership open-mindedness reflects the fact that Soviet society has become "increasingly permeated by an awareness of multiple truths, multiple interests and multiple forces at work both at home and abroad."[18]

The increasingly pragmatic bent and the growing awareness of the ambiguity and contingent character of truth and of the "immense heterogeneity" of the factors affecting policy can be explained in terms of recent Soviet experience. In earlier periods, objectives were clear (the Five-Year Plans, the taming of nature, the defeat of the fascist hordes, and the post-war reconstruction), enemies were obvious (the "Whites," the Bank of England, Hitler, the Japanese militarists, Wall Street, the German "revanchists"), and methods were agreed upon (central planning, tight Party controls and indoctrination, collectivization, isolation from alien influences). Today, in both domestic and foreign policy, the situation seems confused. Allies have turned into enemies (China) and enemies into "acceptable partners" (the United States); fraternal brothers in the "national liberation movements" of the Third World have proven both unreliable and ungrateful while bourgeois class enemies in the Western business community eagerly lend themselves to the task of solving Soviet economic difficulties. Internally, agriculture remains a very serious problem (despite huge investments), industrial labor productivity remains low, central planning remains inefficient and wasteful, political dissidents are active as never before, the nationalities remain a problem, the workers want more bourgeois creature comforts, intellectuals remain restive under Party controls, and the economic gap between "socialist" and "capitalist" societies remains as large as ever.

There has been progress: both the Kremlin leaders and the average Russian can boast of accomplishments and opportunities as never before in history. However, the obdurate character of the regime's many problems seems to be eroding the Politburo's faith in traditional remedies. "Realistic" elements in the Party leadership seem to have come to the view that, in all spheres, only less doctrinaire, more open-minded policies can offer the possibility of success. Of course, there are still those who cling to the "fundamental truths" of doctrine and who continue to insist that the traditional, ideologically sanctioned way is the only way. And sometimes their views seem vindicated, as in the case of Czechoslovakia. However, the more pragmatic, more flexible stance urged by the "realistic" elements in the Party leadership continues to receive a hearing.

Recent changes in the USSR's international position has also encouraged the development of these new perspectives. As we described earlier, substantial modifications and improvements in Soviet military capabilities have created a totally new strategic environment. The USSR today is more secure militarily than at any previous time in its history. Not only is it physically capable of protecting against external attack but its armed forces have the strategic power capability of devastating the most powerful of its potential enemies. As a result of its vast military strength, the Great Power role of the USSR is recognized and respected around the world. The international prestige of this once backward and outlaw nation has never been higher.

Given this new power and status, traditional anxieties have been fading. Not only has the Soviet fear of annihilation declined—its enormous weapons arsenal makes such a contingency highly remote—but earlier convictions that hostile outside powers desired the extinction of the USSR seem to have diminished. Previously, writes Arbatov, it was American policy "to counteract, as a minimum 'to contain,' but in the long run to crush the Soviet Union once and for all." Now, "despite all fundamental differences," the United States and the USSR share "spheres of parallel or coinciding interests."[19] Earlier assumptions regarding two antagonistic systems locked into mortal combat seem to have been abandoned. The imperatives of nuclear technology demanded some degree of cooperation so as to maintain internal peace. Furthermore, the USSR has acquired a stake in its relations with the West. This last point was well illustrated by a comment made by Premier Kosygin regarding recent financial problems. Commenting on the inability of the Western powers to cope with their monetary difficulties, the Soviet leader observed, "I must state that the Soviet Union is not the least interested in international monetary chaos. . . . it is clear that we feel the effects of this monetary crisis in our trade."[20] Once the eager prophet and expectant beneficiary of capitalist economic breakdown, Moscow today is heavily dependent on Western economic stability.

The greatly improved "correlation of forces" and the USSR's growing international prestige have produced a more relaxed, more self-confident leadership. Fears of "capitalist encirclement" have greatly diminished. The changed security environment has also had implications for the revolutionary dimension of Soviet policy. Given its new sense of security, the Kremlin has little reason to believe that revolutions abroad are of any significance to the basic interests of the USSR. The strength of the Soviet Union and the divisions in the Western camp (including the influence of the "realistic" elements in Western political circles) are seen as sufficient to deter any deliberate imperialist attack. Thus, the expansion of the Communist system is not vital to the protection of Soviet security. In this context, the tasks of local Communist parties are to seek to influence the foreign policies of their governments in a direction favorable to the USSR, and to support the CPSU in its ideological struggle against Peking in the international Communist movement. Given the reduced danger from without, whatever interest Moscow had in the international class struggle has virtually disappeared. The "supreme international duty" of the Soviet Union can safely be confined to the improvement of Soviet industrial productivity and living standards.[21]

What all this seems to suggest is that under the influence of changing circumstances and experience—a new weapons environment, a markedly improved strategic power position and great international prestige —traditional Bolshevik beliefs have been substantially modified. Historically and ideologically conditioned assumptions, fears, and expectations have been contradicted by "life itself." Having survived and prospered in fifty years of living together with the "capitalist warmongers," the Kremlin leaders no longer seem to doubt the ability of their system to endure; and they seem less certain that the intentions of others are unequivocally belligerent. They are less suspicious of Westerners with whom they now share "parallel interests"—avoiding nuclear conflict and enlarging trade. And they are convinced that Soviet power and diplomacy can effectively deal with other states.

The sentiments and ideological beliefs of the past—the suspiciousness, secretiveness, xenophobia, self-doubt, fears, conceits, and messianic attitudes—are under pressure. They are being challenged by the new psychological environment in which the Soviet leadership today finds itself. Traditional backwardness and vulnerability have been replaced by great power and prestige. In a Russia more secure, more self-confident, less anxious, and more interested in cooperation than in the past, traditional Bolshevik attitudes have eroded and more moderate perspectives seem increasingly to hold sway. The USSR is now seen as participating in rather than warring against the international system.

The emergence of these new, less militant, less rigid, more open-ended perspectives is highly significant. Along with the increasing influence of moderate "realistic" elements within the Party and the generally conciliatory policies of recent years, these developments seem to indicate the gradual evolution of a more temperate, more reasonable, and more cooperative policy outlook on the part of the Kremlin leadership. However, while serious—and promising—these trends should be kept in perspective. Awareness of the history, traditions, avowed beliefs, and past policies of the USSR should caution against a premature judgment regarding their long-run influence.

It should be remembered that the present Brezhnev regime is essentially conservative, seeking to run Soviet society in established ways. For example, the advance of the civilian sector of the economy has been very slow and Soviet living standards remain below those of most of

Eastern Europe. Political controls remain stringent. The Kremlin authorities have continuously resisted demands to modify governmental policy. Public-spirited citizens who have championed the cause of reform—like Sakharov, Solzhenitsyn, Amalrik, Grigorenko, Yakir, Medvedev, Litvinov and many others—are accused of "grovelling before the capitalist system" and subjected to political pressure, imprisonment, incarceration in mental hospitals, and, in some instances, expulsion. The practices and traditions of the internal Soviet political system have remained largely unchanged. Thus, while some of the leaders seem to be groping for new methods, as a whole they remain apprehensive that reforms will generate forces that will get out of hand. For example, their fear that economic decentralization may encourage pressures for political decentralization (as it did in Czechoslovakia) deters them from seriously considering basic changes in the economic system.

Furthermore, the political strength of the traditional elements in the Party leadership remains predominant. The rise of Marshal Grechko and KGB chief Andropov to Politburo status clearly does not augur well for the future of détente. These two leaders of the security-anxious "hard" wing of the Party are suspicious of any improvement of relations with the West; they regard internal vigilance and great military power as the only sure means of protecting the vital interests of the USSR. Brezhnev was finally successful in having his "Peace Program" adopted but, during the period before the 24th Party Congress (which had been delayed for a year), there were considerable signs of a sharp debate in which Party traditionalist and military interests seriously questioned the proposed policy of "normalization" of relations with the United States. The strength of the conservative elements continues to be formidable.

While moderate perspectives and forces may be asserting themselves with increasing vigor, the dominant mood of the leaders remains generally cautious. Their policies reveal contradictory trends. On one hand, the Kremlin recognizes the dangers of unabated arms competition and has agreed to limit offensive and defensive arms. Leonid Brezhnev has signed a pact promising to join with the United States in "urgent consultations" should local conflict situations arise anywhere in the world which involve the risk of nuclear war (U.S.–USSR Accord on Avoiding Atomic War, June, 1973). Thus, the "rules of the game" of peaceful coexistence, codified in 1972, are slowly being enlarged.

On the other hand, the Soviet Union has been probing for tactical gains especially in the Middle East. Further, the major build-up of Soviet military power detailed earlier cannot be ignored. And, although Brezhnev's détente policy is certainly to be welcomed, its destabilizing effects (or intentions) cannot be overlooked. As a result of the general relaxation of international tensions, the perceived need to maintain the NATO military alliance system has sharply declined both in the United States and in Europe. Should such trends continue, the Soviet Union will shortly become not just the predominant but virtually the only military power in Europe.

As to the future of Soviet policy, much depends on the changing "correlation of forces" in the Kremlin—which coalition of interests and sentiments secures predominant influence. There are those for whom the traditional Bolshevik view remains compelling, whether as a psychological survival of an earlier period or as a reflection of internal political needs. (The persistence and audacity of Soviet political dissidents undoubtedly reinforces the convictions of many regarding the need for doctrinal orthodoxy.) Among the ideologically inspired, there are groups for whom the USSR remains, in the words of former American Ambassador to Moscow Charles Bohlen, more of a cause than a country.[22] However weak, the crusading spirit remains alive in the breasts of all good Party members. In addition, there are the conservative Party leaders who still retain a fundamental mistrust of the West and warn against compromises in foreign policy which express "opportunism and betrayal of the workers' interest."[23] There are also the generals, admirals, and Russian nationalists who want the Soviet Union to enjoy the fruits of its newly acquired status as a Great Power. Well before 1917, Russians were quoted as saying to a Western visitor: "You may be stronger now, richer than we are, but we shall be stronger tomorrow than you—yes, and all the world; for the future belongs with the Slav! . . . Would you know another name for Russia? Very well, then, call her 'The Inevitable.' "[24] For some, the future is now and "The Inevitable" is upon us. In contrast, there are those who appear to recognize the need to exercise restraint in the USSR's military rivalry with the United States, to control and moderate the political competition between the two powers, and to concentrate increasing resources on improving and modernizing the domestic economy as the best way to promote Soviet interests in the long run.

Which tendency will prevail? As we have noted, Soviet policy and perhaps even Soviet politics are influenced by the changing character of the international environment and, particularly, by the policies of the United States. Cannot Washington, therefore, seek to shape Soviet choices? It can (and probably does), but such efforts are not likely to be very fruitful. Our knowledge of the dynamics of Soviet policymaking is too limited to predict the impact of American policy with much accuracy. It would appear, on the surface at least, that a "hard" American policy (seen as expressing hostility or evil intentions) would strengthen the argument, position, and influence of the conservative elements in the Party. Such has been the case in the disarmament negotiations where the assertive policies of the military on each side tends to bolster the position of their counterparts on the other. Marshal Grechko's budgets and weapons stockpiles are always cited by the American Defense Department to justify its budgetary claims, and vice versa. Somewhat paradoxically, the military interests of each side thrive on the accomplishments of their adversary.

At the same time, however, we do not know enough about internal Kremlin politics to judge whether a moderate American position on, say, negotiations for a reduction of military forces in Europe, would strengthen the position of Soviet moderates and generate a reasonable counter-proposal or would simply convince Kremlin militants that the position of the United States was crumbling and that their best option would be to remain firm. Concessions may make Washington appear reasonable and "sober," or politically weak, or even devious. A "tough" posture may stimulate a harsh Soviet response and bolster the position of the Kremlin "hawks," as it apparently did at the time of the U-2 crisis which resulted in the scuttling of the 1960 Paris summit conference. But another tough stand, the American mining of North Vietnamese harbors (a less overt but nevertheless direct challenge), did not prevent the Soviet leadership from receiving President Nixon in the Kremlin in 1972.

Obviously, the impact of American policy on the Soviet policymaking process is unpredictable. The United States has probably tried to strengthen the position of the more moderate elements in the Kremlin and Soviet leaders have undoubtedly tried to bolster our "realists." (There seems to be a loose cross-national coalition of "realists" who, like the military, interact and reinforce each other's position.) Yet the ability of each side to manipulate the internal politics of the other is rather slight.

The future remains uncertain. Soviet policy will continue to defend its security interests in Eastern Europe and against the threat of China; it will also strive for at least an equal role in world affairs with the United States. The competition for political influence will undoubtedly continue. Moscow will persist in seeking to translate its global power and prestige into tangible political gains; the crucial question remains, at what costs and risks? Though the situation today seems more hopeful, these issues still await answers.

Perhaps the most fitting note on which to conclude would be to quote the comment made by the first American ambassador to the USSR at the end of his mission in 1936. In regard to our relations with the Soviet Union, he wrote,

> We should neither expect too much or despair at getting anything at all. We should take what we can get when the atmosphere is favorable and do our best to hold on to it when the wind blows the other way.[25]

And then to hope, along with a more recent ambassador, that, at long last, "Reason has begun to prevail. . . ."[26]

Notes

[1]Ulam, *Expansion and Coexistence, op. cit.,* pp. 399, 400.

[2]Arnold L. Horelick and Myron Rush, *Strategic Power and Soviet Policy* (Chicago: The University of Chicago Press, 1966), p. 107. For a fuller explanation of this neglected view, see Rush, "Soviet Policy and International Tension," in Robert A. Goldwin, ed., *Beyond the Cold War* (Chicago: Rand NcNally and Co., 1965), pp. 138–153.

[3]Dinerstein, *Fifty Years of Soviet Foreign Policy, op. cit.,* p. 53.

[4]The Central Committee of the CPSU on June 30, 1956, issued a decree in which it identified Stalinism as the product of historical conditions—capitalist encirclement ("bitter attacks by the Imperialist states"), rapid industrialization,

the struggle against class enemies. As an official Party history observes, "The complicated international and domestic situation called for iron discipline, a high degree of vigilance and the strictest centralization of leadership." *History of the Communist Party of the Soviet Union* (Moscow: Foreign Languages Publishing House, 1960), p. 670.

[5] Linden, *op. cit., passim.*

[6] See Moore, *op. cit.*, p. 389.

[7] Neal Ascherson, "Willy Brandt's *Ostpolitik:* What's at Stake," *The New York Review of Books* (April 20, 1970), p. 28.

[8] *Soviet Documents on Foreign Policy, op. cit.*, Vol. II, 1925–1932, p. 408.

[9] "Lenin's Cause Lives and Triumphs. Report by Comrade L. I. Brezhnev at the Joint Ceremonial Session of the C. P. S. U. Central Committee, the U. S. S. R. Supreme Soviet and the Russian Republic Supreme Soviet on April 21, 1970. Dedicated to the 100th Anniversary of the Birth of Vladimir Ilyich Lenin," *Pravda*, April 22, 1970; translated in *CDSP*, Vol. XXII, No. 16 (May 19, 1970), p. 9.

[10] S. Trapeznikov, "The Construction of Communism and the Horizons of Science," *Pravda* (January 5, 1973); *ibid.*, Vol. XXV, No. 1 (January 31, 1973), p. 12. Trapeznikov, director of the Science and Educational Institutions Department of the Party's Central Committee, has been identified as "one of the most influential representatives of neo-Stalinism" by Andrei Sakharov. (*Progress, Coexistence and Intellectual Freedom, op. cit.*, p. 56.) The fact that someone with so conservative a political orientation publicly takes on pragmatic, reasonable, non-doctrinaire views suggests that either a) this is a spurious pose adopted for less visible (probably political) reasons or b) that as an academic politician with close ties to Brezhnev, Trapeznikov is, perhaps reticently, simply following the current leadership line.

[11] L. I. Brezhnev, "on the 50th Anniversary of the Union of Soviet Socialist Republics," *Pravda*, December 22, 1972; *ibid.*, Vol. XXIV, No. 51 (January 17, 1973), p. 18. Brezhnev defined Communism as "the most organized and most hard-working society in the history of mankind. Those who live in this society will be the hard-working, conscientious, highly organized and highly class-conscious people." Little wonder that human psychology has to be "remade."

[12] *The New York Times*, June 23, 1973, p. 9. He went on to say: "But if I say that applies to us I also have every right to say, gentlemen, that that is certainly something that applies to yourselves as well."

[13] Soviet diplomatic circles, it was reported, believed that the Watergate scandal was partly the result of a right-wing conspiracy aimed at undermining President Nixon's policy of improving relations with the Soviet Union.

[14] Arbatov, "Amerikanskaya vneshnaya politika no poroge 70-kh godov," *op. cit.*, p. 34.

[15] G. Arbatov, "O Sovetskikh–Amerikanskikh otnosheniyakh [On Soviet–American Relations]," *Kommunist*, No. 3 (February, 1973), pp. 109–110, 106.

[16] *Ibid.*, p. 105.

[17] Dallin, *op. cit.*, p. 258.

[18] *Ibid.*, p. 263. One Soviet writer has recently observed that "a state's policy does not automatically derive from its economic system. It has a relative independence and, under certain conditions, can break away from its economic base for a particular length of time." It is in these terms, it is argued, that American "realism" and Chinese "anti-Sovietism" can be explained. Prof. Maj. Gen. Ye. Sulimov, "The Scientific Nature of the CPSU's Foreign Policy," *Krasnaya zvezda*, December 20, 1973, pp. 2–3.

[19] Arbatov, "O Sovetskikh–Amerikanskikh otnosheniyakh," *op. cit.*, pp. 106, 109.

[20] Associated Press dispatch on Kosygin news conference held in Vienna after four-day visit to Austria, *Riverside Press*, July 5, 1973.

[21] See Richard Lowenthal, "Soviet and Chinese Communist World Views,"

in Donald W. Treadgold, ed., *Soviet and Chinese Communism, Similarities and Differences* (Seattle: University of Washington Press, 1967), pp. 393–398.

[22]Charles E. Bohlen, *Witness to History, 1929–1969* (New York: W. W. Norton and Co., 1973), p. 542.

[23]Quoted in Sidney Ploss, "New Politics in Russia,?" *Survey*, Vol. 19, No. 4 (89) (Autumn, 1973), p. 33.

[24]Albert J. Beveridge, *The Russian Advance* (New York: Harper and Brothers Publishers, 1904), p. 109.

[25]Message of William C. Bullitt to Secretary of State Cordell Hull, quoted in Bohlen, *op. cit.*, p. 34.

[26]"What Brezhnev Wants from U.S.: Interview with Jacob D. Beam, former Ambassador to Moscow," *U.S. News and World Report*, May 28, 1973, p. 41.

Index